A Who's Who of
Lancashire
County Cricket Club

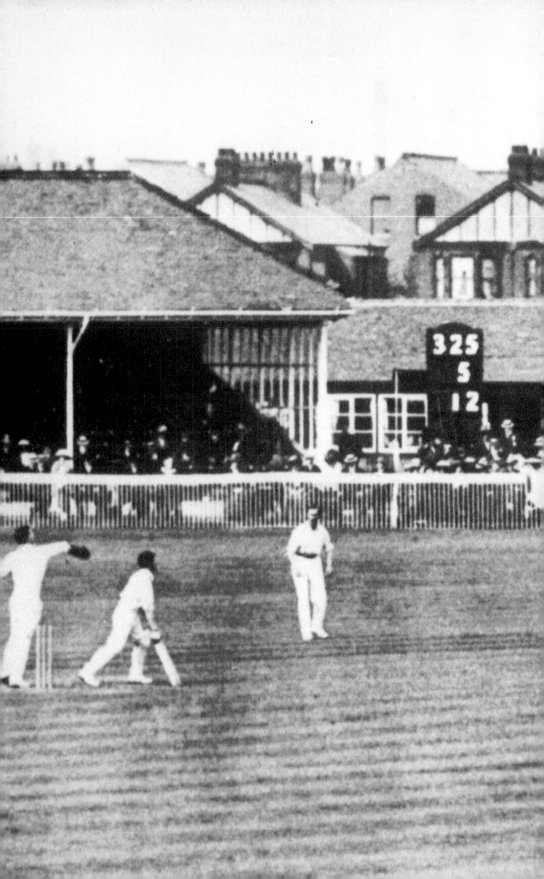

A Who's Who of Lancashire
County Cricket Club
1865-1990

Robert Brooke
& David Goodyear

BREEDON
BOOKS
SPORT

First published in Great Britain by
The Breedon Books Publishing Company Limited
44 Friar Gate, Derby DE1 1DA
1991

ISBN 0 907969 85 2

Printed and bound in Great Britain by The Bath Press Limited, Bath
and London.
Jacket printed by Arkle Print Ltd of Northampton.

Contents

Acknowledgements

The authors wish to thank the following: Roy Tattersall for agreeing to write the Foreword and for the loan of his personal photographs; Keith Hayhurst for the loan of his personal photographs; officials of Lancashire County Cricket Club for their kind support of this project; the *Manchester Evening News*; the publishers, especially Anton Rippon; Rev Malcolm Lorimer; Philip Bailey; Brian Hunt; and last but most important, all the past and present players of Lancashire CCC, without whom this book would not have been possible.

Photographs

Most of the photographs in this book have been supplied from private collections. Other contributers are Mark Leach, Sporting Pictures (UK) Ltd and Bob Thomas.

Foreword
by Roy Tattersall

WHEN I was asked to write a foreword for the *Who's Who of Lancashire CCC*, I was a bit puzzled about what was expected. Then it occurred to me how times and things have changed at Old Trafford since the end of World War Two.

I reported to Old Trafford early in April 1947, after having success in trial matches in 1946, it was a great thrill and honour to join such a big-name club and meet the big-name cricketers and officials.

The ground and accommodation had suffered due to the war years. In fact a reconstruction fund was formed and matches played to raise extra money in order to repaint the surrounds and make better seating facilities and also to replace steel fencing which had been used for the war effort. The offices were in various parts of the Pavilion.

What a transformation has taken place at Old Trafford. It is easy to get lost now, with all the alterations and new buildings which have appeared. New office blocks, large dining-rooms, indoor cricket and squash areas, library and souvenir shop, plus executive boxes, the latest Red Rose Suite and new Press box area etc.

When Test matches and other big games are played here, the practice ground is filled with large marquees to accommodate the various sponsors and their friends and clients.

When going through the large car-park, it is interesting to see the numerous array of sponsored players' cars, plus all the sporting equipment supplied to them. We travelled in all sorts of 'old bangers' and on trains which were often full and had standing-room only. There were no motorways for quick journeys and coach travel was not to be compared with the luxury vehicles of today. However, we still enjoyed our cricket and made many lasting friends.

The game itself has changed so much over the years. Certainly one big improvement is the present-day fielding,

I think this is partly due to the limited-overs game, but it is strange to see medium and fast bowlers having no slip fielders or starting a three-day county match without a third man.

The absence of spin bowlers is a lost art and I am sure is detrimental to this great game.

With all the changes that have taken place at most county grounds, it is also good to notice big improvements at small club level — the grass roots of cricket. Better wickets and pavilions, coaching and so on all help to make this grand game more enjoyable. The years roll by and records keep being broken, but the main item is that thousands of people over many parts of the world are still attracted to the game of cricket.

Roy Tattersall

Glossary

BB	best bowling
HS	highest score
LB	leg-break bowler
LBG	leg-break and googly bowler
LFM	left-armed fast-medium bowler
LHB	left-handed batsman
OB	off-break bowler
RAS	right-armed spin bowler
RF	right-armed fast bowler
RFM	right-armed fast-medium bowler
RHB	right-handed batsman
RM	right-armed medium-paced bowler
SLA	left-armed slow bowler
*	not out

All details on cricket performances are for first-class matches unless otherwise stated. Figures include the England tour to Australia 1990-91, but not England 'A' to Pakistan and Sri Lanka.

A Brief History
of Lancashire CCC

N O RESUME of the exploits of Lancashire County
Cricket Club could be complete without reference
to the earliest days of cricket in the county, a difficult
task indeed, since Lancashire seems to have had no part
whatsoever in the general development of the game in its
'adolescence', *ie* the eighteenth century.

There is disagreement as to the first definite reference
to cricket, but it is beyond dispute that the eighteenth
century was a period of growth and development towards
the modern game and, in Southern England at least, it
was in a comparatively flourishing state.

Not only in the south, however. As early as the 1750s
there are definite references to cricket being played in
Yorkshire and Durham, and it is known that in August
1781, a team from Haughton, near Denton, travelled into
Cheshire to play Bradbury.

As for cricket actually played in Lancashire, however,
apart from a somewhat mysterious reference to a match
staged on a field in Cazneau Street, Liverpool, late in the
eighteenth century, nothing certain is known until 1807,
when a group of Liverpool gentlemen formed 'The Original
and Unrivalled Mosslake Fields Cricket Society'.

Thus it seems that Lancashire cricket had its roots in
Liverpool and it was some time before the rest of the county
caught up, possibly because 'superior society' was busy
making money, whilst the masses were forced to work most
of the hours God sent, simply to avoid starvation. Sunday
was often the only free day and this was probably used
to beg the Almighty for the strength to carry on the unequal
struggle for survival for a further seven days. Sport, of
any sort, simply had no place.

Cricket did grow, albeit at a slow pace, and at last, in
1864, some leading members of Manchester Cricket Club
organized a meeting at Manchester's Queen's Hotel for the
express purpose of forming a county club. Thirteen clubs
were represented, all from the southern part of the county,
and they made 12 January 1864 a red letter (or red rose?)
day as Lancashire County Cricket Club was officially
established.

There were no proper county matches during the first

The Gentlemen of Lancashire team of the mid-1870s. Back row (left to right): Harris (umpire), Roger Walker, John Leach, R.Stubbs, H.W.Gardner, A.Appleby, J.R.Hillkirk. Seated: W.Potter, Ed Porter, J.F.Leese, Josh Makinson. On ground: A.N.Hornby.

season and it was not until Middlesex visited Old Trafford on 20, 21, 22 July 1865 that Lancashire could really claim to be in business. They did pretty well in the first match. Middlesex cricket was dominated in the early days by 'The seven proud Walkers,' bachelor brothers who stood for all that was good in contemporary cricket. This meant privilege for wealth or position, dominance of amateur over professional as of right, the latter to know his place and do all the donkey work.

In fairness, the Walkers were good cricketers and in this match Mr R.D.Walker was easily the top scorer with 84 and 28, whilst Mr V.E.Walker took all ten second-innings wickets for 104 runs. Perhaps there were too many

The Lancashire team of around 1878. Back row (players only, left to right): A.Appleby, A.Watson, J.E.Kershaw, W.McIntyre, R.Pilling. Front row: R.G.Barlow, O.P.Lancashire, A.N.Hornby, A.G.Steel, E.B.Rowley, V.Royle.

passengers amongst their amateur friends, however, since the Lancashire club began its career in the best possible way, with a 62-run victory.

The ensuing seasons were sometimes a struggle, especially with regard to fielding a regular side of the desired quality. Some who made fleeting appearances seem to have possessed somewhat elusive ability, as well as dubious personal qualities. One wonders at such people as J.Harrop, a singular individual whose main concern after the only game of a somewhat unsuccessful county 'career' was that readers of the *Salford and Manchester Gazette* may have erroneously thought he was a professional. Poor Mr Harrop. One thought that the playing of the game was the only really important matter.

The loss to the team of such people as Mr Harrop could not fail to strengthen it, of course, and the influx of good-class professionals like Barlow, Watson and William McIntyre, in support of amateurs who were actually worth a place, both in ability and attitude, meant that on-field progress was steady and unerring.

More matches were being won than lost and in 1879

Lancashire, County Champions (with Nottinghamshire) in 1879. Back row: (left to right): Rowbotham, G.Nash, R.Pilling, James A.C.MacLaren, A.Watson, R.G.Barlow. Seated at back: J.Crossland, C.Haigh, A.N.Hornby (captain), F.Taylor. Seated at front: W.Robinson, V.Royle, J.Briggs.

most of the cricket Press (though not *Wisden*) expressed the view that Lancashire and Nottinghamshire were joint champion county. Two seasons later there was no argument and the Press was adamant that Lancashire, for the first time, was undisputed champion county.

It was easy to explain such success. A.N. ('Monkey') Hornby was an inspiring captain as well as the leading batsman, and after the three-pronged bowling spearhead of Barlow, Nash and Watson had done its work, the batting support for Hornby was usually just about adequate. They also had a splendid wicketkeeper in Dick Pilling, whilst one imagines that apart from his useful batting, 'Boy' Briggs saved any number of runs in the field.

It was generally felt that Lancashire should share the title with Nottinghamshire in 1882 (although the magazine *Cricket* awarded the accolade to Lancashire alone). But the following seasons saw a slight decline, until 1889 saw them awarded a share of the title, along with Surrey and Nottinghamshire. This was the last time the Championship was decided by

Lancashire group of 1881. Back row (left to right): G.Nash, J.Crossland, J.Smith (umpire), R.Pilling, A.Watson. Middle row: Mr A.G.Steel, Revd V.Royle, Mr A.N.Hornby, Mr A.Appleby. Front row: W.Robinson, R.G.Barlow, Mr O.P.Lancashire, J.Briggs.

Lancashire team in 1889. Back row (left to right): Clarke (umpire), A.W.Mold, A.Ward, A.G.Paul, F.H.Sugg, Draper (umpire). Middle row: R.Pilling, R.G.Barlow, A.N.Hornby (captain), J.Eccles, A.Watson. Front row: G.R.Baker, F.Ward, J.Briggs.

Yorkshireman Albert Ward enjoyed a long career with Lancashire. As one of a professional quartet he supplied the backbone of Lancashire's batting around the turn of the century.

the Press; for 1890 the counties themselves worked out the method for deciding positions, thus ensuring that the only future disagreements would be over the method used.

Lancashire continued to hold their own in the 'new' Championship competition, but not until 1897, after two seasons as runners-up, did they take their bow as 'official' county champions.

The 50-year-old 'Monkey' Hornby had resumed the

Archie MacLaren, now unable to turn out regularly but in a class of his own when he did play.

Lancashire team in 1901. Back row (left to right): Lunt (scorer), A.W.Mold, J.Sharp, W.R.Cuttell, S.Webb, J.J.Broughton, W.J.Hibbert. Middle row: A.Ward, H.G.Garnett, A.C.MacLaren, A.Priestley, J.Hallows. Front row: J.T.Tyldesley, C.Smith.

captaincy that season. His predecessor, Archie MacLaren, was unable to turn out regularly but remained in a class of his own when he did appear. The batting backbone was supplied by the professional quartet of Albert Ward, Baker, J.T.Tyldesley and Sugg, however. All scored regularly and achieved averages comfortably in the 30s. Charles Smith was a competent wicketkeeper and useful late-order run-getter. But so often the bowling actually won the matches, and Johnnie Briggs, Cuttell, Mold and Hallam were a quartet which compared with the best.

Lancashire remained amongst the top dogs and 1904 saw them champions again. *Wisden* described the season ' . . .without exaggeration . . .the brightest in the history of Lancashire cricket.' They were led by Archie MacLaren, who was past his best with the bat, but having success as county leader, and with 16 wins in 26 matches, and no defeats, *Wisden's* claim was undoubtedly soundly based.

Johnnie Tyldesley enjoyed a marvellous season, with 2,237 runs (averaging 69.90 in the Championship alone) and he was followed in the batting list by that most cultured of amateurs, R.H.Spooner. Jack Sharp, L.O.S.Poidevin, A.H.Hornby and the skipper scored plenty of runs in their

Lancashire in 1904, when they were County Champions. Back row (left to right): J.Sharp, W.R.Cuttell, W.Worsley, W.Findlay, A.Kermode, L.O.S.Poidevin, J.Hallows, W.Brearley, J.S.Heap. Front row: J.T.Tyldesley, A.H.Hornby, A.C.MacLaren, R.H.Spooner, H.G.Garnett.

different ways, whilst Willis Cuttell, the volatile Mr Walter Brearley, and the Australian, Kermode, did well with the ball.

Poor Johnnie Briggs was now dead after a melancholy period in Cheadle Asylum, but a successor seemed to have been discovered in Jimmy Hallows. Like Briggs, Hallows bowled left-arm, at a somewhat quicker pace, but most successfully and was also a splended left-handed batsman. In 1904 he achieved Lancashire's first Championship 'double', and was probably the one player who did most towards the winning of the title. Unfortunately there was already a little cloud, in the form of a delicate constitution. *Wisden* felt that everything depended on his future health 'still a source of some anxiety'.

How distressingly prophetic was the almanack. The second day of the home match with Kent in May 1910 was abandoned due to the funeral of King Edward VII; on the same day, just a few miles from Old Trafford, Jimmy Hallows was dying. Were the potential spectators aware of this one wonders? One hopes so, and that Hallows was the one uppermost in their thoughts.

There were to be no more titles that side of World War One, and by 1913 Lancashire had sunk to eighth position, whilst the club had been allowed to assume a pretty parlous financial state. There were ructions the following winter, with the county committee subjected to a great deal of criticism from, amongst others, the current captain, A.H.Hornby.

Hornby expressed his views in the Press, an action which should surely have led to his dismissal. Fortunately for Hornby, his father was still President of the club, and he was an amateur, of course. Positive efforts were made to improve the financial situation but on the field, 1914 proved a most depressing season with Lancashire slipping to a comparatively ignominious 11th position.

Plenty of games were drawn, but more were now being lost than won. The batting in 1914 was headed by Johnnie Tyldesley with a record markedly inferior to that of his best years, whilst although brother Ernest was his main support, he was in no sense the batsman he was to become after 'the war to end all wars'.

Jack Sharp and Harry Makepeace also reached 1,000 runs but the rest of the support was poor indeed, and there was no compensation to be found in the bowling. Cecil Parkin and Harry Dean performed reasonably well, but neither was regularly available and the attack mainly revolved around Huddleston and Whitehead, both of whom were expensive. Jimmy Heap completely lost form and Lol Cook was not yet the bowler he later became. Ignoring the ghastly happenings in France, the war may almost have been welcomed as an opportunity for retrenchment.

The resumption of cricket in 1919 saw Lancashire amongst the leading counties and building towards the most successful period in its history. The leading bowlers of the immediate post-war period were Dick Tyldesley, Parkin and Dean, and the presence of such lethal attackers made it somewhat surprising that the first title was not won until 1926, when Dean had departed and Parkin disqualified himself.

There had been a very considerable gain, however, in the lithe and athletic form of the Tasmanian, Ted McDonald. Getting through a remarkable amount of work, McDonald became the county's leading bowler, both shock and stock, for the rest of the decade. He received admirable support from the unathletic but mightily effective leg spinner, Dick Tyldesley, and what little extra help was needed was supplied mainly by Frank Sibbles and Jack Iddon.

Lancashire in 1926. Back row (left to right): J.Iddon, E.Tyldesley, J.W.H.Makepeace, C.Hallows, F.B.Watson. Third row: Nash (umpire), W.E.Howard, R.Tyldesley, McDonald, F.M.Sibbles, A.Woolley, Moore (scorer), Buswell (umpire). Second row: H.Rylance (secretary), O.P.Lancashire (chairman of committee), L.Green (captain), S.S.E.F.Stockton (president), P.T.Eckersley (vice captain), T.A.Higson (high treasurer). Front row: G.Duckworth, M.L.Taylor.

The 1928 season saw the county complete a hat-trick of titles and, if the bowling was insufficient, then the top four batsmen with their averages were Ernest Tyldesley (76), Frank Watson (68), Charles Hallows (66) and Jack Iddon (56). Harry Makepeace remained to add rarely-needed stiffening in the event of threatened collapse, whilst George Duckworth was not only one of the most vociferous of wicketkeepers, he was also among the best. No doubt Leonard Green had an easy task as captain but three titles in three seasons, with 42 wins against three defeats, surely indicates some competence in the job.

The 1929 season saw a new skipper, Peter Eckersley, and a 'slump' to runners-up, but although they gained only ten victories the following season, Lancashire were again unbeaten and returned to top spot. Ernest Tyldesley, Watson and Iddon again scored well, but Charles Hallows

Lancashire, the County Champions of 1927. Back row (left to right): E.Paynter, G.Duckworth, F.M.Sibbles, J.Iddon, F.Webster, M.L.Taylor. Front row: C.Hallows, P.T.Eckersley, Maj. L.Green (captain), E.Tyldesley, E.K.Watson, R.Tyldesley.

was past his best and Makepeace retired. Dick Tyldesley was the most successful bowler with a slightly fading McDonald now in a supporting role.

Both soon departed and with the exception of a slightly surprising first place in 1934, the seasons from 1931 until the war saw a run of comparative mediocrity. In 1934, Ernest Tyldesley enjoyed an 'Indian Summer', and Jack Iddon, with 2,381 runs, his best-ever season with the bat. Watson and Eddie Paynter also scored well but perhaps most credit was due to Len Hopwood, who in his own unspectacular manner achieved his first 'double' and was by far the most successful bowler.

The late 1930s saw the replacement of old stalwarts by a new generation. Eddie Paynter became the leading batsman, whilst Cyril Washbrook and 'Buddy' Oldfield gave promise of future attractive prolific scoring.

With regards to Oldfield, this promise was never really fulfilled. The unlucky, and quite elderly, Bill Farrimond replaced Duckworth behind the stumps with great proficiency, but unhappily the bowling in the late '1930s never quite made it with regard to class and effectiveness. Pollard was striving well when war came, and Phillipson

Lancashire in 1936. Back row (left to right): E.Paynter, J.L.Hopwood, R.Pollard, N.Oldfield, F.Booth, F.M.Sibbles, Washbrook. Front row: G.Duckworth, W.H.L.Lister, F.Watson, J.Iddon.

was a talented all-rounder, but there seemed no successor to Dick Tyldesley, until Len Wilkinson made his most impressive mark in 1938. He suggested infinite possibilities as a leg spinner, with 145 wickets at the age of 21, but after a disappointing 1939 season, any future hopes, or fears, were put on ice by the Führer.

Championship cricket resumed in 1946 and Lancashire seemed to have been affected more than most by the war. *Anno Domini* had finished the career of Hopwood, Paynter and Farrimond, whilst Iddon had been killed in a road accident. What could not have been foreseen were the decisions by Oldfield, and all-rounder Bert Nutter, to go into the Leagues and the complete loss of form of Len Wilkinson. Lionel Lister's decision to relinquish the captaincy also caused problems. His replacement, Jack Fallows, did his best but age and shortage of ability were against him.

Lancashire attempted to head off anticipated problems with a number of signings, and the promotion of players from the Second XI. In the first group, the acquisitions

Lancashire in 1948. Back row (left to right): E.H.Edrich, A.Wharton, J.T.Ikin, G.A.Edrich, M.J.Hilton. Front row: W.Place, C.Washbrook, K.Cranston (captain), R.Pollard, W.B.Roberts, T.L.Brierley.

of Phil King, Tom Brierley and Eric Edrich smacked of panic, but Geoff Edrich, who came with his brother from Norfolk, proved to be a decided success, whilst Winston Place, Jack Ikin, Alan Wharton, Bill Roberts and Eric Price, all developed within the county, did enough to inspire a cautious optimism.

The remainder of the 1940s saw many further changes in personnel. Ken Cranston, skipper in 1947 and 1948, flashed across the scene like a meteor, but most of the new players became more permanent fixtures. Throughout this period of change, one pre-war player, Cyril Washbrook, was at a most impressive peak, scoring runs with the regularity and style of a Tyldesley, and he had a sound phalanx of support from such talented run-getters as Place and Ikin.

Unfortunately, the bowling still caused problems. Len Wilkinson played no part in the post-war scene, whilst by 1949 Dick Pollard was feeling the strain of so much thundering up to the wickets. Bill Roberts did well, but lacked 'devil', whilst Eddie Phillipson soon lost his pre-war hostility.

Lancashire at The Oval in 1950. Back row (left to right): K.J.Grieves, R.Tattersall, A.Barlow, R.Berry, M.J.Hilton, J.B.Statham, T.E.Dickinson. Front row: J.T.Ikin, C.Washbrook, N.D.Howard, W.Place, G.A.Edrich.

In all the circumstances, perhaps Lancashire's slump to 11th place under the youthful Nigel Howard in 1949 did not come as a surprise. It was certainly more surprising when the following season saw Lancashire joint champions with Surrey. Howard suddenly showed big advances in both batting and leadership, whilst Australian Ken Grieves made big strides as an all-rounder who could catch just about anything.

The real advance was in the slow bowling, however. The tall Roy Tattersall, who converted to off-spin in 1949, took 163 Championships wickets (average 12.19), and the young left-armer, Malcolm Hilton, had 125 (15.04). They received admirable support from Grieves and Bob Berry, and late in the season a big impression was made by a young paceman who occasionally flung himself flat on his face in a quest for speed. Brian Statham's wickets in August were the icing on the cake, and ensured a share of the title.

For the rest of the 1950s, Lancashire, as did all counties, laboured in the knowledge that Surrey, were the best led and probably most talented side around. Their home wicket also seemed doctored to suit their own particular abilities and they won an unprecedented seven successive titles.

Malcolm Hilton (left), whose career took off when he gained 125 wickets with his slow left-arm bowling. Cyril Washbrook (right) succeeded Nigel Howard as captain in 1954.

Lancashire wasted time trying to decide who, out of Hilton and Berry, should be the side's left-armer and the indecision at the top can have helped neither bowler. The choice eventually fell on Hilton but the unsympathetic treatment meted out to both him and Tattersall probably contributed to the early demise of both players.

Statham was probably the only bowler in the 1950s who fully realized expectations but, until the arrival of Ken Higgs, the county were unable to find him an adequate opening partner. Cyril Washbrook succeeded Howard as skipper in 1954 but the batting consisted mainly of players from the 1940s, or earlier, and until the arrival of Marner and Pullar suggested better days, there was a startling lack of fresh talent in this department.

Lancashire were second once during the 1950s, and third three times, but Washbrook's paternalistic approach to leadership failed to set things alight and they can hardly be said to have made the most of the available talent.

Ken Higgs, whose arrival at last saw an adequate opening partner for Brian Statham.

If the 1950s saw the Lancashire train spend much time going nowhere, then the early 1960s saw it go off the rails. Under Bob Barber, a talented cricketer, but too young and pliable to lead a county team like Lancashire, they finished second in 1960 and 13th in 1961. In 1962, under Joe Blackledge, there was a further disastrous plunge to 16th; and in Grieves' two seasons of leadership they were 15th in 1963 and 14th in 1964.

The amount of talent stifled or wasted in this period

Bob Barber, who showed great batting ability but did not prove the right man to lead a county like Lancashire.

was horrific. Tommy Greenhough's leg-breaks flourished briefly before they faded, whilst although Pullar, Marner, Bond and Barber showed real batting ability, none was as lastingly effective as his talent decreed.

Membership disatisfaction came to a head in 1964, when

A sad moment for Lancashire cricket as Brian Statham leaves the field after his final appearance, in the 1968 Roses Match at Old Trafford when he took 6-34 to underline just how much he would be missed.

the committee resigned *en bloc*, after strict interpretations of the rules had brought accusations of gerrymandering. Elections resulted in a number of new faces and a new outlook, with a new committeeman in Cedric Rhodes, who was soon to become Chairman of the club and the mastermind behind the resurgence of Lancashire cricket.

Several experienced players left Lancashire at this time but one man, who throughout the long period of in-fighting and fratricide had remained respected by all sides and had

West Indian Clive Lloyd, a magnificent all-round cricketer who was an inspired signing for Lancashire.

retained his form to a remarkable degree, stayed at Old Trafford. In 1965, Brian Statham was appointed captain.

Although not marked with any real success, Statham's spell as skipper was a period of comparative peace and tranquility, laying the foundations so avidly built upon when Jack Bond took over in 1968. During this time, such players as Clive Lloyd, David Lloyd, Barry Wood, Harry Pilling,

Left-hander David Lloyd emerged as Lancashire proved the kings of one-day cricket. Lloyd succeeded Jack Bond as skipper in 1973.

Farokh Engineer, David Hughes and Jack Simmons arrived on the scene.

Bond led the side for five seasons, during which time Lancashire's best Championship position was third, in 1970 and again in 1971. In the same period, however, they also won the Gillette Cup three times and the John Player Sunday League twice.

David Lloyd succeeded Bond in 1973, and the 1975 season

Frank Hayes, a Lancashire batting star before injury brought a premature end to his career.

saw the Gillette Cup won for a record fourth time. But the peak had now been passed and when Lloyd resigned in 1977, another lengthy drift into mediocrity was already well underway.

Captains came and went, but only when the long-serving David Hughes, an early hero of the limited-overs triumphs with his brave hitting and tight left-arm spin, was appointed in 1987 was a recovery really in evidence. Under Hughes, Lancashire have finished second, ninth, fourth and, in 1990, sixth in the Championship.

Old Trafford in the 1970s, showing the ground packed for a big match.

John Abrahams, a stylish, gritty batsman who was captain for two years in the mid-1980s.

The Sunday League has seen successive placings of ninth, third, first and sixth, and in 1988 the Refuge Assurance Cup was won. Then, in 1990, came the winning of the Benson & Hedges Cup, followed a few weeks later by

Graeme Fowler, a valuable batsman and popular figure.

triumph in the NatWest Trophy. Lancashire had uniquely won both major limited-overs knockout competitions in the same season.

A number of young players are now fighting to make their mark, and more are needed. Outstanding is Michael Atherton, for whom the possibilities seem infinite. The 1991 season starts with Lancashire cricket again on the march.

Paul Allott, has proved a fine servant to Lancashire despite suffering niggling injuries.

With the enlightened guidance lately apparent, they should
certainly maintain a high position among the counties.
Possibly they could go much further.

ABRAHAMS, John

LHB; OB,
Born: Salt River, Cape Town, South Africa, 21
July 1952.
Education: Heywood Grammar School.
First-class debut: 1973, Lancashire v Kent,
Folkestone.
251 matches for Lancashire 1973-88. Capped
1982. Captain 1984-85. Benefit (£52,500) 1988.
HS: 201* v Warwickshire, Nuneaton, 1984.
(unbroken 6th-wicket stand of 226 with Jack
Simmons)
BB: 3-27 v Worcestershire, Old Trafford, 1981.
1,000 runs (4); 1,261 (39.40) 1983 best.

The son of South African League professional,
Cecil Abrahams, John Abrahams gave several
seasons valuable service, being somewhat
surprisingly appointed county captain for two
seasons. His captaincy fortunes were mixed,
apart from winning the Benson & Hedges Cup
in 1984 against a poorly-directed Warwickshire
side, when Abrahams was made man-of-the-
match by P.B.H.May, despite a 'duck' and no
wickets! As a batsman John Abrahams was
stylish and gritty but lacked the ability, or power,
to force his game. His gentle off-spin was often
valuable. Since leaving Lancashire, Abrahams
has played most successfully for Shropshire. His
League cricket has been for Heywood, Egerton,
Milnrow, and Radcliffe in England; he also
played for Mowbray CC (Tasmania) and
Western Creek (Canberra).

AINSCOUGH, Thomas

LHB.
Born: Parbold, Lancashire, 23 Februry 1865.
Died: Parbold, 20 November 1927, aged 62.
Education: Ampleforth.
Debut for Lancashire: 1894 v Surrey, Old Trafford.
2 matches for Lancashire 1894-1906 (amateur).
HS for Lancashire: 24 v Kent, Old Trafford, 1906.
First-class debut: 1891, Liverpool & District v
Yorkshire, Liverpool.
HS: 61 Liverpool & District v Yorkshire, 1892.
Full first-class record: 194 runs (24.25).

Tom Ainscough served as Second XI captain
and also on the County Committee but played
most of his cricket in the Liverpool area, and
club cricket for Ormskirk.

AINSWORTH, Jerry Lionel

SLA; tail-end batsman.
Born: Formby, Lancashire, 11 September 1877.
Died: Falmouth, Cornwall, 30 December 1923,
aged 46.
Education: Marlborough.
First-class debut: 1899, Lancashire v Warwick-
shire, Old Trafford.
4 matches for Lancashire 1899 as amateur.
HS: 11 v Nottinghamshire, Trent Bridge, 1899.
BB for Lancashire: 6-84 v Nottinghamshire,
Trent Bridge, 1899.
BB: 7-61 v Philadelphia, Manheim, 1898.

Jerry Ainsworth, of Liverpool, first came to
notice for his bowling feats on tour in America
in 1898 with P.F.Warner's team, but he had
shown excellent all-round form for the Marlborough XI in 1894 and 1895. After four most
successful games for Lancashire in 1899 he
decided he had no wish to play further county
cricket. His last first-class match was in the
Bombay Presidency, August 1904, for Europeans
v Parsis, when he made little impact. Jerry
Ainsworth, whose brother George played a single
first-class match in 1902, for H.D.G.Leveson
Gower's team, was well known as an owner and
breeder of racehorses and greyhounds.

ALDERSON, Ralph

RHB.
Born: Newton-le-Willows, Lancashire, 7 June
1919.
Died: Glazebury, Leigh, Lancashire, 2 April
1988, aged 68.
First-class debut: 1948, Lancashire v Oxford
University, The Parks, Oxford.
2 matches for Lancashire, 1948-49 (professional).
HS: 55 v Kent, Old Trafford, 1949, adding 120
for fourth wicket with G.Edrich.

After a war-interrupted career, Alderson was a

13 Tests for England 1981-85; HS: 52* v Australia, Old Trafford, 1981; BB: 6-61 v West Indies, Headingley, 1984. Test record: 213 runs (14.20); 4 catches; 26 wickets (41.69).
13 matches for Wellington (NZ) 1985-86 to 1986-87
Other tours: Lancashire to West Indies 1986-87; to Zimbabwe 1988-89; England to India/Sri Lanka 1981-82; 1984-85.
13 limited-overs matches for England.
Full first-class record: 3,297 runs (17.17); 129 catches; 638 wickets (25.31).

Minor Counties umpire 1964-68 and subsequently joined the Lancashire coaching staff.

ALLOTT, Paul John Walter
RHB; RFM.
Born: Altrincham, Cheshire, 14 September 1956.
Education: Altrincham Grammar School; Durham University.
First-class debut: 1978, Lancashire v Gloucestershire, Bristol.
196 matches for Lancashire, 1978-90. Capped 1981. Benefit 1990.
HS: 88 v Hampshire, Southampton, 1987.
BB: 8-48 v Northamptonshire, Northampton, 1981.
Took 75 wickets (23.88) in 1981 — still best season.

Allot joined Lancashire after playing for native Cheshire in 1976. Tall (6ft 4ins), strongly-built and enthusiastic, he suffered nagging injuries which precluded his advance to authentic Test player, but he is a good servant to Lancashire.

APPLEBY, Arthur
LHB; LFM.
Born: Enfield, near Clayton-le-Moores, Lancashire, 22 July 1843.
Died: Enfield, 24 October 1902, aged 59.

Education: Grange School, Thorpe Arch, Yorkshire.
First-class debut: 1866, Lancashire v Surrey, Liverpool.
58 matches for Lancashire 1866-87 (amateur).
HS: 99 v Yorkshire, Sheffield, 1871 (took 8-141 in match).
BB: 9-25 v Sussex, Hove, 1877.
Played 12 times for Gentlemen v Players, 1867-87.
Toured North America with R.A.Fitzgerald, 1872.
Full first-class record: 1,249 runs (11.45); 336 wickets (15.68).

Arthur Appleby bowled fastish round-arm, left-handed, and although his trade as a corn merchant and mill owner at his native place precluded his appearing in first-class cricket as often as he should, he was of great value to Lancashire for some 20 years. Appleby was a useful, free-hitting left-handed batsman — one of the unfortunates to have 99 as his best score — and until putting on weight in his 30s, he was a keen fielder with a strong throw. Appleby, who stood in as county captain on occasions, played for, and later became president of, Enfield CC.

ARNOLD, James Frederick
RHB.
Born: Withington, Manchester, 2 March 1869.
Died: Worthing, Sussex, 26 March 1944, aged 75.
First-class debut: 1896, Lancashire v Leicestershire, Liverpool.
3 matches for Lancashire 1896 (amateur).
HS: 37 v Leicestershire (debut).

ARROWSMITH, Robert
RHB; SLA.
Born: Denton, Manchester, 21 May 1952.
Education: Two Trees School, Denton.
First-class debut: 1976, Lancashire v Warwickshire, Blackpool.
43 matches for Lancashire 1976-79.

HS: 39 v Derbyshire, Chesterfield, 1979.
BB: 6-29 v Oxford University, The Parks, 1977.

After leaving the staff in 1979 he played League cricket for Milnrow and Delph, and Minor Counties for Northumberland 1983-85.

ASHWORTH, John Thomas
Batsman, sometimes opened.
Born: New Hall, Haslingden, Lancashire, 27 February 1850.
Died: Werneth, Oldham, 20 October 1901.
First-class debut: 1871, Lancashire v Kent, Old Trafford.
2 matches for Lancashire 1871, 1873 as amateur.
HS: 19 v Kent (debut).

ATHERTON, Michael Andrew
RHB; LB.
Born: Manchester, 23 March 1968.
Education: Manchester Grammar School; Downing College, Cambridge.
Debut for Lancashire: 1987 v Warwickshire, Southport.

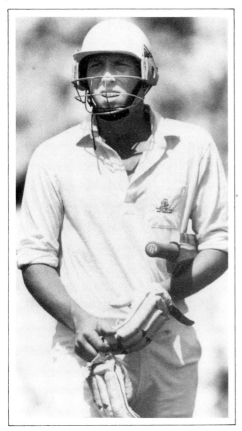

39 matches for Lancashire 1987-1990. Capped 1989.
HS: 191 v Surrey, The Oval, 1990.
BB: 6-78 v Nottinghamshire, Trent Bridge, 1990.
During best score above added 364 with Neil Fairbrother (Lancashire 3rd-wicket record).
1,000 runs (1); 1,053 (75.21) in 1990.
13 Tests for England 1989-1990-91. HS: 151 v New Zealand, Trent Bridge, 1990. Test record: 1,087 runs (45.29); 3 centuries.
First-class debut: 1987, Cambridge University v Essex, Cambridge.
Cambridge University 1987-89 (Blue each year). Captain 1988-89.
7 limited-overs matches for England.
Full first-class record: 5,677 runs (43.33). 15 centuries; 102 wickets (41.61); 29 catches.

A very sound, well-organised batsmen with an intelligent approach to all facets of his method, Atherton usually opened — with success — for England, but bats number-three for Lancashire. He also has great potential as a leg-spin bowler if given sufficient work. Thought of by many as an England and Lancashire skipper of the near future.

ATKINSON, Graham

RHB; OB.
Born: Lofthouse, near Wakefield, Yorkshire, 29 March 1938.
Debut for Lancashire: 1967 v Warwickshire, Edgbaston.
62 matches for Lancashire 1967-69. Capped 1967.
HS for Lancashire: 124 v Essex, Chelmsford, 1967.
BB for Lancashire: (and only Lancashire wicket) 1-19 v Sussex, Old Trafford, 1967.
1,000 runs for Lancashire: (1) 1,301 (3,097) 1967.
First-class debut: 1954, Somerset v Pakistanis, Taunton.
271 matches Somerset (professional) 1954-66. Capped 1958.
14,468 runs for Somerset (32.08).
HS: 190 Somerset v Glamorgan, Bath, 1960.
BB: 4-63 Somerset v Hampshire, Taunton, 1960.
1,000 runs (8) for Somerset; 2,035 (36.33) 1962 best.
Full first-class record: 17,654 runs (31.13); 27 centuries.

An opening batsman with a very sound method, his Somerset career, although statistically impressive, exhibited a progressive loss of confidence to play shots — a tendancy not halted with Lancashire. He was a League professional with Lowerhouse (1970-73) and subsequently went into Rugby League administration.

AUSTIN, Ian David

LHB; RM.
Born: Haslingden, Lancashire, 30 May 1966.
Education: Haslingden High School.
First-class debut: 1987, Lancashire v Derbyshire, Derby.
31 matches for Lancashire 1987-90.

HS: 64 v Derbyshire, Old Trafford, 1988.
BB: 5-79 v Surrey, The Oval, 1988.
Scored 61* v Combined Universities, Fenner's, 1990 B&H Cup, & 80 in same competition v Worcestershire, Worcester 1987. 4-25 v Surrey at Old Trafford 1990 B&H.

He played for Haslingden before joining Lancashire. Represented NCA (North) in 1985 Bermuda Youth Tournament.

BAILEY, David

RHB; OB.
Born: West Hartlepool, County Durham, 9 September 1944.
Education: Malvern College.
First-class debut: 1968, Lancashire v Cambridge University, Fenner's.
27 matches for Lancashire 1968-69.
HS: 136 v Kent, Old Trafford, 1969.
5 first-class matches for Minor Counties XI 1973-81. Captain 1981.
Full first-class record: 1,265 runs (28.68); 1 century.
BB: 3-67 Minor Counties v Sri Lankans, Reading, 1981.

A deep-thinking cricketer, Bailey played Minor Counties cricket for his native Durham from 1961-68, and for Cheshire 1973-83. Amongst his clubs were Accrington, Alderley Edge, Bowdon, Didsbury and Northwich. His younger brother, John Bailey, played for Durham and in first-class matches for the Minor Counties 1967-69.

BAKER, George Robert

RHB; RM.
Born: Malton, Yorkshire, 18 April 1862.
Died: Wing, Buckinghamshire, 6 February 1938, aged 75.
Debut for Lancashire: 1887 v Sussex, Old Trafford.
228 matches for Lancashire 1887-1899 (professional). Benefit (£1,850) v Yorkshire, 1898.
HS: 186 v Sussex, Hove, 1897.
BB: 6-18 v Gloucestershire, Bristol, 1896.
1,000 runs (1); 1,233 (33.32) 1897.
First-class debut: 1884, Yorkshire v Kent, Sheffield.
7 matches for Yorkshire 1884 (professional).
Full first-class record: 7,563 runs (21.48); 4 centuries; 153 catches; 145 wickets (24.93).

George Baker was a right-handed high-order batsman with a free style, a fair medium-pace

bowler and fine fielder anywhere. After playing for local Yorkshire clubs, Malton and Welham, and making 7 appearances for his native county, Yorkshire, in 1884, Baker became professional for Bury in 1885 and from 1887 played for Lancashire under the residential qualification. Although his form tended to be somewhat uneven, Baker was a great servant to his adopted county and was held in such esteem that between 1894 and 1898 he was regularly chosen for Players v Gentlemen matches.

George Baker had been a useful Rugby footballer and athlete and whilst with Lancashire he set up in business as a sports outfitter in Bury. After retiring from county cricket, Baker was coach at Harrow for 12 years and remained connected with the school even after retirement due to ill health. In later years he was groundsman and greenkeeper for Anthony de Rothschild at Leighton Buzzard.

BANHAM, Stanley Tattersall

RHB; WK.
Born: Bacup, Lancashire, 21 September 1913.
Died: Peterborough, Northamptonshire, 29 December 1984, aged 71.
First-class debut: 1939, Lancashire v West Indians, Old Trafford.
1 match Lancashire 1939 — did not bat.

Banham was a 2nd XI wicketkeeper whose only first-class appearance was marred by rain. He played League cricket for Bacup.

BARBER, Horatio William

LHB; RM.
Born: Salford, Lancashire, 27 February 1843.
Died: St Leonard's, Sussex, 27 April 1869, aged 26.
Education. Rossall: Oxford University.
First-class debut: 1866, Lancashire v Surrey, Edge Hill, Liverpool.
3 matches for Lancashire 1866-67 (amateur).
HS for Lancashire: 15 v Yorkshire, Old Trafford, 1867.
Played two first-class matches for North of England teams 1867.
HS: 20 North of England v Nottinghamshire, Trent Bridge, 1867.
Full first-class record: 69 runs (6.90).

Little is really known of this member of the Manchester Broughton CC.

BARBER, John Benjamin

Born: Stretford, Manchester, 6 February 1849.
Died: Southwark, London, 21 Februry 1908, aged 59.

Education: Winchester.
First-class debut: 1874, Lancashire v Kent, Maidstone.
3 matches for Lancashire 1874-76 (amateur).
HS: 12* v Kent (debut).

Barber later played for Mitcham CC for many years.

BARBER, Robert William

LHB; LB.
Born: Withington, Manchester, 26 September 1935.
Education: Ruthin; Magdalene College, Cambridge.
First-class debut: 1954 Lancashire v Glamorgan, Old Trafford.
155 matches for Lancashire 1954-62 (amateur).
Capped 1958. Captain 1960-61.
HS for Lancashire: 175 v Kent, Folkestone, 1961.
BB for Lancashire: 7-35 v Derbyshire, Chesterfield, 1960.
Scored 104 before lunch on third day v Nottinghamshire, Worksop, 1961.
1,000 runs (4); 1,516 (29.72) 1961 best.
124 matches for Warwickshire 1963-69. Capped 1963.
Further century before lunch: 138, Warwickshire v Australians, Edgbaston, 1964 (first day).
Performed hat-trick, Warwickshire v Glamorgan, Edgbaston, 1963.
Played for Cambridge University 1955-57; Blue 1956-57.

28 Tests for England, 1960-68. HS (& also in first-class cricket): 185 v Australia, Sydney, 1965-66. BB: 4-132 v New Zealand, Edgbaston, 1965. Test record: 1,495 runs (35.59): 1 century; 9 catches; 42 wickets (43.00).
Tours: MCC to New Zealand 1960-61; India 1961-62; South Africa 1964-65; Australia 1965-66.
Full first-class record: 17,631 runs (29.43); 17 centuries; 549 wickets (29.46).

After a brilliant record at Ruthin and a good record at Cambridge, Bob Barber was expected to assume the Lancashire leadership and remain as a back-bone of the side for many years. Unhappily, the introverted and sensitive Barber found all too much for him and after two seasons of captaincy he was dismissed in favour of Joe Blackledge. After another season, with the feelings of frustration unabated, he removed to Warwickshire and almost immediately blossomed as a brilliant, and daring opening batsman, and until business prevented regular appearances he was one of the most exciting and audacious of all cricketers. Barber was also a fine fielder with a good arm.

BARCHARD, Harry George
RHB.
Born: Crumpsall, Manchester, 25 June 1860.
Died: Seaton, Devon, 28 July 1935, aged 75.
Education: Uppingham; Oxford University.
First-class debut: 1888, Lancashire v Oxford University, Old Trafford.
1 match for Lancashire 1888 (amateur).
HS: 40 v Oxford University (debut).

BARCROFT, Peter
RHB.
Born: Sharneyford, Bacup, Lancashire, 14 August 1929.
Died: Bacup, 26 August 1977, aged 48.

First-class debut: 1956, Lancashire v Glamorgan, Old Trafford.
3 matches for Lancashire 1956 (professional).
HS: 29 v Essex, Old Trafford, 1956.

Barcroft, a batsman from Lancashire League club Bacup, won a limited trial too late in life.

BARDSLEY, Robert Vickers, CMG, OBE
RHB; LB.
Born: Prestwich, Manchester, 28 June 1890.
Died: Colwaltham, Pulborough, Sussex, 26 July 1952, aged 62.
Education: Shrewsbury School; Merton College, Oxford.
Debut for Lancashire: 1910 v Northamptonshire, Old Trafford.

7 matches for Lancashire 1910-20 (amateur).
HS for Lancashire: 15 v Warwickshire, Blackpool, 1910.
Played for Oxford University 1910-13, Blue 1911-12-13.
HS: 72 Oxford University v Cambridge University, Lord's, 1913.
BB: 3-15 Oxford University v Cambridge University, Lord's, 1912.
Played last first-class match in 1922 for Free Foresters.
Full first-class record: 964 runs (18.53); 19 catches; 12 wickets (28.66).

An outstanding all-rounder at Shrewsbury, where he captained the XI in 1907-08-09, Bardsley never quite fulfilled his promise as a first-class player, although he always played well in the University match at Lord's. A sporting all-rounder, Bardsley also played for Oxford at billiards and golf. A career diplomat, he served in the Sudan and was Governor of the Blue Nile Province from 1928 to 1932.

BARDSWELL, Gerald Roscoe
RHB; RM.
Born: Woolton, Liverpool, 7 December 1873.
Died: New Orleans, USA, 29 December 1906, aged 33.
Education: Uppingham; Oriel College, Oxford.
Debut for Lancashire: 1894 v Somerset, Old Trafford.
21 matches for Lancashire 1894-1902 (amateur).
Joint-captain 1899 with A.C.MacLaren.
HS for Lancashire: 50 v MCC, Lord's, 1899.
BB for Lancashire: 4-37 v Middlesex, Lord's, 1894.
Oxford Blue 1894-96-97 (injured 1895). Captain 1897.
HS: 97 Oxford University v Surrey, The Oval, 1897.
BB: 6-36 Oxford University v Leicestershire, Oxford, 1894.
Full first-class record: 1,585 runs (20.06); 104 catches; 63 wickets (25.68).

Gerry Bardswell first attracted note at Uppingham, where he was in the XI for five seasons, and with his bowling (right-arm medium with high action) he took more than 200 wickets. He later lost his bowling but became a useful batsman and, perhaps above all, a brilliant slip fielder. Bardswell went on tours to America, West Indies and Portugal, and also achieved a good reputation, mainly with the bat, with Formby CC. He was a member of the Lancashire and MCC committees and president of Manchester & District League at the time of his death, which came as a surprise, although he had undergone a major operation a few months previously.

BARLOW, Alfred
RHB; WK.
Born: Little Lever, Lancashire, 31 August 1915.
Died: Middleton, Lancashire, 9 May 1983, aged 67.
First-class debut: 1947, Lancashire v Cambridge University, Old Trafford.
74 matches for Lancashire 1947-51 (professional). Capped 1950.

HS: 44 v Derbyshire, Old Trafford, 1950.
55 dismissals (34 catches; 21st) in 1950, his only full season.
Toured India/Ceylon with Commonwealth XI 1950-51.

Alf Barlow, a cheerful individual who enjoyed life, was a talented wicketkeeper connected with the Middleton club, who probably missed some good years due to the war and had to compete with several other 'keepers of similar standard.

BARLOW, Edwin Alan
RHB; OB.
Born: Ashton-under-Lyne, Lancashire, 24 February 1912.
Died: Gretton, Gloucestershire, 27 June 1980, aged 68.
Education: Shrewsbury School; Brasenose College, Oxford.
Debut for Lancashire: 1932 v Nottinghamshire, Trent Bridge.

7 matches for Lancashire 1932 (amateur).
HS for Lancashire: 40 v Gloucestershire, Cheltenham, 1932.
BB for Lancashire: 4-33 v Middlesex, Old Trafford, 1932.
Oxford Blue 1932-33-34.
HS: 46 Oxford University v Leicestershire, Oxford, 1934.
BB: 6-44 Oxford University v Yorkshire, Oxford, 1932 (on first-class debut)
Full first-class record: 582 runs (13.85); 21 catches; 102 wickets (27.38).

Barlow had a very good first season in 1932, with 56 wickets (26.98) in all first-class matches, but his form then deteriorated. He also played Liverpool CC.

BARLOW, Richard Gorton

RHB; LM.
Born: Barrow Bridge, Bolton, Lancashire, 28 May 1851.
Died: Blackpool, 31 July 1919, aged 68.
First-class debut: 1871, Lancashire v Yorkshire, Sheffield.
249 matches for Lancashire 1871-91 (professional). Benefit (£1,000) v Nottinghamshire, Old Trafford, 1886.
HS: 117 v MCC, Lord's, 1885.
BB: 9-39 v Sussex, Old Trafford, 1886.
Carried bat throughout completed innings 11 times; 26/116 v Kent, Maidstone, 1874; 34/187 v Nottinghamshire, Trent Bridge, 1876; 34/99 v MCC, Lord's, 1878; 10/47 v Yorkshire, Old Trafford, 1880; 66/269 v Australians, Old Trafford, 1882; 5/69 v Nottinghamshire, Trent Bridge, 1882; 44/93 v Nottingamshire, Liverpool, 1882; 58/240 v Gloucestershire, Clifton, 1882; 62/183 v Gloucestershire, Clifton, 1885; 51/215 v Kent, Maidstone, 1889; 29/131 v Surrey, The Oval, 1890.
Reached 50 in 290 minutes during 51 v Kent, Maidstone, 1889 — slowest half-century in county cricket. Scored 5 in 150 minutes v Sussex, Old Trafford, 1876, and 5* in 150 minutes v Nottinghamshire, Trent Bridge, 1882. Also 17 in 215 minutes v Nottinghamshire, Old Trafford, 1888. In innings of 5* v Nottinghamshire, Trent Bridge, 1882, was 0* for 70 minutes; ***Match 'double': 71 and 39*; 5-27, 5-92 v Surrey, Old Trafford, 1883.
Achieved three hat-tricks for Lancashire: v Derbyshire, Old Trafford, 1879; v Derbyshire, Derby, 1881; v Nottinghamshire, Old Trafford, 1886. Also did hat-trick for Players v Gentlemen, The Oval, 1884.

17 Tests for England 1881-82 to 1886-87; HS: 62 v Australia, Sydney, 1881-82. BB: 7-40 v Australia, Sydney, 1882-83. Test record: 591 runs

(22.73); 14 catches; 34 wickets (22.55).
Three tours, England to Australia, 1881-82, 1882-83, 1886-87.
Full first-class record: 11,217 runs (20.61); 4 centuries; 268 catches; 951 wickets (14.50).

Dick Barlow was one of Lancashire's greatest personalities and most dedicated of cricketers. He was a remarkably steady right-handed batsman who, with A.N.Hornby, formed an opening partnership celebrated in lore and fable. He was also a medium-paced left-handed round-arm bowler and a good fielder at all times, but especially to his own bowling. He played for Bolton when he was 12, and was subsequently professional with Farsley, and then Saltaire. After he retired from cricket he became an umpire, serving on the first-class list from 1895 until 1914, and umpiring one Test match in 1899. Barlow was much more than a cricketer; he lived cricket completely, much to the detriment of his marriage. His house was a shrine to the game and a special stained-glass window owned by Barlow, featuring himself, A.N.Hornby and Dick Pilling is now at Old Trafford. Although he left school at 14, Barlow was a talented and inventive man. He was a sports outfitter, first in Manchester and then Blackpool, and he designed wicket-covers, an air-tight valve, and a laceless football. At soccer, Barlow played in goal for Lancashire and Northern representative teams, and later, as a referee, he took charge when Preston North End beat Hyde United 26-0 in the 1887 FA Cup competition. Finally, he was a real fitness buff - a teetotaller and non-smoker.

BARNES, John Reginald

RHB; LB.

Born: Aughton, Ormskirk, Lancashire, 18 May 1897.

Died: Grange-over-Sands, Lancashire, 22 July 1945, aged 48.

Education: Marlborough.

First-class debut: 1919, Lancashire v Nottinghamshire, Trent Bridge.

89 matches for Lancashire 1919-30 (amateur).

HS for Lancashire: 123* v Middlesex, Lord's, 1922.

HS: 133 MCC v Cambridge University, Lord's, 1929.

Full first-class record: 3,643 runs (29.86) 40 catches; 4 centuries.

Jack Barnes had an excellent all-round record at Marlborough, whom he skippered in 1915, but although his county record was reasonable he never played regularly enough to make the most of his free-driving style. In 1925 the county tried to persuade Barnes to succeed Jack Sharp as captain but his work as a cotton merchant in Liverpool took precedence, although he did lead the side occasionally. Barnes enjoyed great success in club cricket, for Ormskirk and latterly Liverpool. Unusually, Barnes served in both world wars; he won the MC with the Royal Flying Corps in World War One, and from 1941 until ill-health in 1944 forced his demobilisation he was on the RAF groundstaff.

BARNES, Sydney Francis

RHB; RFM or RM.

Born: Smethwick, Staffordshire, 19 April 1873.

Died: Chadsmoor, Staffordshire, 26 December 1967, aged 94.

Debut for Lancashire: 1899 v Sussex, Hove.

46 matches for Lancashire 1899-1903 (professional).

HS for Lancashire: 35 v Essex, Old Trafford, 1903.

BB for Lancashire: 8-37 v Essex, Leyton, 1903

(14-70 in match). Also match figures 14-59 v Derbyshire, Derby, 1903.

100 wickets (1); 131 (17.85) 1903.

27 Tests for England 1901-02 to 1913-14. HS: 38* v Australia, Melbourne, 1907-08. BB: 9-103 v South Africa, Johannesburg, 1913-14 (17-159 in match, best Test Match figures until beaten by J.C.Laker in 1956). Took 49 wickets (10.93) in rubber v South Africa 1913-14 (and missed Fifth Test), still the record for a series. Took 34 wickets (22-88) in rubber v Australia 1911-12, a series record until beaten by M.W.Tate in 1924-25. Test record: 242 runs (8.06); 12 catches; 189 wickets (16.43).

First-class debut: 1894, Warwickshire v Gloucestershire, Clifton College.

4 matches for Warwickshire 1894-96 (professional). Played for Wales 1927-30
HS: 93, MCC v Western Australia, Perth, 1907-08.
BB: 9-103 in Test above.
Full first-class record: 1,573 runs (12.78); 72 catches; 719 wickets (17.09).

Syd Barnes, an aloof, independent character, spent only two full seasons with Lancashire before deciding, after a serious dispute with the county, that he preferred League and Minor Counties cricket. Playing for Staffordshire from 1904-34 (with gaps), Barnes took 1,441 wickets (8.15), whilst in League cricket he took 4,069 wickets (6.03). Barnes' first club cricket was for Smethwick; from 1895-96 he played for Rishton, and then appeared for Church and Burnley. From 1906 to 1914 he was with Porthill Park and 1915 to 1923 saw him with Saltaire in the Bradford League. He later spent time with Castleton Moor and signed his last professional contract in 1938, aged 65.
  Syd Barnes is regarded as one of the greatest of all bowlers. A fast bowler with an occasional slower break-back in his youth, at his peak he was fast-medium, with pace variations, and absolute control over length, flight and direction. His best ball was a fast leg-break, pitching leg and snapping away to the edge or off stump. Over 6ft tall, he had a high action which enabled him to extract life from the deadest wickets. Barnes, who lived to 94 and worked as writer of legal documents for Staffordshire County Council almost up to his death, became a legend in his own lifetime. In 1949 he was an original Honorary Member of MCC, and in 1965 a Syndey Barnes Cricket Society was formed in Staffordshire.

BARRELL, Ben

All-rounder.
Born: Orford, Suffolk, 14 May 1885.
Died: Bootle, Lancashire, 14 July 1969, aged 84.
First-class debut: 1911, Lancashire v All-India, Old Trafford.
3 matches for Lancashire 1911-23 (professional).
HS: 25 v Essex, Old Trafford, 1923.
BB: 3-10 v All-India (debut).

Ben Barrell was a stalwart of the Huyton Cricket Club for many years.

BARRON, William

LHB; occasional WK.
Born: Herrington, County Durham, 26 October 1917.

First-class debut: 1945, Lancashire v Yorkshire, Bradford.
1 match for Lancashire 1945 (professional).
Scored 2 and 1 in only match.
118 matches for Northamptonshire 1946-51. Capped 1946.
HS: 161* Northamptonshire v Cambridge University, Fenner's, 1948.
1,000 runs (2) for Northamptonshire; 1,123 (26.11) 1946 best.
Full first-class record: 4,772 runs (25.51); 6 centuries; 5 wickets (40.00); 98 catches; 1 stumped.

Bill Barron, who played for Durham County 1937-45, and then enjoyed a useful career with Northamptonshire, scored 64 for Lancashire v Yorkshire in a two-day game in 1945 but failed in his only first-class game, when a weakness on off-stump was exploited by Bowes and Ellis Robinson. He played club cricket for Philadelphia and, latterly, British Timken (Northampton). A good soccer player, Barron played for amateur giants Bishop Auckland, and professionally for Wolves and Northampton Town.

BAUCHER, Frederick William

RHB; WK.
Born: Wigan, Lancashire, 6 November 1878.
Died: Blundellsands, Lancashire, 7 June 1947, aged 68.
First-class debut: 1903, Lancashire v Sussex, Old Trafford.
One match for Lancashire as amateur 1903.
HS: 8 v Sussex (debut).

Baucher also played for Bootle CC.

BAXTER, Arthur Douglas

RHB; RFM.
Born: Oxford Terrace, Edinburgh, Scotland, 20 January 1910.
Died: Edenbridge, Kent, 28 January 1986, aged 76.
Education: Loretto
Debut for Lancashire: 1933 v West Indians, Old Trafford.
3 matches for Lancashire 1933-34 as amateur-
Did not score in only innings.
BB for Lancashire: 6-50 v West Indians (debut)
First-class debut: 1929, Scotland v Ireland, Dublin.
Played for Middlesex in 1938, and for Scotland from 1929-37.
HS: 26* Scotland v South Americans, Edinbugh, 1932
BB: 7-33 H.D.G.Leveson Gower's XI v Oxford Univesity, Reigate, 1935 (match figures 13-72 best).
Tours: Australia & New Zealand with MCC under E.R.T.Holmes 1935-36.

Full first-class record: 273 runs (7.18); 10 catches; 189 wickets (21.74).

'Sandy' Baxter was a pacy practitioner of fast inswing and occasionally produced a devastating fast 'leg-break'. Baxter, who first played first-class cricket for his native Scotland, was never able to appear regularly, otherwise he may well have reached the top (or batsmen may have fathomed him out!). His action, when he appeared to bowl off the wrong foot, was not conducive to a long career, whilst he was an indifferent batsman and poor fielder. In 1930, Baxter played for Devon.

BEATTIE, Fred Demetrius
RHB.
Born: Manchester, 18 August 1909.
Died: Bangor, North Wales, 20 March 1989, aged 79.
Education: Rossall.
Debut for Lancashire: 1932 v Derbyshire, Buxton.
5 matches for Lancashire 1932 (amateur).
HS: 36 v Sussex, Hove, 1932.
First-class debut: 1930, Minor Counties v Lancashire, Old Trafford.
Also represented Minor Counties v Oxford University, 1933.
Full first-class record: 172 runs (17.20).

Beattie, who was President of Lancashire CCC 1975-76, also played for Sale CC.

BEDDOW, Alan Michael
RHB; RM.
Born: St Helens, Lancashire, 12 October 1941.

Education: Cowley Grammar School, St Helens.
First-class debut: 1962, Lancashire v Sussex, Old Trafford.
33 matches for Lancashire 1962-66 (professional).
HS: 112* v Oxford University, The Parks, 1965.
BB: 3-10 v Derbyshire, Southport, 1965.

Beddow played for Blackhall CC as a professional and was also a Rugby League player for St Helens.

BENNETT, Albert
RHB; LB.
Born: St Helens, Lancashire, 21 May 1910.
Debut for Lancashire: 1932 v Glamorgan, Blackburn.
16 matches for Lancashire 1932-33 (professional).
HS: 51 v Glamorgan, Swansea, 1933.

BB: 4-49 v Leicestershire, Leicester, 1933.
Full first-class record: 254 runs (16.93); 12 catches; 24 wickets (37.75).
He played once for New South Wales 1930-31, then came to Lancashire on birth qualification and also played for St Helens Recs before returning to Sydney.

BENNETT, Henry Simpson

RHB; WK.
Born: Bakewell, Derbyshire, 3 September 1869.
Died: Chapel-en-le-Frith, Derbyshire, 18 February 1965, aged 96.
First-class debut: 1894, Lancashire v Derbyshire, Old Trafford.
1 match for Lancashire 1894 (professional).
HS: 11 v Derbyshire (debut).

Bennett replaced Richard Thomas for one match in 1894 'the season of the four wicketkeepers'.

BENNETT, Robert

RHB.
Born: Bacup, Lancashire, 16 June 1940.
Education: Rossall.
First-class debut: 1962, Lancashire v Pakistanis, Old Trafford.

49 matches for Lancashire 1962-66. Capped 1963.
HS: 112 v Nottinghamshire, Trent Bridge, 1962.

Robert Bennett, who also played for Bacup, is currently Chairman of Lancashire CCC.

BENTON, Charles Henry

RHB.
Born: Glossop, Derbyshire, 8 January 1868.
Died: Knutsford, Cheshire, 19 May 1918, aged 50.
Education: Harrow.
First-class debut: 1892, Lancashire v Oxford University, Old Trafford.
29 matches for Lancashire 1892-1901 (amateur).

HS: 68 v Oxford University, Old Trafford, 1893.

C.H.Benton also played for Cheshire, and for Gentlemen of Cheshire v Ludlow in 1899 he scored 297. A civil engineer, he served on the MCC committee and died by his own hand.

BERRY, Robert

LHB; SLA.
Born: West Gorton, Manchester, 29 January 1926.
First-class debut: 1948, Lancashire v Kent, Old Trafford.
93 appearances for Lancashire 1948-54 (professional). Capped 1950.
HS for Lancashire: 27* v Gloucestershire, Cheltenham, 1953.
BB: 10-102 v Worcestershire, Blackpool, 1953. (Match figures of 14-125; same match figures v Somerset, Old Trafford, 1953).
98 wickets (18.97) in 1953.
Played 94 matches for Worcestershire 1955-58. Capped 1957; 54 matches for Derbyshire 1959-62. Capped 1961. First player to be capped by three counties.
HS: 40 Derbyshire v Nottinghamshire, Ilkeston, 1960.

Two Tests for England v West Indies 1950. Took 5-63 and 4-53 in 1st Test, Old Trafford. Test record: 6 runs (3.00); 2 catches; 9 wickets (25.33). Full first-class record: 1,463 runs (7.58); 138 catches; 703 wickets (24.73).

Toured Australia/New Zealand with MCC 1950-51; India with Commonwealth XI 1953-54.

The diminutive Bob Berry was a delightful character and excellent left-arm slow bowler relying on flight and variation rather than spin. He was unfortunate at having to compete with Bill Roberts and, especially, Malcolm Hilton before he moved to Worcestershire and finally Derbyshire. A promising Test debut was not built upon and a bleak tour of Australia in 1950-51 sealed his fate as a Test player. He was a good outfielder with a strong throw. A prominent pigeon fancier, he subsequently became a licensee. Berry's club cricket was with Longsight CC.

BIDDOLPH, George Henry

RHB; RMF.
Born: Manchester, 28 March 1858.
Died: Melbourne, Victoria, Australia, 21 April 1937, aged 59.
First-class debut: 1885, Lancashire v Derbyshire, Old Trafford.
1 match for Lancashire 1885 (amateur).
HS: 18 (debut).

BIGG, George Ashburner

Born: Barrow-in-Furness, Lancashire, 24 July 1861.
Died: Barrow-in-Furness, 27 October 1931, aged 70.
First-class debut: 1887, Lancashire v Derbyshire, Old Trafford.
1 match for Lancashire 1887 (amateur).
HS: 16 in only innings.
BB: 1-13 in only bowl.

An amateur from Ulverston CC, Bigg was described as 'a small man who wore glasses'.

BIRD, George

RHB
Born: Crouch Hall, Hornsey, 30 July 1849.
Died: Esher, Surrey, 28 October 1930, aged 81.
Education: Highgate.
Debut for Lancashire: 1880 v Nottinghamshire, Trent Bridge.
1 match for Lancashire 1880 (amateur).
Scored no runs.
First-class debut: 1872, Middlesex v Surrey, Princes.
13 matches for Middlesex 1872-77 (amateur).
HS: 75 MCC v Kent, Canterbury, 1875.

Full first-class record: 477 runs (14.45).

George Bird was a batsman of graceful style who scored runs aplenty in cricket just below first-class standard. He posessed of a very long throw. George Bird's son was M.C.Bird (Lancashire); another son, A.C.Bird, played for MCC.

BIRD, Morice Carlos

RHB; RM.
Born: St Michael's Hamlet, Liverpool, 25 March 1888.
Died: Broadstone, Dorset, 9 December 1933, aged 45.
Education: Harrow.
First-class debut: 1907, Lancashire v Essex, Leyton.

5 matches for Lancashire 1907 (amateur).
HS for Lancashire: 10 v Middlesex, Old Trafford, 1907.
BB for Lancashire: 2-9 v Derbyshire, Old Trafford, 1907.
Played 127 matches for Surrey 1909-21 (amateur). Captain 1911-13.

Toured South Africa with MCC 1909-10 and 1913-14. Also Argentina 1911-12.

10 Tests for England 1909-10 to 1913-14. HS: 61 v South Africa, Durban, 1913-14. BB: 3-11 v South Africa, Johannesburg, 1909-10. Full Test record: 280 runs (18.66); 5 catches; 8 wickets (15.00).

HS: 200 MCC v Orange Free State, Blomfontein, 1913-14.

BB: 5-48 Surrey v All-India, The Oval, 1911 (10-98 match figures).

Full first-class record: 6,938 runs (23.76); 7 centuries; 112 catches; 149 wickets (25.68).

Morice Bird first made his name when scoring 100* and 131 for Harrow v Eton at Lord's in 1907, the only such feat in the series of matches. A tall, forcing batsman, he never really fulfilled the promise he showed at school, but gave good service for Surrey until World War One. He subsequently became a coach, at Harrow and The Oval. His father, George Bird, also played for Lancashire.

BIRLEY, Francis Hornby.

RHB; RA (spinner).
Born: Chorlton, Manchester, 14 March 1850.
Died: Dormans Land, Surrey, 1 August 1910, aged 60.
Education: Winchester; University College, Oxford.
First-class debut: 1870, Lancashire v Hampshire, Old Trafford.
4 matches for Lancashire 1870-72 (amateur).
HS: 18 v Hampshire, Southampton, 1870.
BB: 3-76 v Hampshire, Old Trafford, 1870.
1 match for Surrey 1879.

An excellent soccer player, Birley appeared for Oxford University in the 1874 FA Cup Final, and for Wanderers when they won the Cup 1876-77. He was also capped twice for England at soccer.

BIRTWELL, Alexander Joseph

RHB; LB.
Born: Burnley, Lancashire, 17 December 1908.
Died: Nelson, Lancashire, 20 November 1974, aged 65.
First-class debut: 1937, Lancashire v Worcestershire, Liverpool.
14 matches for Lancashire 1937-39 (amateur).
HS: 31 v Kent, Old Trafford, 1937.
BB: 4-78 v Essex, Clacton, 1937.

A Burnley solicitor, Birtwell played for many years in the Lancashire League, for Nelson, Colne, Burnley and Lowerhouse.

BLACKLEDGE, Joseph Frederick

RHB.
Born: Chorley, 15 April 1928.
Education: Repton.
First-class debut: 1962, Lancashire v Glamorgan, Cardiff.
26 matches for Lancashire 1962 (amateur).
Captain 1962.
HS: 68 v Glamorgan (debut).

Blackledge, with no first-class experience, was recruited from club cricket with Chorley to succeed Bob Barber as skipper. Lancashire finished in 16th position, Blackledge became overwhelmed after a promising start with the bat and resigned after a single season.

BLACKSTOCK, Richard

RHB; RF (round-arm); occasional WK.
Born: Oxton, Cheshire, 13 July 1838.
Died: Oxton, 3 February 1893, aged 54.
Debut for Lancashire: 1865 v Middlesex, Old Trafford.
1 match for Lancashire 1865 (amateur).
HS for Lancashire: 18 v Middlesex (debut).
First-class debut: 1858, Gentlemen of North v Gentlemen of South, The Oval.
HS: 47 North v Surrey, The Oval, 1863.
BB: 1-11 Lancashire v Middlesex (debut).

Blackstock was a stalwart of Birkenhead Park CC.

BLAKE, Wilfred

RHB; RM (round-arm).
Born: Embsay, Skipton, Yorkshire, 29 November 1853.
First-class debut: 1877, Lancashire v Yorkshire, Huddersfield.
1 match for Lancashire 1877 (professional).
HS: 26 in only innings.
2 matches for Yorkshire 1880 (professional).

A round-arm bowler and good fielder as well as a sound batsman, Wilf Blake was a well-known professional, engaged variously with Keighley, Bacup, Lockwood, Lowerhouse and Burnley. It has been impossible to trace his death.

BLEACKLEY, Edward Overall

Born: Salford, Lancashire, 10 March 1898.
Died: Ealing, 17 February 1976, aged 77.
Education: Harrow.
Debut for Lancashire: 1919 v Derbyshire, Chesterfield.
2 matches for Lancashire 1919 (amateur).
HS: 21 v Derbyshire (debut).
First-class debut: MCC v Oxford University, Oxford 1919.
Full first-class record: 31 runs (6.20).

Bleackley did well for Harrow. He subsequently entered the Army, reaching rank of major.

BLOMLEY, Benjamin

RHB; WK.
Born: Chadderton, Lancashire, 10 June 1879.
Died: Chadderton, 12 March 1949, aged 69.
First-class debut: 1903, Lancashire v Warwickshire, Old Trafford.
69 matches for Lancashire 1903-23 (professional).
HS: 41 v Nottinghamshire, Trent Bridge, 1921

(added 72 in 50 minutes for 10th wicket with Fred Taylor).

A solid character who gave many years faithful service, Blomley was an authentic No.11 batsman who took his art very seriously. In 1922 he received a grant of £500 in lieu of a benefit.

BODDINGTON, Robert Alan

RHB; WK.
Born: Kersal, Manchester, 30 June 1892.
Died: Fifield, Oxford, 5 August 1977, aged 85.
Education: Rugby; Trinity College, Oxford.
First-class debut: 1913, Lancashire v Worcestershire, Old Trafford.
52 matches for Lancashire 1913-24 (amateur).
HS for Lancashire: 58* v Surrey, The Oval, 1913.
Oxford (No Blue) 1914.
HS: 69, Oxford University v Kent, Oxford, 1914.
Full first-class record: 801 runs (12.51); 76 caught, 21 stumped.

A good wicketkeeper, unlucky not to win his

Blue at Oxford, Boddington was on the Lancashire committee for many years. His son, Myles Boddington, played first-class cricket for the RAF in 1946.

BODEN, Reginald George

Batsman.
Born: Ashby-de-la-Zouch, Leicestershire, 13 September 1884.
Died: Bowness-on-Windermere, 11 February 1966, aged 77.
First-class debut: 1907, Lancashire v Cambridge University, Cambridge.
One match for Lancashire 1907 (professional).
HS: 5 (debut).

Little is known about this player.

BOLTON, Alan

RHB; OB.
Born: Darwen, Lancashire, 1 July 1939.

First-class debut: 1957, Lancashire v Cambridge University, Liverpool, 1957.
40 matches for Lancashire 1957-61 (professional).
HS: 96 v Leicestershire, Leicester, 1959.

A neat batsman who should perhaps have expected more opportunities, Bolton returned to Darwen CC after 1961 and faded from the cricket scene.

BOND, John David

RHB; occasional LB.
Born: Kearsley, Lancashire, 6 May 1932.
Education: Bolton School.
First-class debut: 1955, Lancashire v Surrey, Old Trafford.
344 matches for Lancashire 1955-72 (originally as professional). Capped 1961. Benefit (£7,400) 1970. Captain 1968-72.
HS: 157 v Hampshire, Old Trafford, 1962.
1,000 runs (2); 2,112 (37.05) 1962 best.
17 matches for Nottinghamshire (as captain-player-coach) 1974.

A somewhat surprising appointment as captain on Brian Statham's retirement, Jackie Bond was an outstanding success, especially in limited-overs cricket. During his reign, Lancashire were Sunday League champions twice, won the Gillette Cup three times, and finished third in the Championship twice. After a season as Lancashire coach, he spent an unhappy season in 1974 as Notts player-manager. After a spell coaching schoolboys, Bond was Lancashire's manager from 1980-86 and since 1988 has been a first-class umpire. As a batsman Bond showed promise as a schoolboy with his native club, Kearsley, and then moved to Radcliffe. His batting never quite recovered from the broken wrist he received from West Indian paceman Wes Hall in 1963; during the previous two seasons he had at last blossomed as a busy stroke maker and prolific scorer after a lengthy apprenticeship. Bond was also a fine fielder away from the bat.

BOOTH, Arthur

RHB.
Born: Droylsden, Lancashire, 8 January 1926.
First-class debut: 1950, Lancashire v Nottinghamshire, Liverpool.
4 matches for Lancashire 1950-51 (professional).
HS: 49 v Hampshire, Liverpool, 1951.

He made his mark by scoring 253 against Lincolnshire at Grimsby in the 1950 Minor Counties competition, but was never given a run in the first team and his form faded in 1951. He played for Haslingden, Ashton and Werneth in the local Leagues.

BOOTH, Brian Joseph

RHB; LBG.
Born: Blackburn, 3 October 1935.

First-class debut: 1956, Lancashire v Scotland, Paisley.
117 matches for Lancashire 1956-63 (professional). Capped 1961.
HS: 183* v Oxford University, Old Trafford, 1961.
BB: 7-143 v Worcestershire, Southport, 1959.
1,000 runs (2); 1,642 (30.98) 1961 best.
232 matches for Leicestershire 1964-73. Capped 1964. Testimonial 1973.
1,000 runs (6) for Leicestershire.
Full first-class record: 15,298 runs (27.91); 18 centuries; 135 catches; 146 wickets (32.03).

Useful all-rounder unlucky in the period, Booth was with the county. He subsequently enjoyed fair success with Leicestershire.

BOOTH, Frank Stanley

RHB; RFM.
Born: Cheetham Hill, Manchester, 12 February 1907.
Died: Shoreham-by-Sea, Sussex, 21 January 1980, aged 72.

First-class debut: 1927, Lancashire v Derbyshire, Old Trafford.
140 matches for Lancashire 1927-37 (professional).

HS: 54 v Essex, Blackpool, 1930.
BB: 7-59 v Gloucestershire, Gloucester, 1935.
100 wickets (1); 101 (23.46) 1934.

A tall, well built man, he appeared irregularly for Lancashire until 1933 and injuries caused curtailment of career. He also played for East Lancashire in the Lancashire League.

BOUSFIELD, Edwin James

RHB; occasional WK.
Born: Chorlton, Manchester, 21 May 1838
Died: Torquay, Devon, 8 January 1895, aged 56.
Debut for Lancashire: 1865 v Middlesex, Old Trafford.
12 matches for Lancashire 1865-78.
HS: 32 v Sussex, Hove, 1869.
First-class debut: Gentlemen of North, 1860.
Full first-class record: 321 runs (12.84).

Bousfield played club cricket in Manchester.

BOWDEN, Ernest

Batsman (late-order); RFM.
Born: Lancaster, 13 June 1892.
Died: Slyne, Lancashire, 14 October 1972, aged 80.
First-class debut: 1914, Lancashire v Northamptonshire, Northampton.
4 matches for Lancashire 1914 (amateur).
HS: 10 v Northamptonshire (debut).
BB: 6-78 v Essex, Old Trafford, 1914.

An amateur pace bowler with the Littleborough club.

BOWER, William Henry

RHB; WK.
Born: Bradford, Yorkshire, 17 October 1857.
Died: Nelson, Lancashire, 31 January 1943, aged 85.
Lancashire debut: 1885 v Yorkshire, Huddersfield.
4 matches for Lancashire 1885-86 (professional).
HS: 23 v Yorkshire, Huddersfield 1885.
First-class debut: 1883, Yorkshire v Nottinghamshire, Sheffield.
1 match for Yorkshire 1883.

A slightly-built but hard-hitting batsman, he once hit a delivery from W.G.Grace through the tennis-court window at Lord's.

BOWES, John Barton

RHB; RMF.
Born: Stretford, Manchester, 2 January 1918.
Died: Manchester, 22 May 1969, aged 51.

First-class debut: 1938, Lancashire v Northamptonshire, Northampton.
10 matches for Lancashire (professional) 1938-48.
HS: 39 v Northamptonshire (debut).
BB: 4-103 v South Africans, Old Trafford, 1947.

A 6ft 4†ins-tall paceman whose career was cruelly interrupted by war. He was a professional for Colne before the war and after retirement became an umpire (1955-57, 1960-63 in the Minor Counties; 1958-59 first-class). He subsequently took employment outside cricket.

BOWLING, Kenneth

RHB.
Born: Fulwood, near Preston, Lancashire, 10 November 1931.
First-class debut: 1954, Lancashire v Derbyshire, Old Trafford.

1 match for Lancashire 1954 (professional).
HS: 4* (debut).

A nephew of Jack Iddon, Bowling played at various times for Leyland Motors and Honley.

BOWMAN, Richard

RHB; RF.
Born: Cleveleys, Lancashire, 26 January 1934.

Education: Fettes & University College, Oxford.
Lancashire debut: 1957 v West Indians, Old Trafford.
9 matches for Lancashire 1957-59 (amateur).
HS for Lancashire: 58 v Oxford University, The Parks, 1959.
BB for Lancashire: 2-28 v Sussex, Worthing, 1957.
First-class debut: 1955, Oxford University v Lancashire, Oxford.
Played for Oxford University 1955-57 (Blue 1957).
HS: 75, Oxford University v Essex, Westcliffe, 1957.
BB: 7-60 v Oxford University in same match above.
Full first-class record: 454 runs (16.21); 51 wickets (37.29).

A talented if somewhat impulsive cricketer, Dick Bowman was in the running for the county captaincy after the dismissal of Bob Barber. Bowman was a Free Forester and also played for Whalley CC.

BOYES, Richard

RHB; WK.
Born: Burnley, Lancashire, 17 June 1849.
Died: Burnley, 4 January 1896, aged 46.
First-class debut: 1877, Lancashire v MCC, Lord's.
1 match for Lancashire 1877 (professional).
HS: 10 (debut).

Boyes played as a professional for Colne and Sefton. He worked as a hatter in Burnley and died there when a chimney fell on him.

BRADBURY, Thomas Farrell

Born: Barton-on-Irwell, Lancashire, 1856.
Died: Cadishead, Lancashire, 26 April 1934.
First-class debut: 1881, Lancashire v Surrey, The Oval.
1 match for Lancashire (amateur) 1881.
HS: 6* (debut).

Little is known of this amateur who batted last and failed to bowl in his only match. He was a Surrey colt who played only when H.C.R.John failed to appear.

BRADDOCK J

Opening Batsman.
First-class debut: 1873, Lancashire v Derbyshire, Derby.
1 match for Lancashire 1873 (professional).
HS: 11 (debut).

Nothing is known of this player other than that he was a professional at Sefton CC when he played for Lancashire.

BRAMHALL, Stephen

RHB; WK.
Born: Warrington, Lancashire, 26 November 1967.
First-class debut: 1990, Lancashire v Northamptonshire, Northampton.
2 matches for Lancashire 1990.
HS: 1* v Sri Lankans, Old Trafford, 1990.
Bramhall plays for Cheshire in the Minor Counties Championship.

BREARLEY, Walter

RHB; RF.
Born: Bolton, Lancashire, 11 March 1876.
Died: Marylebone, London, 13 January 1937, aged 60.
Education: Tideswell Grammar School, Derbyshire.
First-class debut: 1902, Lancashire v Sussex, Hove.

106 matches for Lancashire 1902-11 (amateur).
HS: 38 v Northamptonshire, Old Trafford, 1908.
BB: 9-47 v Somerset, Old Trafford, 1905 (took 17-137 in the match, the first instance of 17 wickets in match for Lancashire). Also 9-80 v Yorkshire, Old Trafford, 1909.
Four wickets in four balls v Somerset, Old Trafford, 1905 (see BB above).

100 wickets (3); 154 (15.46) 1908 best.
Four Tests for England 1905-12 HS: 11* v Australia, The Oval, 1905. BB: 5-110 in same Test match. Test record: 21 runs (7.00); 17 wickets (21.11).
Full first-class record: 907 runs (5.88); 844 wickets (19.31); 52 catches.

Walter Brearley was a heftily-built amateur who generated great pace from a short run and showed very great stamina despite allegedly training on tankards of ale. A volatile character, he had frequent disputes with the Lancashire authorities, resulting in his being left out of the side in 1902, 1906 and 1907. He played for Farnworth Parish Church and Farnworth Village, then Bolton, Bury and Manchester. In 1912 he joined Cheshire and made his final Test appearance when connected with that county. He lived in London in later life and often coached at Lord's.

BRIERLEY, Thomas Leslie

RHB; WK.
Born: Southampton, 15 June 1910.
Died: Vancouver, Canada, 7 June 1989, aged 78.
Education: Stretford Grammar School.
Debut for Lancashire: 1946 v Cambridge University, Cambridge.

46 matches for Lancashire 1946-48 (professional). Capped 1946.
HS: 116* v Glamorgan, Liverpool, 1947.
Lancashire assistant coach 1948.
181 matches for Glamorgan 1931-39 (professional). Capped.
1,000 runs (1); 1,183 (23.66) for Glamorgan, 1938.
Full first-class record: 6,244 runs (18.97); 215 catches; 91 stumped.
Coach to Vancouver CC 1949-51; British Colombia 1952; later groundsman at Shawnigan Lake CC.
5 matches for Canada 1951-54. Toured England with Canadian XI 1954.
This much-travelled and most interesting personality, who joined Lancashire on a residential qualification, was too late to make maximum impact.

BRIGGS, Jack

RHB; SLA.
Born: Haslingden, Lancashire, 8 April 1916.
Died: Rawtenstal, Lancashire, 1 June 1984, aged 68.
First-class debut: 1939, Lancashire v Leicestershire, Leicester.

4 matches for Lancashire 1939 (professional).
HS: 0* in only two innings.
BB: 4-48 v Derbyshire, Old Trafford, 1939.

Briggs remained on staff after the war before becoming professional with Haslingden.

BRIGGS, John (Johnnie)

RHB; SLA.
Born: Sutton-in-Ashfield, Notts, 3 October 1862.
Died: Cheadle, Cheshire, 11 January 1902, aged 39.
First-class debut: 1879, Lancashire v Nottinghamshire, Trent Bridge.
391 matches for Lancashire 1879-1900 (professional). Benefit (£1,000) 1894.
HS: 186 v Surrey, Liverpool, 1885.
BB: 10-55 v Worcestershire, Old Trafford, 1900.
Also had figures of 9-29 v Derbyshire, Derby, 1885; and 9-88 v Sussex, Old Trafford, 1888.
100 wickets (11); 155 (16.51) 1897 best.
Took 166 wickets (15.89) in all matches 1893 and 165 (19.71) in 1896.
Three times achieved match double for Lancashire: 129* & 5-25, 5-16 v Sussex, Old Trafford, 1890; 115 & 8-113, 5-96 v Yorkshire, Old Trafford, 1892; 112 & 5-51, 6-64 v Surrey, The Oval, 1893; Bowled 630 deliveries in match v Sussex, Old Trafford, 1897 (county record).
33 Tests for England 1884-85 to 1899; HS: 121 v Australia, Melbourne, 1884-85. BB: 8-11 v South Africa, Cape Town, 1888-89 (match figures of 15-28, most wickets in a day in a Test). Hat-trick v Australia, Sydney, 1891-92. First Test bowler to take 100 wickets (in 25th Test v Australia, Sydney, 1894-95). Test record: 815 runs (18.11); 1 century; 12 catches; 118 wickets (17.74).
Undertook record six Test tours to Australia: 1884-85, 1886-87, 1887-88, 1891-92, 1894-95, 1897-98. Also toured South Africa 1888-89.
Full first-class record: 14,092 runs (18.27); 10 centuries; 259 catches; 2,221 wickets (15.95).

'Johnnie' or 'Boy' Briggs remains one of the best loved of all Lancashire's cricketers. He was seemingly an easy-going, ever-smiling little man, who rarely took life or himself seriously; he also loved cricket and his enthusiasm was infectious both amongst the other players and in relation to the spectators. Standing about 5ft 5ins tall, for some time he was regarded almost wholly as a batsman, free-hitting with a slashing off-drive, and a brilliant cover point. But he soon became a wonderful slow-medium left-arm bowler, with an easy action, plenty of spin and, in his early years, a well-concealed quicker ball. Briggs, who lived in Lancashire most of his life, incredibly had his first professional engagement

Johnnie Briggs

for Hornsea in 1876, aged 13. He then went on to Northern CC (Liverpool) and in 1880 began a long association with Manchester CC.

The details of Briggs' ultimate demise are tragic. During the Headingley Test against Australia in 1899, Briggs suffered an (epileptic) fit during the evening of the first day and was taken to Cheadle Asylum, where he was detained several months. He returned to the county side most successfully in 1900 but his illness recurred in March 1901 and he was returned to Cheadle where he died.

Johnnie Briggs' father was a League professional, whilst his brother Joe played for Nottinghamshire. His nephew, Jim Briggs of Leamington Spa, was a collector of cricketana connected with Johnnie Briggs; his collection was lost after his death in about 1970.

BROCKLEBANK, Sir John Montague (Baronet)

RHB; LB.
Born: Hoylake, 3 September 1915.
Died: Rabat, Malta, 13 September 1974, aged 59.
Education: Eton; Magdalene College, Cambridge.

Lancashire debut: 1939 v Yorkshire, Headingley.
4 matches for Lancashire 1939 (amateur).
HS for Lancashire: 4 v Yorkshire (debut).
BB for Lancashire: 3-61 v Nottinghamshire, Trent Bridge, 1939.
First-class debut: 1936, Cambridge University v Indians, Cambridge.
Played for Cambridge University 1936 (Blue); Free Foresters 1947-49; Bengal 1947-48.
HS: 23 Cambridge University v Somerset, Taunton, 1936.
BB: 6-92 (10-139 match) Cambridge University v Oxford University, Lord's, 1936.
Full first-class record: 112 runs (9.33); 7 catches; 68 wickets (29.38).

Sir John Brocklebank may well have been a top-class bowler had opportunities presented themselves, but it was not to be, the only tour for which he was chosen, MCC to India in 1939-40, being cancelled owing to war. He subsequently became a successful businessman, being chairman of Cunard 1959-65. His brother, T.A.L.Brocklebank played for Cambridge University, whilst his uncle was Sir Stanley Jackson of Yorkshire and England. He played for Liverpool CC.

BROOKE, Francis Ralph Russell

RHB; WK.
Born: Bowdon, Cheshire, 2 October 1884.
Died: Greywell, Basingstoke, Hampshire, 20 June 1960, aged 75.
Education: Harrow.
Lancashire debut: 1912 v Sussex, Old Trafford.
29 matches for Lancashire 1912-13 (amateur).
HS for Lancashire: 61 v Sussex, Old Trafford, 1912.
HS: 115 Europeans v Parsis, Poona, 1911-12.
Played for The Army 1919-29; also played for Europeans in India, 1910-11 to 1926-27; and for Ceylon XI 1925-26 and 1926-27.
Full first-class record: 2,197 runs (25.54); 2 centuries; 85 catches, 21 stumped.

A fine wicketkeeper, Brooke was unable to play much for Lancashire due to service as Regular Army officer.

BROOKS, Abraham Worthington

WK.
Born: Swannington, Lancashire, 7 October 1853.
Died: Breighmer Fold, Bolton, Lancashire, 7 May 1925, aged 71.
First-class debut: 1877, Lancashire v Yorkshire, Huddersfield.
1 match for Lancashire 1877 (professional).
HS: 6 (debut).

Brooks was a little-known deputy wicketkeeper.

BROUGHTON, John Jarvis

RHB.

Born: Grantham, Lincolnshire, 8 September 1873.
Died: Orrell, Lancashire, 3 April 1952, aged 78.
First-class debut: 1901, Lancashire v South Africans, Old Trafford.
6 matches for Lancashire 1901-02 (professional).
HS: 99 v Essex, Leyton, 1901 (in second match).

Broughton made a promising start with 26 and 2-28 on his debut, and 99 in his second match, but he then faded away, leaving after 1902 to sign professional for Burnley.

BROWN, William

RHB; LM.
Born: Brierley Hill, Staffordshire, 13 June 1866.
Died: details unknown.
First-class debut: 1894, Lancashire v Kent, Old Trafford.
2 matches for Lancashire 1894 (professional).
HS: 7 v Sussex, Old Trafford, 1894.

Brown was a professional who played in Minor Counties cricket for Staffordshire and League cricket for Bacup.

BROWN, William

Batsman; MF.
Born: 1892.
First-class debut: 1919, Lancashire v Sussex, Hastings.

10 matches for Lancashire 1919-22 (professional).
HS: 39 v Northamptonshire, Old Trafford, 1919.
BB: 4-22 v Kent, Gravesend, 1919.

An all-rounder who was a useful batsman and medium-fast bowler, Brown left Lancashire after 1922 and signed for Haslingden. He also played for Littleborough.

BULCOCK, Leslie

RHB; RM/OB.
Born: Colne, Lancashire, 5 January 1913.
Education: Park School, Colne.
First-class debut: 1946, Lancashire v Sussex, Old Trafford.
1 match for Lancashire 1946 (professional).
HS: 1 (debut).
BB: 2-41 (debut).

An experienced League player with spells at Baildon Green, Bingley, Colne, Egerton, Heywood, Walkden and Windhill.

BULLOUGH, John

RHB; RA (Spin).
Born: Bolton, Lancashire, 1893.
Died: Westhoughton, Lancashire, 3 June 1967, aged 74.
First-class debut: 1914, Lancashire v Nottinghamshire, Trent Bridge.
8 matches for Lancashire 1914-19 (professional).
HS: 17 v Middlesex, Old Trafford, 1914.
BB: 5-123 (including hat-trick) v Derbyshire, Derby, 1914.

Jack Bullough of Bolton had trials for Lancashire either side of World War One. He later played for Harwich, Atherton, Leyland Motors and West Houghton.

BURROWS, William

RM (round-arm).
Born: Preston, Lancashire, 31 December 1844.
Died: details not known.
First-class debut: 1867, Lancashire v Surrey, The Oval.
14 matches for Lancashire 1867-73 (professional).
HS: 39 v Sussex, Hove, 1869.

Burrows, a good batsman, round-arm bowler and good fielder behind the wickets, was a hay and straw dealer in Blackburn.

BURTON, Clifford

RHB; RFM.

Born: Moston, Manchester, 15 June 1931.
Died: Oldham, Lancashire, 20 May 1978, aged 46.
First-class debut: 1956, Lancashire v Worcestershire, Dudley.
2 matches for Lancashire 1956 (professional).
Failed to score or take a wicket.
Amateur League player with Werneth and Royton, later professional for Kendal.

BUTTERWORTH, Henry Rhodes Whittle

RHB; LB.
Born: Rochdale, Lancashire, 4 February 1909.
Died: Hollingworth Lake, Littleborough, Lancashire, 9 October 1958, aged 49.
Education: Rydal; Jesus College, Cambridge.
Lancashire debut: 1931 v Warwickshire, Old Trafford.
25 matches for Lancashire 1931-36 (amateur).
HS: 107 v Sussex, Old Trafford, 1932.
BB for Lancashire: 6-85 v All-India, Old Trafford, 1932.
First-class debut: 1929, Cambridge University v Sussex, Cambridge.
Cambridge Blue 1929.
During his best score above he added 278 with Jack Iddon, still the 6th-wicket record for Lancashire. He also played for Littleborough CC.

BUTTERWORTH, Wilfred Selkirk

RHB; WK.
Born: Rochdale, Lancashire, 11 October 1855.
Died: Rochdale, 9 April 1908, aged 52.
Education: Lancing.
First-class debut: 1876, Lancashire v Nottinghamshire, Trent Bridge.
9 matches for Lancashire 1876-82.
HS: 22 v Derbyshire, Old Trafford, 1878.
Butterworth, who played for the Rochdale club, went to Texas shortly after making his last appearance for Lancashire and he is thought to have stayed there for many years.

CAMPBELL, George Augustus

Batsman (middle-order).
Born: Tunbridge Wells, Kent, 7 July 1847.
Died: Brackley, Northamptonshire, 12 September 1930, aged 83.
Education: Wellington School.
First-class debut: 1866, Lancashire v Surrey, Liverpool.
1 match for Lancashire 1866 (amateur).
HS: 10 (debut).
A little-known amateur whose son-in-law, H.F.J.Eaton, played for Cambridge University in 1885.

CARLISLE, Frederick

Batsman (middle-order).
Born: Liverpool, 4 November 1849.
Died: Pevensey, Sussex, 22 October 1920, aged 70.
Education: Harrow.
First-class debut: 1869, Lancashire v Surrey, The Oval.
2 matches for Lancashire 1869 (amateur).
HS: 18 v Surrey (debut).

Carlisle also played for Cheshire.

CHADWICK, Edmund Leach

RHB.
Born: Rochdale, Lancashire, 31 August 1847.
Died: Parkstone, Dorset, 6 August 1918, aged 70.
Education: Marlborough; Bruce Castle, Tottenham.
First-class debut: 1875, Lancashire v MCC, Lord's.
13 matches for Lancashire 1875-81.
HS: 42 v Nottinghamshire, Old Trafford, 1877.
He played for Castleton CC, scoring 213 for them against Rusholme in 1877. Cousin of H., J., R., R.G. and W.E.Leach.

CHADWICK, Mark Robert

RHB; RM.
Born: Milnrow, Rochdale, Lancashire, 9 February 1963.

Education: Roch Valley High School, Milnrow.
First-class debut: 1983, Lancashire v Essex, Old Trafford.
33 matches for Lancashire 1983-87.
HS: 132 v Somerset, Old Trafford, 1985.
Toured West Indies with Lancashire 1986-87.

CHAMPION, Albert

LHB: RMF (round-arm).
Born: Hollins End, Handforth, Yorkshire, 27 December 1851.
Died: Wortley, Sheffield, 30 June 1909, aged 57.
Lancashire debut: v Nottinghamshire, Trent Bridge, 1886.
1 match for Lancashire 1886 (professional).
HS for Lancashire: 4.
First-class debut: 1876, Yorkshire v Surrey, Sheffield.
14 matches for Yorkshire 1876-79.
HS: 29 Yorkshire v Middlesex, Sheffield, 1876.

When he played for Lancashire his clubs included Western CC, Manchester, Batley and Longsight.

CHAPPELL, Ian Michael

RHB; LB.
Born: Unley, South Australia, 26 September 1943.
Education: Prince Alfred College, Adelaide.
Lancashire debut: 1963 v Cambridge University, Old Trafford.
1 match for Lancashire 1963 (professional).
HS: 3 (only innings).
First-class debut: South Australia v Victoria, Adelaide, 1961-62, scoring 59 (highest of match for his side).
109 appearances for South Australia, 1961-62 to 1979-80. Captain 1970-71 to 1979-80.
75 Test matches for Australia 1964-65 to 1979-80. Captain 30 times. HS: 196 v Pakistan, Adelaide, 1972-73. BB: 2-21 v West Indies, Brisbane, 1968-69. Test record: 5,345 runs (42.42); 14 centuries; 105 catches; 20 wickets (65.80).
HS: 209 Australians v Barbados, Bridgetown, 1972-73.
Full first-class record: 448 innings; 19,680 runs (48.35); 59 centuries; 312 catches; 1 stumping; 176 wickets (37.57).

This extraordinary personality, whose grandfather Vic Richardson, and brothers Greg and Trevor Chappell all played for Australia, was a combative right-handed batsman, very competitive and attractive even when patently out-of-touch, and an occasional leg-spinner. Above all he was a determined, successful captain prepared to go to the limits of the game's rules and spirit; a shrewd pragmatist and fierce supporter of his players. Not surprisingly he was

a strong supporter of players' rights in the Kerry Packer era; also, it is no surprise that as a cricket broadcaster he invariably gets the better of that most hard-headed of pundits, Geoff Boycott.

Chappell made his single Lancashire appearance whilst professional for Ramsbottom; it is perhaps a pity that a county career — or specifically, a county captaincy career (for any county) never materialised. That would surely have been truly memorable.

CLARKE, J

Batsman; Bowler.
First-class debut: 1905, Lancashire v England XI, Blackpool.
1 match for Lancashire 1905 (professional).
0 in only innings.

Nothing else is known of this player.

CLAYTON, Geoffrey

RHB; WK.
Born: Mossley, Lancashire, 3 February 1938.
Lancashire debut: 1959 v Yorkshire, Middlesbrough, (friendly match).

183 matches for Lancashire 1959-64 (professional). Capped 1960.

HS for Lancashire: 84 v Sussex, Hove, 1963.

Set Lancashire record of nine dismissals (8 ct, 1st) in match, v Gloucestershire, Gloucester, 1959; equalled by Chris Maynard in 1982, beaten by Warren Hegg in 1989.

92 dismissals in 1962 beaten in season only by George Duckworth (97 in 1928).

First-class debut: for Combined Services 1957.

89 matches Somerset 1965-67. Capped 1965.

HS: 106 Somerset v Middlesex, Taunton, 1965.

Full first-class record: 6,154 runs (17.63); 603 catches; 65 stumpings.

Clayton, an abrasive and often contrary character, standing only 5ft 5ins, was dismissed by his county after the 1964 season because he was felt to be a disruptive influence. Lancashire cricket soon began its long upward surge with Jack Bond, so perhaps the county officials were correct, yet who could say what effect Bond, and a successful, positive team would have had on Clayton. Certainly he was a fine wicketkeeper who, at his best and with his mind on the job,

missed little. Early in his career he appeared to have the credentials, and ability, to do a decent opening batting job, although he never found consistency. Moving to Somerset, he showed glimpses of his best and worst, and dismissal from the staff after not missing a match in 1967, set the somehow appropriate seal on his career.

COCKBAIN, Ian

RHB; SLA.

Born: Bootle, Lancashire, 19 April 1958.

Education: Bootle Grammar School.

First-class debut: 1979, Lancashire v Leicestershire, Old Trafford.

46 matches for Lancashire 1979-83.

HS: 98 v Warwickshire, Southport, 1982.

Ian Cockbain, who plays for his local club, Bootle, has played with great distinction for Cheshire since 1984.

COLE, Terence George Owen

RHB; SLA.

Born: Llanrhaiadr, Denbighshire, 14 November 1877.

Died: Stoke Court, Taunton, Somerset, 15 December 1944, aged 67.

Education: Harrow; Trinity Hall, Cambridge.

Lancashire debut: 1904 v Leicestershire, Leicester.

1 match for Lancashire 1904 (amateur).
Scored 0 in only innings.
First-class debut: 1898, Cambridge University v
C.I.Thornton's XI, Cambridge.
Played for Cambridge University 1898, Derby-
shire 1913 and Somerset 1922.
Toured West Indies with Lord Brackley's team
1904-05.
HS: 68 Brackleys XI v Jamaica, Kingston,
1904-05.

Cole showed great promise as a slow left-arm
bowler at Harrow, but the art soon left him and
he became a useful batsman instead. A much
travelled amateur, Cole played for Denbighshire
in 1905 as well as three first-class counties. Cole
played most successfully for Liverpool and after
World War One is found appearing for Somerset
Stragglers. In 1899 he scored 252 for Trinity Hall
v St John's College at Cambridge, adding 346
in 2½ hours for the first wicket with
W.P.Robertson.

COLLINS, Roy
RHB; OB.
Born: Clayton, Manchester, 10 March 1934.
First-class debut: 1954, Lancashire v Hampshire,
Portsmouth.

119 matches for Lancashire 1954-62 (profes-
sional). Capped 1961.
HS: 107*v Somerset, Bath, 1961.
BB: 6-63 v Sussex, Old Trafford, 1961.

Roy Collins, whose wife's sister married Jim
Cumbes, was a strongly built and talented all-
rounder who never seemed to make the most
of his abilities as an aggressive batsman and
useful off-spinner. He was unfortunate that his
spell with Lancashire coincided with some pretty
dire on and off-field happenings; perhaps these
affected him more than was apparent. As late
as 1961, Collins scored 858 runs (26.00) and took
52 wickets (29.73) and even in his last season he
had flashes of inspiration, hitting 25 sixes in the
season, including seven in an innings of 69
against Hampshire at Southampton.

Roy Collins played for Cheshire until 1970,
and enjoyed a varied League career with Leek,
Longsight, Lowerhouse and Rochdale, but his
seemingly pre-ordained niche as hard-hitting,
off-spinning all-rounder was never filled by him.

COOK, Lawrence Whalley
RHB; RMF.
Born: Preston, Lancashire, 28 March 1885.
Died: Wigan, Lancashire, 2 December 1933, aged
48.

First-class debut: 1907, Lancashire v Yorkshire, Old Trafford.

203 matches for Lancashire 1907-23 (professional). Benefit (£1,657) 1923.

HS: 54* v Middlesex, Old Trafford, 1921.

BB: 8-39 v Northamptonshire, Northampton, 1911.

100 wickets (3); 150 (14.96) 1920 best. Dismissed Wilfred Rhodes with first ball in first-class cricket.

Achieved innings analysis of 7-8 in 14 overs v Derbyshire, Chesterfield, 1920.

'Lol' Cook, a steady bowler — sometimes more — gave yeoman service interrupted by war before leaving after 1923 and becoming professional with Rawtenstall. Brother William also played for Lancashire.

COOK, William

RHB; RFM.

Born: Preston, Lancashire, 16 January 1882.

Died: Burnley, Lancashire, 18 December 1947, aged 65.

First-class debut: 1905 Lancashire v Gloucestershire, Old Trafford.

11 matches for Lancashire 1905-07 (professional).

HS: 46 v Derbyshire, Old Trafford, 1905.

BB: 7-64 v Gloucestershire, Old Trafford, 1905. (Match figures of 11-118 on first-class debut).

Billy Cook made a marvellous start to his county career but soon disappeared from the Lancashire side, preferring a career in the Leagues. Over a long period of time he appeared with distinction in the Lancashire League for Burnley, Lowerhouse, Enfield and Colne. Billy Cook was also a good soccer player, appearing for Preston North End and Oldham Athletic, although his winter career was effectively ended by an injury sustained whilst playing for the Football League in 1919. He was something of a controversial character, too, once being suspended for 12 months by the FA for refusing to leave the field after being sent-off. Lol Cook was his better known cricketing brother.

COOKE, Noel Henry

RHB; OB.

Born: West Derby, Liverpool, 5 January 1935.

Education: Liverpool College.

First-class debut: 1958, Lancashire v Nottinghamshire, Old Trafford.

12 matches for Lancashire 1958-59 (professional).

HS: 33 v Combined Services, Old Trafford, 1958.

BB: 2-10 v Gloucestershire, Blackpool, 1958.

Noel Cooke, who played for Cheshire in 1962 and 1963, played club cricket, mainly in the Liverpool area, for Eagley, Neston, Hightown and Sefton. He was a fine hockey player who appeared for Lancashire.

COOPER, Fred

RHB.

Born: Bacup, Lancashire, 18 April 1921.

Died: Stourbridge, Worcestershire, 22 December 1986.

First-class debut: 1946, Lancashire v Oxford University, Oxford.

4 matches for Lancashire 1946 (professional).

HS for Lancashire: 33* v Leicestershire, Blackpool, 1946.

40 matches for Worcestershire 1947-50.

HS: 113* v Nottinghamshire, Trent Bridge, 1948.

Fred Cooper was a talented batsman whose career was probably adversely affected by some very bad war experiences. He joined his brother, and fellow Lancastrian, Edwin Cooper, at Worcestershire but although showing signs of quality he finally gave up the unequal struggle. Fred Cooper's League cricket was played for Old Hill and Kidderminster, and he also appeared for Scarborough. In later years he was a successful businessman and as a local politician in the Conservative persuasion he became Mayor of Stourbridge.

COPELAND, William

LHB; LM.

Born: Trimdon, County Durham, 10 June 1856.

Died: South Shields, County Durham, 28 January 1917, aged 60.

First-class debut: 1885, Lancashire v Yorkshire, Huddersfield.

1 match for Lancashire 1885 (professional).

HS: 21* (debut).

BB: 1-23 (debut).

Copeland spent most of his career in his native County Durham, for whom he played successfully from 1882-94. He was professional for Sunderland, Durham City, Durham University, Seaham Harbour and South Shields.

CORLETT, Samuel

RHB; RM (round-arm).

Born: Withington Village, Lancashire, 8 May 1852.

Died: Rusholme, Manchester, 2 January 1921, aged 68.

First-class debut: 1871, Lancashire v Kent, Gravesend.

2 matches for Lancashire 1871-75.
HS: 4 (debut).
Did not bowl.

A local professional, Sam Corlett had a number of engagements. In the early 1870s he was engaged at Oxford, and latterly was with Rusholme CC and Birch CC.

COULTHURST, Josiah

LFM.
Born: Blackburn, Lancashire, 24 December 1893.
Died: Lytham, Lancashire, 6 January 1970, aged 76.
First-class debut: 1919, Lancashire v Northamptonshire, Old Trafford.
1 match for Lancashire 1919 (amateur).
Did not bat or bowl.

Coulthurst played in the Lancashire League for East Lancashire, for whom he took 101 wickets (9.78) in 1919, still a record for the club for an amateur. Later he appeared for Whalley CC. Bad weather prevented him either batting or bowling in his only first-class match.

COWARD, Cornelius

RHB; RMF.
Born: Preston, Lancashire, 27 January 1838.
Died: Preston, 15 July 1903, aged 65.
First-class debut: 1865, Lancashire v Middlesex, Islington.
36 matches for Lancashire 1865-76 (professional). Benefit 1878.
HS: 85 v Middlesex, Old Trafford, 1866.
Appeared in other first-class matches, for teams such as The North, and The Players.
Full first-class record: 1,210 runs (14.93); 12 catches.

Slightly-built Cornelius Coward was a stylish-looking batsman with good off-side strokes who never scored the runs of which he was capable. In his best score of 85 above he scored his runs out of 133, being last out after going in at 48-6. Coward had professional engagements at two Catholic establishments, Stonyhurst College and Clongowes Wood College in Ireland. Given benefits in 1878 and 1879, he was a first-class umpire after his retirement. Brother Frederick also played Lancashire.

COWARD, Frederick

RHB; RM (round-arm).
Born: Preston, Lancashire, 11 February 1842.
Died: Broadgate, Preston, 15 December 1905, aged 63.
First-class debut: 1867, Lancashire v MCC, Lord's.

7 matches for Lancashire 1867-68 (professional).
HS: 9 v Surrey, Old Trafford, 1867.

Like his brother, Cornelius, he played for Lancashire and had a professional engagement at Stonyhurst College. He was also a publican at Preston.

COWNLEY, John Michael.

LHB; LBG.
Born: Wales, near Sheffield, Yorkshire, 24 February 1929.
Education: Woodhouse Grammar School, Sheffield; Sheffield University.
First-class debut: 1962, Lancashire v Pakistanis, Old Trafford.
2 matches for Lancashire 1962 (amateur).
HS: 25 v Warwickshire, Southport, 1962.
BB: 2-36 v Pakistanis, Old Trafford, 1962.
2 games for Yorkshire 1952 (amateur).
Full first-class record: 64 runs (12.80); 3 wickets (51.66).

Michael Cownley, who represented the Universities Athletics Union in 1950, played for Cheshire in 1961 and whose clubs included Sheffield United and British Ropes, was a talented cricketer but lacked discipline, in that he seemed inclined to hit every ball into the next county!

CRABTREE, Frederick

RHB; WK.
Born: Baildon, Shipley, Yorkshire, 10 March 1867.
Died: Nelson, Lancashire, 28 November 1893, aged 26.
First-class debut: 1890, Lancashire v MCC, Lord's.
1 match for Lancashire 1890 (professional).
HS: 1 (only innings).

Fred Crabtree, who played two non-first-class matches for Yorkshire in 1893, had professional engagements with Todmorden, Saltaire and Nelson. He was with Nelson when he died from an ulceration of the stomach, said to have been caused by a blow, or blows, at cricket.

CRABTREE, Herbert

RHB; RM.
Born: Colne, Lancashire, 25 May 1880.
Died: Colne, 2 March 1951, aged 70.
First-class debut: 1902, Lancashire v Worcestershire, Worcester.
5 matches for Lancashire 1902-08 (professional).
HS: 49 v Gloucestershire, Old Trafford, 1902.

Herbert Crabtree was a tall, hard-driving

batsman and fine slip fielder who was a stalwart for Colne for many years, and for Walsden.

CRAGG, James Stanley

RHB.
Born: Stockport, Cheshire, 18 October 1886.
Died: Manchester, 27 July 1979, aged 92.
First-class debut: 1908, Lancashire v Worcestershire, Worcester.
1 match for Lancashire 1908 (amateur).
HS: 9 (debut).
Cragg, who also played for Stockport CC, was President of Lancashire from 1966 to 1968. His grandson, J.R.A.Cragg, played for Cambridge University in 1970.

CRAIG, Edward John

RHB.
Born: Formby, Lancashire, 26 March 1942.
Education: Charterhouse; Trinity College, Cambridge.
Debut for Lancashire: 1961 v Nottinghamshire, Worksop.
6 matches for Lancashire 1961-2 (amateur).
HS for Lancashire: 89 v Nottinghamshire (debut).

First-class debut: 1961, Cambridge University v Sussex, Cambridge.
Cambridge Blue 1961-62-63.

HS: 208* Cambridge University v L.C.Stevens' XI, Eastbourne, 1961. (in under five hours with 32 4s).
In 1961 (debut season) scored 1,528 runs (42.44), third-highest in debut season after H.Sutcliffe (1,839 in 1919) and F.A.Lowson (1,799 in 1949). Full first-class record: 3,103 runs (36.08); 7 centuries; 43 catches.

Eddie Craig was a man of remarkable intellect who reportedly spent the time between deliveries at Cambridge discussing moral philosophy from slip with his wicketkeeper, Mike Brearley.

CRAIG, Walter Reid

RHB.
Born: Radcliffe Bridge, Pilkington, Lancashire, 29 December 1846.
Died: Hangleton, Sussex, 6 July 1923, aged 76.
Education: Shrewsbury.
First-class debut: 1874, Lancashire v Derbyshire, Old Trafford.
1 match for Lancashire 1874.
HS: 7 (debut).

Craig was a batsman from Longsight CC.

CRANSTON, Kenneth

RHB; RMF.
Born: Aigburth, Liverpool, 20 October 1917.

Ken Cranston

Education: Liverpool College.
First-class debut: 1947, Lancashire v Oxford University, The Parks.
50 matches for Lancashire 1947-48 (amateur).
Capped 1947. Captain 1947-48.
HS for Lancashire: 155* v Hampshire, Bournemouth, 1947.
BB: 7-43 (10-82 in match) v Surrey, The Oval, 1948.
In his only two seasons as Lancashire player, had outstanding all-round figures: 1947 — 989 runs (41.21); 69 wickets (21.33); 1948 — 936 runs (39.12); 73 wickets (24.58).
Appeared in Scarborough Festival until 1950, making best first-class score 156*, MCC v Yorkshire, Scarborough 1949.
8 Tests for England 1947-48, one as deputy captain v West Indies 1947-48. HS: 45 v South Africa, The Oval, 1947; BB: 4-12 v South Africa, Headingley, 1947, when he took all four wickets in one over. Test record: 209 runs (14.64); 18 wickets (25.61).
Full first-class record: 3,099 runs (34.82); 3 centuries; 47 catches; 178 wickets (28.00).
Ken Cranston made a name for himself in wartime cricket for the Royal Navy and Combined Services but was made Lancashire skipper in 1947 without first-class experience. He was an immediate success in every respect and was chosen for England against South Africa within two months of his Championship debut. After two fine seasons he resigned to resume his practice as a dentist in Liverpool and, although he continued to play club cricket for Neston, a fine natural talent was lost to the first-class game. Ken Cranston was still in dental practice in his 73rd year in 1990.

CRAWLEY, John Paul

RHB.
Born: Maldon, Essex, 21 September 1971.
Education: Manchester Grammar School.
First-class debut: 1990, Lancashire v Zimbabwe.
3 matches for Lancashire 1990.
HS: 76* v Zimbabwe (debut).
John Crawley, the brother of Mark, skippered England Under-19s on their tour to New Zealand in 1991.

CRAWLEY, Mark Andrew

RHB; RM.
Born: Newton-le-Willows, Lancashire, 16 December 1967.
Educated: Manchester Grammar School; Oriel College, Oxford.
First-class debut: 1990, Lancashire v Sri Lankans, Old Trafford.
1 match for for Lancashire 1990.
HS for Lancashire: 48 (debut).
Oxford Blue 1987-88-89-90. Captain 1989.

HS: 140 Oxford University v Cambridge University, Lord's, 1987.
BB: 6-92 Oxford University v Glamorgan, The Parks, 1990 (scored 103* in only innings).
Full first-class record: 1,331 runs (42.93); 17 catches; 27 wickets (58.14).

Crawley, who is also an Oxford soccer Blue, is an outstanding cricket prospect who was lost to Lancashire cricket when he joined Nottinghamshire in 1991. He is the brother of John Crawley.

CROFT, Colin Everton Hunte

RHB; RF.
Born: Lancaster Village, Demerera, British Guiana, 15 March 1953.
Debut for Lancashire: 1977 v Gloucestershire, Old Trafford.
49 matches for Lancashire 1977-82.
HS: 46* v Worcestershire, Worcester, 1977.
BB for Lancashire: 7-54 v Nottinghamshire, Trent Bridge, 1977.
27 Tests for West Indies 1976-77 to 1981-82. HS: 33 v England, Bridgetown, 1980-81. BB: (and best first-class) 8-29 v Pakistan, Port-of-Spain, 1976-77. 33 wickets (20.48) in series v Pakistan 1976-77.
First-class debut: 1971-2, Guyana v Jamaica, Kingston.
West Indies domestic cricket for Guyana 1971-72 to 1981-82.
Toured South Africa with West Indies XIs 1982-83, 1983-84, resulting in ban from Test and West Indian cricket. Kerry Packer cricket 1977-78 and 1978-79.

Full first-class record: 865 runs (10.54); 428 wickets (24.59).

Colin Croft came to Lancashire with a fearsome reputation, but for various reasons — a back injury and perhaps a lack of commitment — he was a big disappointment. Croft had an

unusual chest-on action and, with his faster ball, a suspicion of something 'unusual' in his delivery. He was never 'called', however, and generally caused little comment in this respect. After a troubled period in South Africa, Croft eventually went to the USA.

CROOKE, Frederick James
RHB; RF.
Born: Liverpool, 21 April 1844.
Died: Southsea, Hampshire, 6 August 1923, aged 79.
Education: Winchester.
First-class debut: 1865, Lancashire v Middlesex, Old Trafford.
1 match for Lancashire 1865 (amateur), scoring 35 & 20.
Played Gloucestershire 1874-75.
HS: 56* MCC v Cambridge University, Cambridge, 1874.
Full first-class record: 573 runs (16.85); 10 catches.

He spent many years as a merchant in Calcutta, and captained Calcutta CC, playing for Gloucestershire whilst on leave. In Lancashire he played for Liverpool CC.

CROSFIELD, Sydney Morland
RHB; RA (originally fast, later slow).
Born: Warrington, Lancashire, 12 November 1861.
Died: Las Palmas, Canary Islands, 30 January 1908, aged 46.
Education: Wimbledon School.
First-class debut: 1883, Lancashire v Oxford University, Oxford.
90 matches for Lancashire 1883-99 (amateur).
Joint captain with A.C.MacLaren 1892-93.
HS: 82* v Yorkshire, Bradford, 1891.
Full first-class record: 2,027 runs (14.90); 49 catches.

No more than useful with the bat, and one whose original fast bowling had been modified to slow before disappearing, he was, however, an excellent captain and good judge of the game. He played for Cheshire and in 1887 scored 126 for them against Nottinghamshire Gentlemen at Trent Bridge. Crosfield was also an excellent shot, winning the Grand Prix de Casino at Monte Carlo two years in succession. By profession he was a solicitor.

CROSSLAND, John
RHB; RF.
Born: Sutton-in-Ashfield, Nottinghamshire, 2 April 1852.

Died: Blackburn, Lancashire, 26 September 1903, aged 51.

First-class debut: 1878, Lancashire v Yorkshire, Huddersfield.

71 matches for Lancashire 1878-85 (professional).

HS for Lancashire: 48* v Surrey, Old Trafford, 1882.

BB for Lancashire: 7-14 v Surrey, The Oval, 1881 (11-79 in the match). Achieved hat-trick v Surrey, The Oval, 1881, during best bowling above. Took 97 wickets (av.9.96) 1882.

HS: 51 Barlow's XI v Emmett's XI, Batley, 1883.

BB: 8-57 North v South, Tunbridge Wells, 1883. Match figures of 14-80, North v South, Lord's, 1884.

Full first-class record: 1,172 runs (10.95); 32 catches; 322 wickets (12.48).

Crossland was a hard hitting tail-ender and good fielder with very long throw, but he was most famous as a very fast bowler. Unhappily, his action was regarded in some circles — not all based in southern England — as 'a pure throw'. After 1885 he dropped out of the Lancashire side after MCC decided he was not qualified by residence. Possibly it was all a ruse to solve the problem of his dubious action. Crossland was engaged by Enfield CC in 1876 and stayed there until moving to Manchester CC 1881. Out of season, and after retirement, he worked down the pit at Clayton-le-Moors.

CUDWORTH, Henry

RHB.

Born: Burnley, Lancashire, 6 December 1873.
Died: Burnley, 5 April 1914, aged 40.
First-class debut: 1900, Lancashire v Essex, Leyton.
1 match for Lancashire 1900 (amateur).
HS: 4 v Essex (debut, only innings).
Scored 102 on Lancashire debut in non-first-class match against West Indians, Old Trafford, 1900.

A stalwart of Burnley CC, Harry Cudworth's fine innings against West Indies in 1900 suggested untapped potential.

CUMBES, James

RHB; RFM.

Born: East Didsbury, Manchester, 4 May 1944.
Education: Didsbury Technical High School.

First-class debut: 1963, Lancashire v Worcestershire, Worcester.
9 matches for Lancashire in two spells: 1963-67; 1971.
HS for Lancashire: 5 v Essex, Liverpool, 1971.
BB for Lancashire: 4-42 v Kent, Blackpool, 1966.
29 matches for Surrey 1968-69; 109 matches Worcester 1972-81. Capped 1978; 14 matches Warwickshire 1982.
HS: 43, Worcestershire v Sussex, Hove, 1980.
BB: 6-24 Worcestershire v Yorkshire, Worcester, 1977.
Full first-class record: 499 runs (7.56); 38 catches; 379 wickets (30.20).

Jim Cumbes, one of county cricket's greatest travellers, was possessed of a friendly, easy-going attitude and ready wit which made him one of the game's most popular players and helped him become a successful broadcaster on Midlands local radio. Cumbes, who was an accomplished goalkeeper with Tranmere Rovers, West Bromwich Albion and Aston Villa, joined Warwickshire as player and commercial manager in 1982, but illness curtailed his playing days. After six years at Edgbaston, Cumbes returned to Lancashire as marketing manager — a position he retains in 1991.

CUTTELL, Willis Robert

RHB; LB.
Born: Sheffield, Yorkshire, 13 September 1864.
Died: Nelson, Lancashire, 9 December 1929, aged 65.
First-class debut: 1896, Lancashire v Yorkshire, Old Trafford.
213 matches for Lancashire 1896-1906 (professional).
Joint benefit (£657) 1903 with Charles Smith.
HS: 137 v Nottinghamshire, Old Trafford 1899.
BB: 8-105 v Gloucestershire, Old Trafford 1895.
100 wickets (4); 112 (17.25) 1897 best.
2 Tests for England 1898-99; HS: 21 v South Africa, Johannesburg 1898-99. BB: 3-17 same match. Test record: 65 runs (16.25); 2 catches; 6 wickets (12.16).
Achieved 'double' in all first-class matches 1898; 1,003 runs (25.71); 114 wickets (21.21).
Full first-class record: 5,938 runs (20.90); 5 centuries; 140 catches; 792 wickets (19.59).

After two non-first-class games for Yorkshire in 1890 — the county for which his father, William Cuttell played — Willis Cuttell joined Lancashire when over 30 and enjoyed a fine career. He had professional engagements with Bankers CC, Sheffield, Worksop and Accrington before joining Nelson in 1892. In 1894 he became an amateur with Nelson and worked as a warp dresser. In later years Cuttell was a tobacconist

in Nelson and coached at Rugby school during the summer. Cuttell usually kept an accurate length and direction while able to mix off and leg-breaks without any obvious changes in action. He had plenty of spin, although he usually lacked the flight of many of his contemporaries. He was described as a batsman with a sound defence and a fielder who could stop anything.

DAVIDSON, Ian Charles

RHB; OB.
Born: Roe Green, Worsley, Lancashire, 21 December 1964.
Education: Ellesmere High School; Eccles Sixth Form College.
First-class debut: 1985, Lancashire v Warwickshire, Edgbaston.

2 matches for Lancashire 1985-87.
HS: 13 (debut).
BB: 2-24 (debut).

DAVIES, Harry Donald

RHB.
Born: Pendleton, Manchester, 13 March 1892.

Died: Riem, Munich, Western Germany, 6 February 1958, aged 65. (Killed in air crash at Munich Airport with a number of Manchester United footballers and officials and journalists.)
First-class debut: 1924, Lancashire v Kent, Old Trafford.
11 matches for Lancashire 1924-25 (amateur).
HS: 46 v Kent (debut).

Don Davies, who subsequently became a Lancashire committee member and vice-president, was better known in the world of soccer. He played for Bolton Wanderers, won an England amateur cap and later became one of the most literary of soccer writers under the pseudonym 'Old International' for the *Manchester Guardian*. He also played for Bradshaw CC.

DEAN, Harry

LHB; LFM.
Born: Burnley, Lancashire, 13 August 1884.
Died: Garstang, Lancashire, 12 March 1957, aged 72.
First-class debut: 1906, Lancashire v Leicestershire, Leicester.

256 matches for Lancashire 1906-21 (professional). Benefit (£2,217) 1920.
HS: 49* v Nottinghamshire, Trent Bridge, 1920.
BB: 9-31 v Somerset, Old Trafford, 1909.
Also: 9-35 v Warwickshire, Liverpool, 1909; 9-46 v Derbyshire, Chesterfield 1907; 9-62 v Yorkshire, Liverpool, 1913; 9-77 v Somerset, Bath, 1910; 9-109 v Leicestershire, Leicester, 1911.
Match figures of 17-91 v Yorkshire, Liverpool, 1913 are best-ever for Lancashire; also 16-103 v Somerset, Bath, 1910 and 15-108 v Kent, Old Trafford, 1912.
100 wickets (8); 179 (17.48) 1911 best.
3 Tests for England 1912. HS: 8 v South Africa, Headingley, 1912. BB: 4-19 v Australia, The Oval, 1912.

Harry Dean was a left-arm pace bowler with late swerve and pace variations whose best performances above confirm he could be devastating at times. After leaving Lancashire, Dean played for Cheshire and from 1926 to 1932 was coach at Rossall School.

DeFREITAS, Phillip Anthony Jason
RHB; RFM.
Born: Scotts Head, Dominica, 18 February 1966.
Education: Willesden High School, London.
Lancashire debut: 1989 v Warwickshire, Edgbaston.
33 matches for Lancashire 1989-90. Capped 1989.
HS for Lancashire: 102 v Oxford University, Oxford, 1990.
BB: 7-21 v Middlesex, Lord's, 1989.
59 matches for Leicestershire 1985-88. Capped 1986.
HS: 113, Leicestershire v Nottinghamshire, Worksop, 1988.
20 Tests for England 1986-87 to 1990-91. HS: 40 v Australia, Brisbane, 1986-87 (debut). BB: 5-53 v New Zealand, Trent Bridge, 1990. Test record: 378 runs (13.03). 5 catches. 48 wickets (42.31).
Full first-class record: 3,460 runs (21.62); 4 centuries; 38 catches; 424 wickets (27.36).
55 limited-overs matches for England.
Tours: England to Australia 1986-87 and 1990-91 (late replacement); to New Zealand and Pakistan 1987-88; Lancashire to Zimbabwe 1988-89.

A hard-hitting middle-order batsman, aggressive seam bowler (mainly of inswing) and a fine fielder with a strong throw, DeFreitas has proved a fine county cricketer but has not yet quite fulfilled his promise at international level. He was a late call-up for the ill-fated Ashes tour of 1990-91.

DEIGHTON, John Harold Greenway
RHB; RFM.

Phillip DeFreitas

Charles De Trafford

Born: Prestwich, Lancashire, 5 April 1920.
Education: Denstone.
Debut for Lancashire: 1948 v Northamptonshire, Liverpool.
7 matches for Lancashire 1948-50 (amateur).
HS: 79 v Leicestershire, Blackpool, 1949.
BB for Lancashire: 5-52 v Nottinghamshire, Trent Bridge, 1950.
First-class debut: 1947, Combined Services.
20 matches for Combined Services 1947-62.
6 matches for MCC 1948-54; Played for Free Foresters twice 1953 and 1961.
BB: 6-50 (10-91 in match), MCC v Ireland, Dublin, 1954.
Full first-class record: 994 runs (19.88); 17 catches; 127 wickets (24.25).

A major in the Northumberland Fusiliers (he played for that county in 1947), Deighton became an instructor at Sandhurst in 1948, and served in Korea with United Nations forces 1950-52. He was a talented all-rounder but his military career always took precedence over cricket.

De TRAFFORD, Charles Edmund
RHB.
Born: Trafford Park, Manchester, 21 May 1864.
Died: Rothley Temple, Leicestershire, 11 November 1915, aged 87.
Education: Beaumont.
First-class debut: 1884, Lancashire v Derbyshire, Derby.
1 match for Lancashire 1884 (amateur).
No runs or wickets.
In 1888 started playing for Leicestershire, under residential qualification, and led them as a first-class side from 1894-1906, making his final appearance in 1920.
HS: 137, Leicestershire v Derbyshire, Chesterfield, 1913.
Tours: North America with Lord Hawke, 1894; New Zealand, 1906-07; Argentina, 1911-12.
Full first-class record: 9,581 runs (18.67); 6 centuries.

Charles De Trafford, whose family owned the estate on which Old Trafford, stands, was a free-hitting and very aggressive batsman who may have scored more heavily, but less attractively, had he curbed his aggressive impulses. He was also a brilliant fielder. Sir Timothy O'Brien of Middlesex, Ireland and England, was his brother-in-law. Apart from cricket, De Trafford enjoyed hunting and shooting.

DEWHURST, Robert
RHB.
Born: Clitheroe, Lancashire, 11 May 1851.

Died: Blackpool (Central Station), 13 October 1924, Aged 73.
First-class debut: 1872, Lancashire v Yorkshire, Old Trafford.
13 matches for Lancashire, 1872-75 (amateur).
HS: 59 v Derbyshire, Derby, 1875 (adding 101 for seventh wicket with William McIntyre).

Robert Dewhurst, who also appeared for Cheshire in pre-Minor Counties Championship days, was attached for many years to the Lytham Cricket Club, as batsman, right-arm bowler (medium-pace round-arm or slow lobs) and captain. At his death, he was a leading member of Manchester Stock Exchange.

DICKINSON, Thomas Eastwood
LHB; RFM.
Born: Parramatta, New South Wales, Australia, 11 January 1931.
Education: Blackburn Grammar School; Manchester University; Loughborough College.
First-class debut: 1950, Lancashire v Hampshire, Bournemouth.
4 matches for Lancashire 1950-51 (amateur).
HS: 9 v Surrey, The Oval, 1950.
BB for Lancashire: 1-20 v Kent, Old Trafford, 1951.
5 matches Somerset 1957.
BB: 5-36, Somerset v Glamorgan, Weston-super-Mare, 1957.
Full first-class record: 21 runs (3.50); 20 wickets (20.95).

Tom Dickinson showed such promise as a youth that an opening attack of he and Brian Statham was regarded as a likely, and exciting, proposition. He chose an academic career, however, and eventually became a schoolmaster and chief examination marker in mathematics in Bristol. Originally he played for the local East Lancashire club before moving to Bristol, where he appeared for Keynsham CC.

DIXON, J
Details of his birth and death unknown.
First-class debut: Lancashire v Nottinghamshire, Trent Bridge 1878.
1 match for Lancashire 1878 (amateur).

In his only match this unknown batted number 11, scoring 2 and 0, and did not bowl.

DOBELL, Percy
RHB.
Born: Huyton, Liverpool, 29 April 1864.
Died: Freshfield, Liverpool, 5 January 1903, aged 38.

Education: Birkenhead.
First-class debut: 1886, Lancashire v Surrey, The Oval.
7 matches for Lancashire 1886-87 (amateur).
HS: 28 v Kent, Old Trafford, 1886.
Played first-class matches for Liverpool & District 1886-88.
Full first-class record: 142 runs (9.46).

Dobell also played for Huyton CC.

DOUTHWAITE, Harold
RHB.
Born: Lancaster, 12 August 1900.
Died: Lancaster, 9 July 1972, aged 71.
Education: Lancaster Grammar School; Peterhouse, Cambridge.
First-class debut: 1920, Lancashire v Warwickshire, Old Trafford.
3 matches for Lancashire 1920-21 (amateur).
HS: 29 v Warwickshire (debut).

Harold Douthwaite had great success at Lancaster Grammar School, exceeding 1,000 runs in 1919, but although playing in the Freshmen's trials of 1920 he never appeared in a first-class match for Cambridge. He became a stalwart of Lancaster CC, played soccer for Cambridge and the Corinthians, winning England Amateur caps, and eventually played Rugby Union football for Vale of Lune.

DUCKWORTH, George
RHB; WK.
Born: Warrington, Lancashire, 9 May 1901.
Died: Warrington, 5 January 1966, aged 65.
Education: Warrington Grammar School.
First-class debut: 1923, Lancashire v Gloucestershire, Gloucester.
424 matches for Lancashire 1923-38 (professional). Capped 1924. Benefit (£1,257) 1934.
HS: 75 v Leicestershire, Liverpool, 1929.
922 dismissals (634 catches; 288 stumped) for Lancashire, a county record.
8 dismissals in match twice: 5 catches, 3 stumped v Kent, Maidstone, 1928; and 3 catches, 5 stumped v Warwickshire, Old Trafford, 1936. Lancashire record at the time.
97 dismissals for county 1928 (69 catches 28 stumped), a Lancashire record for season.
24 Tests for England 1924-36. 60 Test dismissals (45 catches; 15 stumped).
Full first-class record: 4,945 runs (14.58); 1,095 dismissals (754 catches; 341 stumped).

George Duckworth was a delightful character, stocky of build but remarkably agile, and with the loudest appeal known to first-class cricket.

After retirement he played for Cheshire and subsequently became a sports journalist, specialising in cricket and Rugby League. He was also a farmer, hotelier and successor to W.Ferguson as baggage master to England Test and touring teams, besides managing three Commonwealth touring teams to India.

A Warrington man through and through, he played for the local club at an early age. He died there, sadly at a relatively early age when seemingly still fully retaining all his faculties, and with much to give the game. George Duckworth's grandson, Hugh De Prez, has played for Cheshire on occasions in recent seasons.

DUNLOP, George Colquhoun Hamilton
Batsman.
Born: Edinburgh, Scotland, 28 July 1846.
Died: Crichton, Dumfries, Scotland, 7 June 1929, aged 82.

Education: Edinburgh Academy.
First-class debut: 1868, Lancashire v Surrey, Old Trafford.
1 match for Lancashire 1868 (amateur).
HS: 16 (debut).

A cotton broker at Liverpool, Dunlop was treasurer of Liverpool CC. He scored plenty of runs at Edinburgh Academy and in 1877 he scored 201 for Birkenhead Park v Rock Ferry.

DURANDU, Arthur

RHB.
Born: Great Crosby, Liverpool, 25 December 1860.
Died: Great Crosby, 4 February 1903, aged 42.
First-class debut: 1887, Lancashire v Kent, Old Trafford.
1 match for Lancashire 1887 (amateur).
HS: 5 (debut).

Arthur Durandu was a Liverpool amateur who also played for Northern CC.

DYSON, Jack

RHB; OB.
Born: Oldham, Lancashire, 8 July 1934.
First-class debut: 1954, Lancashire v Glamorgan, Swansea.
150 matches for Lancashire 1954-64 (professional). Capped 1956.
HS: 118* v Scotland, Paisley, 1956.
BB: 7-83 v Somerset, Taunton, 1960.
1,000 runs (1); 1,087 (27.17) 1956 best.
57 wickets (27.40) in 1959.
When Lancashire beat Leicestershire by 10 wickets at Old Trafford in 1956, Dyson (75* & 31*) and Alan Wharton were the only Lancashire players to bat. Lancashire scored 166-0 dec and 66-0. This is the only such happening in English first-class cricket.

Such promise did Jack Dyson show, at various times with both bat and ball, that he must be rated a very big disappointment overall. Not that he always enjoyed the best of forutne. He missed the whole of the 1958 season due to a broken leg received as a Manchester City soccer player, and part of the 1963 season was missed owing to a broken arm. It was not bad luck, however, which caused his 'sacking' in 1960, but '. . .a serious breach of discipline and an act of insubordination and insolence to the captain'. Dyson returned in 1963 but after 1964 was again released, no longer his performances being of the required standard.

Jack Dyson played League cricket for Werneth, and latterly for Newcastle and Hartshill. He gained an FA Cup winners' medal

with Manchester City in 1956 (when he scored in the Final) and after leaving Maine Road in 1961 he appeared for Stirling Albion in the Scottish League.

ECCLES, Alexander

RHB.
Born: Ashton-on-Ribble, Lancashire, 16 March 1876.
Died: Bilsborough Hall, Preston, Lancashire, 17 March 1919, aged 43.
Education: Repton; Trinity College, Oxford.
Lancashire debut: 1898 v Essex, Old Trafford.
123 matches for Lancashire 1898-1907 (amateur).
HS: 139 v Leicestershire, Leicester, 1898.
Played for Oxford University 1896-99. Blue 1897-98-99.
Scored 109 in 1898 Varsity match.
Full first-class record: 5,129 runs (23.20); 6 centuries; 96 catches.

A stylish batsman who never quite fulfilled his early promise, Alex Eccles captained the side on occasions but was not a forceful personality. He also played for Huyton CC.

ECCLES, Henry

RHB; RM.
Born: Huyton Park, Liverpool, 4 March 1863.
Died: Roby, Lancashire, 10 February 1931, aged 67.
Education: Uppingham.

First-class debut: 1885, Lancashire v Surrey, Liverpool.
5 matches for Lancashire 1885-86 (amateur).
HS: 14 (debut).

Henry Eccles played for Liverpool & District in 1889 and club cricket for Huyton CC.

ECCLES, Joseph

RHB.
Born: Accrington, Lancashire, 13 April 1863.
Died: Barton-on-Irwell, Lancashire, 2 September 1933, aged 70.

First-class debut: 1886, Lancashire v Oxford University, Old Trafford.
47 matches for Lancashire, 1886-89 (amateur).
HS: 184 v Surrey, The Oval, 1888.

Eccles played his club cricket with Preston CC and Lytham CC.

ECKERSLEY, Peter Thorp

RHB.
Born: Lowton, Newton-le-Willows, Lancashire, 2 July 1904.
Died: Eastleigh, Hampshire, 13 August 1940 (in flying accident).
Education: Rugby; Cambridge University.
First-class debut: 1923, Lancashire v Cambridge University, Fenner's.
256 matches for Lancashire 1923-35 (amateur).
Captain 1929-35.
HS: 102* v Gloucestershire, Bristol, 1927.
Tours: MCC to India 1926-27; Tennyson's team to Jamaica 1927-28; Sir Julien Cahn's team to Argentine 1929-30.
Full first-class record: 5,629 runs (19.54); 1 century; 121 catches.

Peter Eckersley, a brave batsman at his best in a crisis and a very keen fieldsman, did nothing at Cambridge but in 1928 chose cricket rather than politics, stepping down as prospective Parliamentry candidate for Newton. In 1931 he reversed his decision and unsuccessfully contested Leigh but in 1935 he was successful at Manchester Exchange in the Unionist cause. Joining the Fleet Air Arm in 1939, he was one of the first cricketers to die in action.

EDGE, Cyril Arthur

RHB; RFM.
Born: Ashton-under-Lyne, 14 December 1916.

Died: Ormskirk, Lancashire, 4 October 1985, aged 68.
First-class debut: 1936, Lancashire v Worcestershire, Old Trafford.
8 matches for Lancashire 1936-38 (professional).
HS for Lancashire: 1 (2 occasions).
BB: 4-71 v Glamorgan, Old Trafford, 1936.
Last first-class match: Minor Counties v West Indians, Lord's, 1939.
Full first class record: 17 runs (5.66); 29 wickets (30.10).

EDGE, Harold Emerton

Bowler (probably spin).
Born: Market Drayton, Shropshire, 18 June 1892.
Died: Middlewich, Cheshire, 24 January 1944, aged 51.
First-class debut: 1913, Lancashire v Warwickshire, Old Trafford.
1 match for Lancashire 1913 (professional).
HS for Lancashire: 3 (debut).
Played for Wales v MCC, Lord's 1927.
HS: 19* MCC v Wales (above).
BB: 4-115 MCC v Wales (above).
Full first-class record: 27 runs (6.75); 4 wickets (69.00).

Edge was professional for Little Lever and later Colwyn Bay.

EDMONDS, James William

RHB; LFM.
Born: Smethwick, Staffs, 4 June 1951.

Education: Holly Lodge School, Warley.
First-class debut: 1975, Lancashire v Cambridge University, Fenner's.
1 match for Lancashire 1975.
Did not bat
BB: 3-52 v Cambridge University (debut).

Edmonds played for Mitchells & Butlers in the Birmingham League.

EDRICH, Eric Harry

RHB; WK.
Born: Lingwood, Norfolk, 27 March 1914.
Education: Brackendale School, Norwich.
First-class debut: 1946, Lancashire v Derbyshire, Old Trafford.
33 matches for Lancashire 1946-8 (professional).
Capped 1948.
HS: 121 v Yorkshire, Headingley, 1948.
Played for Norfolk 1935-39; 1949-51.

Eric Edrich, the oldest of the famous cricketing brotherhood, perhaps took to county cricket too late. He was a useful player, however, and cheerful team-man. He subsequently emigrated to Australia for personal reasons but eventually returned to his native heath.

EDRICH, Geoffrey Arthur

RHB.
Born: Lingwood, Norfolk, 13 July 1918.

Education: Brackendale School, Norwich.
First-class debut: 1946, Lancashire v Gloucestershire, Gloucester.
322 matches for Lancashire (professional) 1946-58.
Capped 1946. Benefit (£3,500) 1955.
HS: 167* v Nottinghamshire, Trent Bridge, 1954.
1,000 runs (8); 1,977 (41.18) 1952 best
Fine slip fielder with 322 catches for Lancashire.
Toured India with Commonwealth team, 1953-54.
Full first-class record: 15,600 runs (34.82); 331 catches.

Geoff Edrich, another of the famous brotherhood, played for Norfolk 1937-39 and after a difficult war, during which he suffered under the Japanese, he signed for Lancashire with elder brother, Eric. He ended his Lancashire career as 2nd XI captain and left under sad circumstances, after a difference of opinion with regard to discipline amongst the younger players. He played for Cumberland 1960-62 and then coached at Cheltenham.

ELLIOTT, Harold

RHB; WK.
Born: Wigan, Lancashire, 15 June 1904.

Died: Hindley, Wigan, 15 April 1969, aged 64.
First-class debut: 1930, Lancashire v Surrey, Old Trafford.
1 match for Lancashire 1930 (professional)
HS: 4 (only innings).

Harold Elliott served as a first-class umpire from 1939 to 1956 and officiated in 7 Tests 1950-53.

ELLIS, Jeremy

LHB; LM.
Born: Summerseat, Lancashire, 15 February 1866.
Died: Billington, Lancashire, 14 August 1943, aged 77.
First-class debut: 1892, Lancashire v Oxford University, Old Trafford.
6 matches for Lancashire 1892-98 (professional).
HS: 26* v Kent, Old Trafford, 1893.
BB: 8-21 v Leicestershire, Leicester, 1894.

A local professional whose figures suggest that a fair trial was not given. His sons, Walker and Stanley, both played for Lancashire. Jeremy Ellis played for Ramsbottom in the Lancashire League.

ELLIS, Stanley

LHB; ROB.
Born: Ramsbottom, Lancashire, 12 February 1896.
Died: Blackburn, Lancashire, 14 February 1987, aged 91.
First-class debut: 1923, Lancashire v Derbyshire, Old Trafford.
8 matches for Lancashire 1923-24 (professional).
HS: 25 v Gloucestershire, Old Trafford, 1923.
BB: 5-21 v Derbyshire (debut).

He played for Colne in the Lancashire League, then went to Durham, playing for Eppleton, Durham City and Horden Colliery Welfare, and in 66 matches for Durham County, 1929-37. Father Jeremy and brother Walker both played Lancashire.

ELLIS, Walker

RHB.
Born: Summerseat, Lancashire, 27 January 1895.
Died: Eccleston, Lancashire, 25 November 1974, aged 79.
First-class debut: 1920, Lancashire v Sussex, Old Trafford.
36 matches for Lancashire 1920-23 (professional).
HS: 138* v Kent, Old Trafford, 1921.

Walker Ellis, son of Jerry, brother of Stanley (both

Lancashire debut: 1968 v Kent, Canterbury.
175 matches for Lancashire 1968-76. Capped 1968. Benefit (£26,519) 1976.
HS for Lancashire: 141 v Derbyshire, Buxton, 1971.
8 dismissals in a match four times for Lancashire (a record).
Best season: 82 dismissals (78 catches; 4 stumped) in 1970.
First-class debut: 1958-59; Played for Bombay 1959-60 to 1974-75.

46 Tests for India 1961-62 to 1974-75. HS: 121 v England, Bombay, 1972-73. Test record stand for 8th wicket for India (143 with R.Nadkarni) v New Zealand, Madras, 1964-65. Test record: 2,611 runs (31.08). 2 centuries. 66 catches. 16 stumped.
HS: 192 World XI v Combined XI, Hobart, 1971-72.
Full first-class record: 13,436 runs (29.52); 13 centuries; 824 dismissals (704 catches; 120 stumped).
One of the more successful of the early overseas signings by a county, Engineer was often a match-winning batsman, especially in limited overs matches, as well as a slightly inconsistent, but brilliant wicketkeeper. He became an adopted Lancastrian and still follows the county enthusiastically, as well as commentating on matches, usually involving India.

Lancashire) showed great promise when hitting his only first-class century against Kent in 1921. In only his third game he reached three figures in 1¾ hours, but his form deteriorated rapidly. He played for Manchester CC and was later professional with Heaton, Blackley and Barrow.

ENGINEER, Farokh Maneksha

RHB; WK.
Born: Bombay, India, 25 February 1938.
Education: Don Bosco High School, Bombay; Bombay University.

ENTWISTLE, Robert

RHB.
Born: Burnley, Lancashire, 20 October 1941.
First-class debut: 1962, Lancashire v Gloucestershire, Cheltenham.
48 matches for Lancashire 1962-66 (professional).
HS: 85 v MCC, Old Trafford, 1964.
1,000 runs (1); 1,030 (28.61) 1964 best.

Bobbie Entwistle faded disappointingly after showing great promise in 1964, but he scored heavily for Cumberland in the Minor Counties Championship, playing regularly from 1967 to 1984, scoring 7,950 runs (40.56), a record for the county. He played League cricket for Burnley, Darwen, Fleetwood and Netherfield.

FAIRBROTHER, Neil Harvey

LHB; LM.
Born: Warrington, Lancashire, 9 September 1963.
Education: Lymm Grammar School.
First-class debut: 1982, Lancashire v Kent, Old Trafford. Scored 94* before an 'agreed' declaration v Warwickshire, Edgbaston, 1983, the first match in which he batted.
172 matches for Lancashire 1982-90. Capped 1985.
HS: 366 (best score by any English left-hander) v Surrey, The Oval, 1990. (Took 504 minutes, hit 47 4s, 5 6s; added 364 with Michael Atherton for Lancashire 3rd-wicket record).
1,000 runs (7); 1,681 (80.04) 1990 best.

7 Tests for England 1987-90. HS: 33* v New Zealand, Lord's, 1990. Test record: 64 runs (8.00).
Toured New Zealand and Pakistan with England, 1987-88.
Full first-class record: 10,226 runs (41.06); 20 centuries; 111 catches.

A slightly built, quick-footed and stylish left-hander, Fairbrother's Test record is a travesty of his true ability. So regular a scorer on the county circuit is he that, given a decent run in the England team and made to feel part of affairs, he could still make his mark at Test level.

FAIRCLOUGH, Peter Moss

RHB; SLA.
Born: Bickershaw, Lancashire, 25 September 1887.
Died: Stanley Park, Blackpool, 16 November 1952, aged 65.
First-class debut: 1911, Lancashire v Somerset, Liverpool.

20 matches for Lancashire 1911-23 (professional).
HS: 19 v Somerset (each innings of debut match).
BB: 7-27 v Leicestershire, Old Trafford, 1912.

Peter Fairclough, who never established himself in county cricket, played for Blackpool in League cricket.

FALLOWS, John Armstrong
RHB.
Born: Woodley, Cheshire, 25 July 1907.
Died: Macclesfield, Cheshire, 20 January 1974, aged 66.
Education: Worksop College.
First-class debut: 1946, Lancashire v Cambridge University, Fenner's.
25 matches for Lancashire (amateur) 1946.
Capped 1946. Captain 1946.
HS: 35 v Yorkshire, Old Trafford, 1946.

Fallows, son of Lancashire's Treasurer, was appointed captain for the first season after World War Two. From Stockport, he had captained the Manchester club for several years but his season at the helm for Lancashire was hardly successful. His case was not helped by his poor batting and for 1947 he was replaced by the infinitely more talented Ken Cranston. In 1932, Jack Fallows had played for Cheshire; after retiring from playing he was on the Lancashire committee until 1971.

FARNSWORTH, Andrew William
RHB.
Born: Sydney, New South Wales, Australia 1887.
Died: Sydney, 30 October 1966, aged 79.
Lancashire debut: 1919 v Australian Imperial Forces, Old Trafford.
1 match for Lancashire 1919 (professional).
Scored 0 and 3 in only match.
Played for New South Wales 1908-09.
HS: 69 New South Wales v Queensland, Sydney, 1908-09.
Full first-class record: 78 runs (19.50).

Farnsworth, an Australian of Lancashire extraction, was on a visit when he played for Lancashire in 1919.

FARRAR, Harry
LHB; LFM.
Born: Radcliffe, Lancashire, 14 March 1930.
Education: Stand Grammar School, Manchester.
First-class debut: 1955, Lancashire v Scotland, Old Trafford.
1 game for Lancashire (amateur).
Scored no runs and took no wickets in his only appearance.

Harry Farrar, who played for the Little Lever, Stand and Westhoughton clubs, bowled 13 economical overs in his only first-class match but rain interfered and he scarcely had a chance.

FARRAR, Hubert Lister
RHB.
Born: Broughton Park, Lancashire, 2 April 1881.
Died: Bowdon, Cheshire, 4 July 1939, aged 58.
Education: Repton.
First-class debut: 1904, Lancashire v South Africans, Old Trafford.
1 match for Lancashire 1904 (amateur).
Scored 25 and 3 in only appearance.

FARRIMOND, William
RHB; WK.
Born: Daisy Hill, Westhoughton, Lancashire, 23 May 1903.
Died: Westhoughton, Lancashire, 15 November 1979, aged 76.
First-class debut: 1924, Lancashire v South Africans, Liverpool.
134 matches for Lancashire 1924-25 (professional). Capped 1929. Benefit (£1,000) 1939.
HS for Lancashire: 63 v Gloucestershire, Gloucester 1939.
7 dismissals in innings (6 catches; 1 stumped)

v Kent, Old Trafford, 1930, then County Championship record; still joint Lancashire record with Warren Hegg.
4 Tests for England 1930-31 to 1935. HS: 35 v South Africa, Durban, 1930-31. Test record: 116 runs (16.57); 5 catches; 2 stumps.
HS: 174 Minor Counties v Oxford University, The Parks, 1934.
Full first-class record: 2,908 runs (23.64); 255 catches; 77 stumped.

Bill Farrimond was a fine wicketkeeper, technically proficient and eminently unobtrusive. It was unfortunate that his career clashed to a large extent with the more volatile George Duckworth. Farrimond, who played club cricket for Heywood and Westhoughton, was a regular member of the side only in 1938 and 1939, long after his Test career was over.

FINDLAY, William

RHB; WK.
Born: Maviscourt, Liverpool, 22 June 1880.
Died: Tenterden, Kent, 19 June 1953, aged 72.
Education: Eton; Oriel College, Oxford.
Lancashire debut: 1902 v Middlesex, Liverpool.
58 matches for Lancashire 1902-06 (amateur).
HS: 81 v Sussex, Old Trafford, 1906.
Oxford Blue 1901-02-03. Captain 1903.
Toured Argentine with MCC 1911-12.
Full first-class record: 1,984 runs (19.45); 140 catches; 27 stumped.

A well-known administrator, Findlay was Secretary of Surrey CCC 1907-19; he was then Assistant Secretary of MCC until 1936, and Secretary until 1946. Finally, in 1951-52, Findlay was MCC President.

FITTON, John Dexter

LHB; ROB.
Born: Littleborough, Lancashire, 24 August 1965.
Education: Redbrook High School; Oulder Hill School.
First-class debut: 1987, Lancashire v Hampshire, Southampton.
36 matches for Lancashire 1987-90.
HS: 44 v Australians, Old Trafford, 1989.
BB: 6-59 v Yorkshire, Old Trafford, 1988.

FOLLEY, Ian

RHB; LMF (now SLA).
Born: Stoneyholme, Burnley, Lancashire, 9 January 1963.

Education: Mansfield High School; Nelson and Colne College.
First-class debut: 1982, Lancashire v Cambridge University, Fenner's.
135 matches for Lancashire 1982-90. Capped 1987.
HS: 69 v Yorkshire, Old Trafford, 1985.
BB: 7-15 (12-57 match) v Warwickshire, Southport, 1987.
Tours: Lancashire to West Indies 1986-87; Lancashire to Zimbabwe 1988-89.

Becoming a slow bowler in 1987, Folley took 70 wickets (24.40) but subsequently lost form and became somewhat expensive, losing his place in the side. He was also injured but after recovering was offered a contract by Derbyshire in February 1991.

FOWLER, Graeme

LHB; Occasional RM; Occasional WK.
Born: Accrington, Lancashire, 20 April 1957.

Education: Accrington Grammar School; Durham University.
First-class debut: 1979, Lancashire v Derbyshire, Chesterfield.

204 matches for Lancashire 1979-90. Capped 1981.
HS: 226 v Kent, Maidstone, 1984.
BB: 2-34 v Warwickshire, Old Trafford, 1986.
1,000 runs (7); 1,800 (47.36) 1987 best.
Established record for all county cricket during innings of 56 v Warwickshire, Edgbaston, 1989, when remaining on 39 for 90 minutes.
21 Tests for England 1982 to 1984-85. HS: 201 v India, Madras, 1984-85. Test Record: 1,307 runs (35.32); 3 centuries; 10 catches.
Tours: England to Australia 1982-83, to New Zealand and Pakistan 1983-84, to India 1984-85; International XI to West Indies 1982-83, to Jamaica 1983-84; Lancashire to Jamaica 1987, to Zimbabwe 1988-89.
Scored 126 and 128* v Warwickshire, Southport, 1982, using a runner for each innings. With Steve O'Shaughnessy added 201 in 43 minutes for 1st wicket v Leicestershire, Old Trafford, 1983, the fastest double-century stand ever in first-class cricket. Fowler (100) reached his century in 46 minutes and achieved ten consecutive scoring strokes of six runs (a record). Leicestershire were concerned only with increasing their over-rate and used irregular bowlers. (*See* Steve O'Shaughnessy).

Graeme Fowler had a rapid rise to Test status and with his attractive style and self confidence looked set to have a long international career ahead of him. Alas, he lost his place after breaking his neck. His last two England innings saw him score 201 and 69. This wiry and jaunty cricketer, who is also a physical education teacher, has remained a valuable and popular, if inconsistent, county opener and deputy captain.

GADDUM, Frederick Ducange

LHB; SLA.
Born: Didsbury, Manchester, 28 June 1860.
Died: Stockport, Cheshire, 14 October 1900, aged 40.
Education: Uppingham; Rugby; St John's College, Cambridge.
Lancashire debut: 1884 v Kent, Old Trafford.
1 match for Lancashire 1884 (amateur).
HS for Lancashire: 10 v Kent, Old Trafford, 1884.
Played for Cambridge University 1880-82. Blue 1882.
HS: 16 Cambridge University v Surrey, The Oval, 1882.
BB: 4-34 Cambridge University v England XI, Cambridge, 1880.
Full first-class record: 87 runs (6.69); 9 catches; 21 wickets (19.33).

A merchant in Manchester, Gaddum had scant opportunity as a bowler, despite good performances. He played for a club called Ishmaelites CC and died after being knocked off his bicycle.

GALLIAN, Jason Edward Riche

RHB.
Born: Avalon, New South Wales, Australia, 25 June 1971.
First-class debut: 1990, Lancashire v Oxford University, Oxford.
1 match for Lancashire 1990.
HS: 17* v Oxford University (debut).
BB: 1-50 v Oxford University (debut).

GARLICK, Richard Gordon

RHB; RM then OB.
Born: Kirkby Lonsdale, Westmorland, 11 April 1917.
Died: Blackpool, 16 May 1988.
First-class debut: 1938, Lancashire v Northamptonshire, Old Trafford.
44 matches for Lancashire 1938-47 (professional).

HS for Lancashire: 50 v Somerset, Old Trafford, 1946.
BB: 6-27 (10-46 in match) v Derbyshire, Buxton, 1946.
77 matches for Northamptonshire 1947-50. Capped 1949.
HS: 62* Northamptonshire v Worcestershire, Worcester, 1950.
86 wickets for Northamptonshire (23.80) in 1950.

Full first-class record: 1,664 runs (13.86); 332 wickets (26.11).

Tall and moustachioed, Garlick started with Lancashire as a new-ball bowler but achieved most success with off-spin for Northamptonshire. He was an occasionally effective tail-end batsman. After a very successful first-class season in 1950, he went into the Leagues with Fleetwood and also played for St Anne's.

GARNETT, Harold Gwyer

LHB; WK; SLA.
Born: Aigburth, Liverpool, 19 November 1879.
Died: Marcoing, Cambrai, France (killed in action), 3 December 1917, aged 37.

Education: Clifton.
First-class debut: 1899, Lancashire v Australians, Liverpool.
144 matches for Lancashire 1899-1914 (amateur).
HS: 139 v Leicestershire, Leicester, 1901.
BB: 2-18 v Gloucestershire, Bristol, 1903.
1,000 runs (2); 1,758 (35.87) 1901 best.
6 dismissals (all caught) in innings v Warwickshire, Edgbaston, 1914, Lancashire record until 1930.
A surprise choice for A.C.MacLaren's team in Australia 1901-02, he played no Tests.
Full first-class record: 5,798 runs (26.00); 5 centuries; 185 catches; 18 stumped; 8 wickets (28.00).

Harold Garnett was a dashing left-handed batsman who did so well in 1901 — his first full season — that he was invited to tour Australia (possibly as reserve wicketkeeper). He failed utterly and never again graced the international scene. After 1905, business interests in Argentina severely limited his appearances but when playing regularly in 1914, he did so well as a wicketkeeper that he was chosen for the Gentlemen.

GIBSON, Arthur Buchwald Edgar

RHB; RM.
Born: Salford, Manchester, 15 June 1863.
Died: Cambridge, 11 March 1932, aged 68.
Education: Cheltenham.
First-class debut: 1887, Lancashire v Derbyshire, Long Eaton.
2 matches for Lancashire 1887 (amateur).
HS for Lancashire: 16 v Derbyshire (debut).
Toured India with Lord Hawke's team, 1892-93.
HS: 58 Hawke's XI v All-India, Allahabad, 1892-93.
BB: 3-24 Hawke's XI v Bombay Presidency, Bombay, 1892-93.
Full first-class record: 311 runs (13.52); 3 catches; 16 wickets (14.18).

A decision to go to the colonies shortened Gibson's career and whilst in India he played for the Bihar team, scoring 100 against Calcutta in 1889-90. When in England he also played for Lincolnshire and made his final first-class appearance for MCC in 1896.

GOOCH, Peter Alan

LHB; RFM.
Born: Timperley, Cheshire, 2 May 1949.
First-class debut: 1970, Lancashire v Oxford University, The Parks.
4 matches for Lancashire 1970.
Failed to score in three innings.
BB: 4-52 v Kent, Old Trafford, 1970.

Peter Gooch played for Cheshire in the Minor Counties Championship in 1971 and for

Buckinghamshire from 1976-79. After playing League cricket for Ashton he moved south to appear for Bedford Town and Tring Park.

GOOD, Anthony John

RHB; RFM.
Born: Kumasi, Gold Coast (now Ghana), 19 November 1952.
Education: Worksop College.
First-class debut: 1973, Lancashire v Gloucestershire, Old Trafford.

8 matches for Lancashire 1973-76.
HS: 6 v Gloucestershire (debut).
BB: 5-62 v Northamptonshire, Old Trafford, 1976.

Good played for Alderley Edge in League cricket and appeared for Cheshire in the Minor Counties 1977-79.

GOODWIN, Francis Herbert

LHB; SLA.
Born: Rainhill, Lancashire, 4 January 1866.
Died: Garston, Lancashire, 20 January 1931, aged 65.
First-class debut: 1894, Lancashire v Derbyshire, Derby.
3 matches for Lancashire 1894 (amateur).
HS: 10 v Kent, Tonbridge, 1894.

GOODWIN, Frederick

RHB; RFM.
Born: Heywood, Lancashire, 28 June 1933.

First-class debut: 1955, Lancashire v Kent, Old Trafford.
11 matches for Lancashire 1955-56 (professional).
HS: 21* v Derbyshire, Old Trafford, 1955.
BB: 5-35 v Middlesex, Lord's, 1955.

Attached to the Radcliffe club, Fred Goodwin showed brief promise in 1955 but faded from the scene. A professional scocer player with Manchester United (playing in the 1958 FA Cup Final), Leeds United and Scunthorpe United, he later managed Scunthorpe United, Brighton & Hove Albion and Birmingham City and also coached in the North American Soccer League. He eventually emigrated to the USA, where he now lives.

GOODWIN, Keith

RHB; WK.
Born: Oldham, Lancashire, 25 June 1938.
First-class debut: 1960, Lancashire v Glamorgan, Cardiff.
122 matches for Lancashire 1960-74 (professional). Benefit (£6,700) 1973.

HS: 23 v Glamorgan, Swansea, 1965.
73 dismissals (66 catches; 7 stumped) in 1967.
Toured Pakistan with a 'Rest of World' team 1973-74.

The underrated Keith Goodwin had the misfortune to have to compete with Geoff Clayton and then Farokh Engineer and was never really sure of his place.

GREEN, David Michael

RHB; OB.
Born: Llanengan, Caernarfon, 10 November 1939.
Education: Manchester Grammar School; Brasenose College, Oxford.
Lancashire debut: 1959 v Hampshire, Southampton.
135 matches for Lancashire 1959-67 (initially amateur). Capped 1962.
HS for Lancashire: 138 v Northamptonshire, Northampton, 1961.
BB for Lancashire: 3-6 v Leicestershire, Leicester, 1959.

1,000 runs (3); 1,868 (33.35) 1965 best. (HS that season 85; total runs highest for any county in a season without a century).
81 matches for Gloucestershire, 1968-71. Capped 1968.
Oxford Blue 1959-60-61.
HS: 233 Gloucestershire v Sussex, Hove, 1968.
BB 5-61 Oxford University v Sussex, Hove, 1959.
Scored 2,137 runs (40.32) all first-class matches 1968; and 2,037 (32.85) all first-class matches

1965. Only example of 2,000 runs in a season without a century.
Toured Rhodesia with International Wanderers 1972-73.
Full first-class record: 13,381 runs (28.83); 14 centuries; 97 catches; 116 wickets (38.44).

Heavily-built, sometimes tending towards rotundity, David Green established himself as a schoolboy with Bowden, of the Manchester Association, and Lancashire 2nd XI. He became a regular county player in the 1960s, but despite a remarkably consistent 1965 season as an enterprising opening bat, he suffered more bad patches than expected and, troubled by a leg injury, he left to join Gloucestershire in 1968. Similar fortunes followed him to his new county and Green, more sensitive than his general appearance may have suggested, retired, most prematurely, in 1971. He has subsequently been a sports journalist with a *History of Gloucestershire CCC* to his credit. A good Rugby Union player in his Lancashire days, Green represented Sale and Cheshire.

GREEN, Leonard

RHB.
Born: Whalley, Lancashire, 1 February 1890.
Died: Whalley, 2 March 1963, aged 73.

Education: Bromsgrove.
First-class debut: 1922, Lancashire v Oxford University, Oxford.
152 matches for Lancashire 1922-35 (amateur).
Captain 1926-28. (Lancashire champions each season).
HS: 110* v Gloucestershire, Gloucester, 1923.
BB: 2-2 v Oxford University, Oxford, 1931.
Tours: Jamaica with Tennyson's team 1926-27; Argentina with Sir Julien Cahn's team 1929-30.
Full first-class record: 3,981 runs (25.51); 2 centuries; 12 wickets (33.83).

After distinguished Army service with the East Lancashire Regiment, winning the Military Cross during World War One, Major Green became a useful cricketer with Whalley and was finally persuaded to lead the county, which he did with unbroken success. Major Green was a valuable batsman and reliable fielder. He was a long-standing Lancashire committee member and President of the club 1951-52. He also played Rugby Union and hockey at county level.

GREENHALGH, Eric Washington

RHB; RM.
Born: Sale, Cheshire, 18 May 1910.
First-class debut: 1935, Lancashire v Hampshire, Southampton.
14 matches for Lancashire, 1935-38 (professional).
HS: 53* v Hampshire (debut).
BB: 2-75 v Gloucestershire, Bristol, 1938.

Eric Greenhalgh played League cricket for Egerton.

GREENHOUGH, Thomas

RHB; LBG.
Born: Cronkey Shaw, Rochdale, Lancashire, 9 November 1931.
First-class debut: 1951, Lancashire v Hampshire, Liverpool.
241 matches for Lancashire 1951-66, (professional). Capped 1956. Benefit (£4,504) 1964.
HS: 76* v Gloucestershire, Old Trafford, 1962.
BB: 7-56 v Worcestershire, Worcester, 1964.
100 wickets (2); 119 (17.85) 1960 best.
4 Tests for England 1959-60; BB: 5-35 v India, Lord's, 1959. Test record: 4 runs (1.33); 1 catch; 16 wickets (22.31).
Tours: West Indies v MCC 1959-60; Jamaica with Duke of Norfolk's XI 1956-57.
Full first-class record: 1,913 runs (8.39); 84 catches; 751 wickets (22.37).

An intelligent looking leg-spinner with impressive, deep-set eyes, Tommy Greenhough took a long, bounding run and spun the ball sharply, but his career was repeatedly interrupted by hand and leg injuries, and also by a habit of running on the pitch during delivery. He had an unimpressive batting record but possessed a natural ability which was never realised. Greenhough played League cricket for Werneth.

GREENWOOD, Peter

RHB; RM or OB.
Born: Todmorden, Yorkshire, 11 September 1924.

First-class debut: 1948, Lancashire v Cambridge University, Fenner's.
75 matches for Lancashire 1948-52 (professional). Capped 1949.
HS: 113 v Kent, Old Trafford, 1951.
BB: 6-35 v Northamptonshire, Old Trafford, 1949.
Took 75 wickets (25.69) in 1949.

Greenwood showed all-round promise in 1949 but faded quickly — possibly due to his uncertain role — and was squeezed out by other bowlers. He played League cricket for Bradshaw, West Bromwich Dartmouth, Todmorden and Kendall, and League soccer for Chester.

GREGSON, William Russell

RHB; RF.
Born: Lancaster, 5 August 1878.
Died: Lancaster, 18 June 1963, aged 84.
First-class debut: 1906, Lancashire v Essex, Leyton.
5 matches for Lancashire 1906 (professional).
HS: 26 v Derbyshire, Old Trafford, 1906.
BB: 5-8 v Leicestershire, Blackpool, 1906. (including hat-trick; 9-76 in match; also took four wickets in five balls).

Bill Gregson of Lancaster CC made a most promising start to his career but did not appear after 1906. He was described as 'of a cheerful disposition' but it was felt that he generally bowled too short.

GRIEVES, Kenneth John

RHB; LBG.
Born: Burwood, Sydney, New South Wales, 27 August 1925.
Lancashire debut: v Sussex, Old Trafford, 1949.
452 matches for Lancashire 1949-64 (professional). Capped 1949. Benefit (£,5756) 1956. Captain 1963-64.
HS: 224 v Cambridge University, Fenner's 1957.
BB: 6-60 v Kent, Old Trafford, 1949.
1,000 runs (13); 2,253 (41.72) 1959 best.
A magnificent slip fielder, he holds Lancashire record for catches in a match: 8 v Sussex, Old Trafford, 1951.
Joint holder with Richard Tyldesley of record for catches in an innings: 6 v Sussex, Old Trafford, 1951. 63 catches in 1950; 54 catches 1953, first and second best in season for Lancashire. 555 catches for Lancashire in career, record for the county.
1,407 runs; 63 wickets; 32 catches (all in debut season, 1949).
Played for New South Wales 1945-46 and 1946-47.
Toured India with Commonwealth XI 1950-51.
Full first-class record: 22,454 runs (33.66); 29 centuries; 608 catches; 242 wickets (29.78).

Ken Grieves came to England in 1947 to play soccer as a goalkeeper for Bury and League cricket for Rawtenstall (after Keith Miller had declined). He joined Lancashire in 1949, became the fourth player to exceed 1,000 runs in debut season for the county, and eventually achieved almost every honour the county club could bestow, although he was unfortunate that his

two years as captain coincided with unrest behind the scenes. Subsequently he returned to League cricket, playing for Accrington, Stockport, and Milnrow. After leaving Bury FC, he played for Bolton Wanderers and Stockport County.

GRIMSHAW, George Henry

RHB.
Born: Ashton, Lancashire, 1838.
Died: Grafton, Herefordshire, 21 January 1898, aged 59.
First-class debut: 1868, Lancashire v MCC, Lords
1 match Lancashire 1868, (amateur).
HS: 11 (debut).

HAGGAS, Stell

RHB; Occasional WK.
Born: Keighley, Yorkshire, 18 April 1856.
Died: Werneth, Oldham, Lancashire, 14 March
1926, aged 69.
Lancashire debut: 1884 v Oxford University.
3 matches for Lancashire 1884-85 (professional).
HS for Lancashire: 18 v Derbyshire, Derby,
1885.
31 for matches Yorkshire 1878-82.
HS: 43 Yorkshire v Surrey, The Oval, 1878.

A steady bat who also fielded well behind the
wickets, Haggas played for Keighley, Bacup and
Oldham. His son, Walter Haggas, also played
for Lancashire.

HAGGAS, Walter

RHB; WK.
Born: Werneth, near Oldham, Lancashire, 1
April 1881.
Died: Macclesfield, Cheshire, 14 November
1959, aged 78.
First-class debut: 1903, Lancashire v Derbyshire,
Derby.
2 matches for Lancashire 1903 (professional).
HS: 4 v Derbyshire, Derby (debut).

Son of Stell Haggas (Lancashire).

HAIGH, Charles Henry

RHB.
Born: Rochdale, Lancashire, 26 September 1854.
Died: Bollington, Cheshire, 15 March 1915, aged
60.
Education: Bromsgrove.
First-class debut: 1879, Lancashire v Derbyshire,
Derby.
24 matches for Lancashire 1879-87 (amateur).
HS: 80 v Gloucestershire, Clifton, 1882.

A batsman who drove and hit well to leg, Haigh
played club cricket for Manchester, Castleton
and Rochdale.

HALL, Alfred Ewart

RHB; LFM.
Born: Bolton, Lancashire, 23 January 1896.
Died: Johannesburg, South Africa, 1 January
1964, aged 67.
Lancashire debut: 1923 v Oxford University,
Oxford.
9 matches for Lancashire 1923-24 (professional).
HS for Lancashire: 5* v West Indians, Old
Trafford, 1923.

BB for Lancashire: 6-23 v Oxford University
(debut).
Played for Transvaal 1920-21 to 1930-31.
HS: 22 Transvaal v MCC, Johannesburg, 1922-23.
BB: 8-80 Transvaal v Natal, Johannesburg,
1926-27. (took 14-115 in match).
52 Currie Cup wickets 1926-27, a record which
stood until 1952-53.
7 Tests for South Africa 1922-23 to 1930-31.
HS: 5 v England, Cape Town, 1922-23. BB:
7-63 (11-112 match) v England, Cape Town,
1922-23 (both on Test debut). Test record: 11
runs (1.83); 4 catches; 40 wickets (22.15).
Full first-class record: 134 runs (3.72); 13 catches;
234 wickets (19.23).

Hall came to England in 1923 and played for
Werneth. He hoped to play in the County
Championship for Lancashire but MCC refused
his registration as he had played for Transvaal
(counted as a 'county') in the same year.

HALLAM, Albert William

RHB; RM.
Born: East Leake, Nottinghamshire, 12
November 1869.
Died: Loughborough, Leicestershire, 24 July
1940, aged 70.
First-class debut: 1895, Lancashire v MCC,
Lord's.
71 matches for Lancashire 1895-1900 (pro-
fessional).
HS for Lancashire: 31* v Sussex, Old Trafford,
1895.
BB for Lancashire: 6-28 v Leicestershire,
Liverpool, 1896.
194 matches for Nottinghamshire 1901-10
(professional), taking 156 wickets in 1907 and
performing hat-trick for Nottinghamshire v
Leicestershire at Trent Bridge 1907.
HS: 57 v Lancashire, Old Trafford, 1908, adding
119 for 9 wicket with B.Taylor.
Full first-class record: 2,606 runs (9.83); 171
catches; 1,012 wickets (19.02).

Albert Hallam made an excellent start to his
Lancashire career but after taking 100 wickets
in all matches in 1897 he was afflicted by what
seems to have been a 'TB spine' and after only
occasional appearances for three seasons he left
Lancashire after 1900 and joined Nottinghamshire. For Notts he had considerable success,
reaching a peak in 1907 when in all matches
he took 168 wickets (12.69) and with his opening
bowling partner, Tom Wass, virtually bowled
Notts to the Championship. Before joining
Lancashire, Hallam played for Leicestershire. In
1911 he joined Nelson and he subsequently
became coach at Loughborough Grammar
School. Hallam's feats in 1907 won him inclusion
as one of Wisden's five 'Cricketers of the Year'.

Albert Hallam

HALLIDAY, Thomas Maxwell

RHB.
Born: Leyland, Lancashire, 1 July 1904.
Died: Leyland, 28 February 1977, aged 72.
First-class debut: 1925, Lancashire v Glamorgan, Old Trafford.

41 matches for Lancashire 1925-29 (professional).
HS: 109* v Surrey, Old Trafford, 1929.

Halliday showed much promise but returned to Leyland Motors in the Ribblesdale League in 1930.

HALLOWS, Charles

LHB; SLA.
Born: Little Lever, Lancashire, 4 April 1895.
Died: Bolton, Lancashire, 10 November 1972, aged 77.
First-class debut: 1914, Lancashire v Yorkshire, Hull.
370 matches for Lancashire 1914-32 (professional). Benefit (£2,908) 1928.
HS: 233* v Hampshire, Liverpool, 1927.
BB: 3-28 v Northamptonshire, Old Trafford, 1914.
1,000 runs (11); 2,564 (65.74) best.

Also scored 2,185 runs 1924 and 2,119 runs 1927. In addition to HS above, scored 227 v Warwickshire, Old Trafford, 1921; 232 v Sussex, Old Trafford, 1928. Two centuries in match twice — 112* and 103* v Leicestershire, Ashby-de-la-Zouch, 1924; 123 and 101* v Warwickshire, Edgbaston, 1928. Three consecutive hundreds 1927 and 1928 — 120 v Rest of England, The

Oval, 1923; 100 v Northamptonshire, Old Trafford; 101 v Glamorgan, Old Trafford, 1928. Carried bat throughout innings six times: 109*/230 v Sussex, Old Trafford, 1921; 110*/183 v Leicestershire, Old Trafford, 1921; 179*/393 v Essex, Southnend, 1923; 158*/297 v Leicestershire, Leicester, 1925; 65*/103 v Derbyshire, Nelson, 1925; 152*/305 v Yorkshire, Old Trafford, 1929.

Scored 1,000 runs in May 1928 — a unique feat for the county — his scores being: 100, 101, 51*, 123, 101*, 22, 74, 104, 58, 34*, 232.

2 Tests for England 1921-28. HS: 26 v West Indies, Lord's, 1928. Test record: 42 runs (42.00).

2,645 runs (64.51) in all first-class matches 1928. 11 centuries same season.

Full first-class record: 20,956 runs (40.24); 55 centuries.

Charlie Hallows, a nephew of James Hallows, was a tall and very stylish left-hander most at home when opening. He had numerous substantial opening stands with Harry Makepeace and Frank Watson. Although sometimes criticised

for a slow scoring, there was no doubt as to class and, at his peak, he was as heavy a scorer as Lancashire has ever possessed. He must be considered unlucky to have won only two Test caps, but he was competing against the likes of Hobbs and Sutcliffe, and it was said that his fielding was below international standard.

After retirement, Charlie Hallows had numerous League engagement before becoming Worcestershire coach; he retained this job until the age of 70 and he finished up on the coaching staff at Old Trafford, right up to his sudden death.

HALLOWS, James

LHB; LFM (changed to SLA/LM).
Born: Little Lever, Lancashire, 14 November 1873.
Died: Farnworth, Lancashire, 20 May 1910, aged 36.
First-class debut: 1898, Lancashire v MCC, Lord's.
138 matches for Lancashire 1898-1907 (professional).

HS: 137* v Middlesex, Old Trafford, 1904.
BB: 9-37 v Gloucestershire, Gloucester, 1904.
1,000 runs (2); 1,170 (32.50) 1901 best.
100 wickets (1); 108 (18.71) 1904.
With 1,071 runs (39.66) in 1904 became first to achieve 'double' for Lancashire and that form saw him chosen as a *Wisden* 'Cricketer of the Year'.
Full first-class record: 5,065 runs (28.77); 8 centuries; 57 catches; 287 wickets (23.26).

Jimmy Hallows was a gifted all-rounder who first established himself, as a batsman and change bowler, in 1901. Ill-health then interfered with his career but apparently full health in 1904 enabled him to blossom as an all-rounder and complete a most impressive 'double'. Unhappily, the strain told the following season, when he exhibited a marked decline in his bowling effectiveness and, although still producing strong evidence of quality, he made only a handful of appearances in the two following seasons and after 1907 his career was over. Hallows, who suffered an epileptic attack on the field during the 'Roses' game at Old Trafford, in 1905, died after a few weeks' illness in 1910, aged only 36. Hallows, whose early cricket was played with the Temperance XI at Little Lever, and who later played for Little Lever CC, was uncle of Charlie Hallows.

HARDCASTLE, Frank
RHB.
Born: Bolton, Lancashire, 12 May 1844.
Died: Lancaster Gate, London, 5 November 1908, aged 64.
Education: Repton.
First-class debut: probably Lancashire v Yorkshire, Middlesbrough, 1867.
3 matches for Lancashire 1867-69.
HS: 9 v Surrey, The Oval, 1869.

A local amateur, Hardcastle was MP for Westhoughton from 1885 until 1892. It is likely that the 'J.Jackson' in the Lancashire team at Middlesbrough in 1867 was in fact Frank Hardcastle playing under a pseudonym.

HARDCASTLE, Walter Mitchell
RHB; RF.
Born: 10 February 1843. Bolton, Lancashire.
Died: Bolton, Lancashire, 27 April 1901, aged 58.
First-class debut: 1869, Lancashire v Sussex, Old Trafford.
4 matches for Lancashire 1869-74 (amateur).
HS: 11 v Sussex, Old Trafford, 1869 (debut).

HARGREAVES, Frederick William
RHB.
Born: Brookhouse, Blackburn, Lancashire, 16 August 1858.
Died: Wilpshire, Blackburn, 5 April 1897, aged 38.

Education: Malvern.
First-class debut: 1881, Lancashire v Derbyshire, Derby.
1 match for Lancashire 1881 (amateur).
Did not score but took 2 catches.

HARPER, George Minto
RHB; RM.
Born: Kensington, London, 30 August 1865.
Died: Details not known.
Education: Rugby.
First-class debut: 1883, Lancashire v Derbyshire, Old Trafford.
1 match for Lancashire 1883 (amateur).
HS: 1 v Derbyshire (debut).
Did not bowl.

Nothing is known of this amateur's subsequent life and career.

HARRISON, Frank
LB.
Born: 1909.
Died: York, 9 June, 1955.
First-class debut: 1936, Lancashire v Middlesex, Old Trafford.
3 matches for Lancashire 1936 (professional).
HS: 2* v Nottinghamshire, Old Trafford, 1936.
BB: 2-30 v Kent, Liverpool, 1936.

A professional engaged with Westhoughton, subsequently engaged at various clubs. He played for Cornwall 1951-52 (professional).

HARROP, J
Born: Details not known.
Died: Details not known.
Education: Bramham College, Tadcaster.
First-class debut: 1874, Lancashire v Derbyshire, Old Trafford.
1 match Lancashire 1874 (amateur).
HS: 5 (debut).

Harrop, who played in one match as a tail-ender and change bowler, objected to local Press coverage after this appearance, when it was not clear that he was an amateur.

HARRY, Frank
RHB; RMF.
Born: Torquay, Devon, 22 December 1876.
Died: North Malvern Hotel, Malvern, Worcestershire, 27 October 1925, aged 51.
First-class debut: 1903, Lancashire v Gloucestershire, Liverpool.

69 matches for Lancashire 1903-08 (professional).
HS: 88 v Worcestershire, Worcester, 1906.
BB: 9-44 v Warwickshire, Old Trafford, 1906 (15-70 in match).
Took 87 wickets (19.63) in 1906.
7 matches for Worcestershire 1919-20 (amateur).

Harry became professional with Kilmarnock CC after leaving Lancashire in 1908, and later played for South Shields and appeared for Durham in the Minor Counties 1912-14. After World War One he went into business in Great Malvern and appeared for Worcestershire as an amateur. He was a good Rugby Union player with Broughton Rangers.

HARTLEY, Alfred
RHB.
Born: New Orleans, USA, 11 April 1879.
Died: Near Maissemy, France, 9 October 1918 (killed in action). aged 39.

First-class debut: 1907, Lancashire v Middlesex, Old Trafford.
112 matches for Lancashire 1907-14 (amateur).
HS: 234 v Somerset, Old Trafford, 1910.
1,000 runs (3); 1,511 (38.74) 1910 best.

After playing in the 2nd XI in 1907, Hartley quickly won a place in the county side. A steady accumulater of runs rather than a brilliant stroke-player, he was strong in defence and on the on side. His form in 1910 won him a place for the Gentlemen, but thereafter his form declined and in the seasons before World War One, he played little. His father, George, and brother, Charles Robert, both played for Lancashire.

HARTLEY, Charles Robert
RHB.
Born: New Orleans, USA, 13 February 1873.
Died: Brooklands, Cheshire, 14 November 1927, aged 54.
First-class debut: 1897, Lancashire v Gloucestershire, Bristol.
106 matches for Lancashire 1897-1909 (amateur).
HS: 139 v Gloucestershire, Bristol, 1900.
1,000 runs (1); 1,084 (30.11) 1900 best.
Added 150 with Albert Ward v Leicestershire, Leicester, 1900, Lancashire 8th-wicket record until 1979.

Father George and brother Alfred both played for Lancashire. A good Rugby Union footballer, Charles Hartley represented Cheshire and The North.

HARTLEY, Fred
RHB; SLA.
Born: Waterfoot, near Bacup, Lancashire, 24 April 1906.
Died: Stacksteads, Bacup, 24 December 1976, aged 65.
First-class debut: 1924, Lancashire v Gloucestershire, Old Trafford.
2 matches for Lancashire 1924-45 (amateur). Lancashire record of 21 years between appearances.
HS: 2 v Yorkshire, Bradford, 1945.

A League cricket stalwart, playing for Bacup, Church, Bradshaw and Tonge, Fred Hartley enjoyed a remarkable county 'career' with two appearances separated by 21 years. His second and final game was in the Hedley Verity memorial match in 1945.

HARTLEY, George
RHB; WK.
Born: Heywood, Lancashire, 17 March 1849.

Died: Timperley, Cheshire, 9 September 1909, aged 60.
Education: Rossall.
First-class debut: 1871, Lancashire v Yorkshire, Sheffield.
3 matches for Lancashire 1871-72 (amateur).
HS: 24 v Yorkshire (debut).

An amateur resident at Southport, subsequently a merchant in New Orleans, where his sons, Alfred and Charles Robert, both Lancashire cricketers, were born.

HARWOOD, Baron

RHB; RF.
Born: Darwen, Lancashire, 14 August 1852.
Died: Moses Gate, Lancashire, 16 December 1915, aged 63.
First-class debut: 1877, Lancashire v Kent, Old Trafford.
1 match for Lancashire 1877 (professional).
Scored 0* in each innings.
BB: 1-16 in only match (Lord Harris was his only wicket).

Baron Harwood was a professional who played for Darwen.

HAWKWOOD, Clifford

RHB.
Born: Nelson, Lancashire, 16 November 1909.
Died: Burnley, Lancashire, 15 May 1960, aged 50.

First-class debut: 1931, Lancashire v Oxford University, Oxford.
24 matches for Lancashire 1931-35 (professional).
HS: 113 v Yorkshire, Headingley, 1933. (Added 202 for 4th wicket with Len Hopwood, a stand immortalised, with embellishments, by Sir Neville Cardus).

A batsman of the steady school, Hawkwood failed to establish himself in county cricket, although he was a stalwart of the Nelson club.

HAYES, Frank Charles

RHB; Occasionally RM.
Born: Preston, Lancashire, 6 December 1946.
Education: De la Salle College, Salford; Sheffield University.

First-class debut: 1970, Lancashire v Middlesex, Old Trafford.
228 matches for Lancashire 1970-84. Capped 1973. Captain 1979-80. Benefit (£40,768) 1983.
HS: 187 v Indians, Old Trafford, 1974.
1,000 runs (5); 1,283 (37.73) 1974 best.
9 Tests for England 1973-76 (all v West Indies). 106* on Test debut at The Oval, 1973. Test record: 244 runs (18.25).
Tours: West Indies with England, 1973-74; Robins' XI to South Africa, 1972-73, 1974-75,

1975-76; International XI to Rhodesia 1975-76, to Pakistan 1981-82; Overseas XI v Pakistan President's XI, Calcutta, 1980-81.
Full first-class record: 13,018 runs (35.86); 23 centuries; 176 catches.

After playing for Marple CC at the age of 14, Frank Hayes eventually gained a degree at Sheffield University before joining the Old Trafford staff. He made a startling entry to county scene with 94 and 47 on his debut, followed by 2 and 99 in his next match, yet he had to wait until 1973 for his maiden century. A most gifted batsman with an easy and graceful style, whose natural timing enabled him to reach the boundary with minimum effort, he made a triumphant England debut in 1973 but never again approached such Test form, suffering from ill-luck and, seemingly, chronic lack of confidence.

He enjoyed a relatively successful county career as batsman, although his spell as captain was not so successful. A sad early retirement when a brittle-bone condition was diagnosed set a somehow appropriate seal on a career which once held out seemingly infinite possibilities.

HAYES, Kevin Anthony
RHB; RM.
Born: Mexborough, Yorkshire, 26 September 1962.
Education: Queen Elizabeth Grammar School, Blackburn; Merton College, Oxford.
First-class debut: 1980, Lancashire v Oxford University, Oxford.
18 matches for Lancashire 1980-86.

HS for Lancashire: 117 v Somerset, Old Trafford, 1985.
Oxford Blue 1981-82-83-84.
HS: 152 Oxford University v Warwickshire, Oxford, 1982.
BB: 6-58 Oxford University v Warwickshire, Edgbaston, 1983.
Full first-class record: 1,595 runs (23.80); 2 centuries, 17 wickets (31.58); 15 catches.

Kevin Hayes has played Minor Counties cricket for Cumberland since 1988. He also won a soccer Blue at Oxford.

HAYHURST, Andrew Neal
RHB; RM.
Born: Davyhulme, Manchester, 23 November 1962.
Education: Worsley Wardley High School;

Eccles Sixth Form College; Leeds Polytechnic.
First-class debut: 1985, Lancashire v Leicestershire, Old Trafford.

42 matches for Lancashire 1985-89.
HS for Lancashire: 107 v Derbyshire, Derby, 1988.
BB 4-27 Lancashire v Middlesex, Old Trafford, 1987.
22 matches for Somerset 1990.
HS: 170 Somerset v Sussex, Taunton, 1990; and 170 Somerset v Yorkshire, Scarborough,1990.
Full first-class record: 2,44 runs (32.66); 5 centuries; 20 catches; 66 wickets (41.37).
Tours: Lancashire to West Indies 1986-87; to Zimbabwe 1988-89.

HEAD, Francis Somerville

Batsman (high-order).
Born: Kensington, London, 30 June 1846.
Died: Bushey, Hertfordshire, 2 April 1941, aged 94.
Education: Marlborough.
First-class debut: 1868, Lancashire v Surrey, Old Trafford.
6 matches for Lancashire 1868-69 (amateur).
HS: 24 v Surrey (debut).

Head played for Lancashire on a residential qualification. His last first-class match was for MCC in 1881, but he had little success in first-class cricket.

HEAP, James Sutcliffe

LHB; SLA.
Born: Lowerhouse, Burnley, Lancashire, 12 August 1882.
Died: Stoneclough, Bolton, Lancashire, 30 January 1951, aged 68.

First-class debut: 1903, Lancashire v Philadelphians, Old Trafford.
210 matches for Lancashire 1903-21 (professional). Benefit 1921 (£1,804).
HS: 132* v Hampshire, Bournemouth, 1914.
BB: 9-43 v Northamptonshire, Northampton, 1910.
Took 66 wickets (17.37) in 1919.

Recurring back trouble and the belief that he needed favourable conditions to succeed severely limited Heap's appearances and he should almost certainly have played more often. He coached at Shrewsbury School after retirement.

HEAP, John Garsden

Born: Higher Baxenden, Accrington, Lancashire, 5 January 1857.
Died: North Shore, Blackpool, 20 April 1931, aged 74.
First-class debut: 1884, Lancashire v Derbyshire, Derby.
2 matches for Lancashire 1884 (amateur).
HS: 0 (both first-class innings).

HEGG, Warren Kevin

RHB; WK.
Born: Whitefield, Lancashire, 23 February 1968.
Education: Unsworth High School, Bury; Stand College, Whitefield.
First-class debut: 1986, Lancashire v Glamorgan, Lytham.
85 matches for Lancashire 1986-90. Capped 1989.
HS: 130 v Northamptonshire, Northampton, 1987.
Equalled Lancashire record with 7 dismissals (all

caught) in innings v Derbyshire, Chesterfield, 1989. Equalled world record with 11 dismissals (all caught) in same match.
Tours: Lancashire to West Indies 1986-87; to Zimbabwe 1988-89.

Hegg is a talented if sometimes slightly inconsistent wicketkeeper, regarded at the time of writing as one of the best in England.

HENRIKSON, Soren
RHB; RFM.
Born: Rodoure, Copenhagen, Denmark, 1 December 1964.
RHB; RF.
First-class debut: 1985, Lancashire v Surrey, The Oval.
3 matches for Lancashire 1985-86.
HS: 10* v Surrey (debut).
BB: 1-26 v Derbyshire, Buxton, 1986.

Henrikson, who played Denmark, joined Lancashire from Svanholm CC, Copenhagen.

HEWITSON, Joseph
LHB; SLA.
Born: Little Lever, Bolton, Lancashire, 17 October 1865.
Died: Halliwell, Bolton, 4 December 1925, aged 60.
First-class debut: 1890, Lancashire v Oxford University, Old Trafford.
4 matches for Lancashire 1890 (professional).
HS: 56 v Middlesex, Old Trafford, 1890.
BB: 6-57 (10-115 match) v Oxford University (debut).

Against Gloucestershire in 1890, Hewitson incurred the ire of W.G. and E.M.Grace and never again played for Lancashire, although he remained a force at Bolton.

HEYS, William
RHB; WK.
Born: Oswaldtwistle, Lancashire, 19 February 1931.
First-class debut: 1957, Lancashire v Worcestershire, Worcester.
5 matches for Lancashire 1957 (professional).
HS: 46 v West Indians, Old Trafford, 1957.

HIBBARD, Henry
Born: 1854.
Died: St Michael's, Liverpool, 12 February 1902.
First-class debut: 1884, Lancashire v Derbyshire, Old Trafford.
1 match for Lancashire 1884 (professional).
HS: 4 (debut).
BB: 2-35 (debut).

HIBBERD, George
RHB; RF.
Born: Sheffield, Yorkshire, 8 February 1845.
Died: Todwick, Yorkshire, 24 August 1911, aged 66.
First-class debut: 1867, Lancashire v Yorkshire, Blackburn.
1 match for Lancashire 1867.
HS: 2* (debut).

HIBBERT, William John
LHB.
Born: Nottingham, 11 July 1873.
Died: Lincoln, 6 June 1934, aged 60.
First-class debut: 1900, Lancashire v Warwickshire, Edgbaston.
14 matches for Lancashire 1900-01 (professional).
HS: 79 v Warwickshire (debut).

A most promising start — he was the highest scorer in his debut game — was not built upon.

HICKMOTT, William Edward
RHB; LM.
Born: Boxley, Kent, 10 April 1893.

Died: West Malling, Kent, 16 January 1968, aged 74.
Lancashire debut: 1923 v Yorkshire, Old Trafford.
34 matches for Lancashire 1923-24 (professional).
HS: 31* v Nottinghamshire, Trent Bridge, 1924.
BB: 5-20 v Leicestershire, Old Trafford, 1924.
First-class debut: 1914, Kent v Hampshire, Bournemouth.
3 matches for Kent 1914-21.
Full first-class record: 301 runs (10.37); 25 catches; 92 wickets (25.65).

Hickmott played club cricket for Ramsbottom and for Rochdale — for whom he took a record 140 wickets in 1927 — and Wallasey. His uncle, Edward Hickmott, played for Kent.

HICKTON, William
RHB; RFM.
Born: Hardstoft, near Chesterfield, Derbyshire, 14 December 1842.
Died: Higher Broughton, Manchester, 25 February 1900, aged 57.
First-class debut: 1867, Lancashire v MCC, Lord's.
24 matches for Lancashire 1867-71 (professional). Benefit 1883.
HS for Lancashire: 55 v Yorkshire, Sheffield, 1871.
BB: 10-46 v Hampshire, Old Trafford, 1870 (best-ever innings analysis for Lancashire; took 14-73 in the match).
34 matches for Derbyshire 1871-78.

HS: 63 for Derbyshire v Yorkshire, Derby, 1877.
Bill Hickton was a fast round-arm bowler of great effectiveness who was the first Lancashire player to take all 10 wickets in an innings. Against MCC in 1869, Hickton dismissed W.G.Grace twice, bowled each time. Hickton's son, W.H.Hickton, played for Worcestershire.

HIGGS, Kenneth
LHB; RFM later RM.
Born: Kidsgrove, Staffordshire, 14 January 1937.
Education: Tunstall Secondary Modern School, Stoke on Trent.
First-class debut: 1958, Lancashire v Cambridge University, Fenner's.
306 matches for Lancashire 1958-69. Capped 1959. Benefit (£8,390) 1968. (originally professional).
HS: 60 v Gloucestershire, Cheltenham, 1967.
BB: 7-19 v Leicestershire, Old Trafford, 1965.
100 wickets (5); 123 (20.02) 1960 best.
Two hat-tricks for Lancashire: v Essex, Black-

pool, 1960; v Yorkshire, Headingley, 1968. Also hat-trick for Leicestershire v Hampshire, Leicester, 1977.

167 matches for Leicestershire 1972-86. Capped 1972. Captain 1979.

15 Tests for England 1965-68. HS: 63 v West Indies, The Oval, 1966, adding 128 for last wicket with J.A.Snow. BB: 6-91 v West Indies, Lord's, 1966. Test record: 185 runs (11.56); 4 catches; 71 wickets (20.74).

HS: 98 Leicestershire v Northamptonshire, Leicester, 1977 (added 228 with R.Illingworth for Leicestershire 10th-wicket record).

Full first-class record: 3,648 runs (11.29); 311 catches; 1,536 wickets (23.61).

Tours: England to Australia and New Zealand 1965-66; to West Indies 1967-68.

Tall, fair-haired and strongly-built, Ken Higgs was a new-ball bowler who relied on pace and movement from the pitch rather than speed through the air and, barring occasional lapses, he gave Lancashire great service. He was also a useful left-handed tail-ender with a very straight bat, and a good catcher. Higgs joined Lancashire after a season with his native Staffordshire, having played for Meakins CC. After leaving Lancashire he joined Rishton for two seasons but then resumed first-class cricket with Leicestershire. He gave great service to his second county, becoming captain and then coach, a position he relinquished in 1990.

HIGHTON, Edward Frederick William
RHB; RFM.
Born: Formby, Lancashire, 29 August 1924.
Died: Formby, 9 October 1985, aged 61.
Education: King Edward VI School, Southport.
Lancashire debut: 1951, v Essex, Colchester.
1 match for Lancashire 1951 (professional).
HS for Lancashire: 6 (debut).
BB for Lancashire: 1-49 (debut).
1 match for Minor Counties 1950.
HS: 26 Minor Counties v MCC, Lord's, 1950.
BB: 4-87 Minor Counties v MCC (above).

Highton, who made his first-class debut for Minor Counties, played several seasons for Lancashire 2nd XI and club cricket for Formby.

HIGSON, Peter
RHB.
Born: Bramhall, Cheshire, 1 December 1904.
Died: Hove, Sussex, 19 April 1986, aged 81.
Education: Cheltenham.
First-class debut: 1928, Lancashire v Sussex, Old Trafford.
3 matches for Lancashire 1928-31 (amateur).

HS for Lancashire: 13* (debut).
1 match for Minor Counties v Oxford University, Oxford, 1933.
HS: 29 Minor Counties v Oxford University (above).

He was President of Lancashire CCC 1973-74. His father, T.A.Higson snr, and brother, T.A.Higson jnr, played for Lancashire.

HIGSON, Thomas Atkinson, Snr
RHB; OB.
Born: Stockport, Cheshire, 18 November 1873.
Died: Grange-over-Sands, Lancashire, 3 August 1949, aged 75.

Education: Rossall; New College, Oxford.
Lancashire debut: 1905 v England XI, Blackpool.
5 matches for Lancashire 1905-23 (amateur).
HS for Lancashire: 42 v Warwickshire, Edgbaston, 1907.
HS: 46 Derbyshire v Lancashire, Old Trafford, 1899.
BB: 4-74 Derbyshire v Warwickshire, Edgbaston, 1899.
Played for Oxford University 1892 (no Blue).
Full first-class record: 584 runs (12.69); 41 wickets (28.41); 12 catches.

Tommy Higson, a solicitor in Manchester, played for Cheshire in 1890 and after leaving Oxford, he missed several seasons until leading Derbyshire in 1899. He first appeared for Lancashire in 1905, returned to Derbyshire in 1910, and came back, yet again, to Lancashire in 1923. This much-travelled cricketer was also a distinguished administrator, serving on Lancashire's committee for 49 years. He served as Treasurer from 1924-32, when he became Chairman. From 1931-34, Higson was on the Test selection committee. Outside cricket he was

a useful hockey and soccer player. Higson's sons, Peter and Tommy junior, also played for Lancashire. His club cricket was played for Colne and Blackley.

HIGSON, Thomas Atkinson, Jnr

LHB; RM.
Born: Whaley Bridge, Derbyshire, 25 March 1911.
Education: Cheltenham College; Jesus College, Cambridge.
Lancashire debut: 1936, v Warwickshire, Old Trafford.
20 matches for Lancashire 1936-46 (amateur).
HS for Lancashire: 32* v Essex, Old Trafford, 1938.
First-class debut: 1932, Derbyshire v Surrey, The Oval.
6 matches Derbyshire 1932-35.
HS: 51 Derbyshire v Essex, Leyton, 1933.

Tommy Higson, son of the Lancashire Treasurer, played as deputy skipper to Lionel Lister and declined a permanent appointment in 1946. He captained Cheltenham College in 1930 and played in the 1931 Cambridge Freshmen's trial, meeting with success, but he never appeared in a first-class match for Cambridge. Before playing for Lancashire he appeared for his native Derbyshire. Higson, President of Lancashire 1977-78, was son of T.A.Higson snr, and brother of P.Higson, both Lancashire cricketers.

HILDYARD, Lyonel D'Arcy

RHB.
Born: Bury, Lancashire, 5 February 1861.
Died: Rowley, Hull, Yorkshire, 22 April 1931, aged 70.
Education: Somerset County School; Magdalen College, Oxford.
Lancashire debut: 1884 v Oxford University, Oxford.
8 matches for Lancashire 1884-85 (amateur).
HS for Lancashire: 39 v Somerset, Taunton, 1884.
Played for Somerset 1882-83. Played for Oxford University. Blue 1884-85-86.
HS: 62* Oxford University v Surrey, The Oval, 1885.
Full first-class record: 811 runs (17.25); 26 catches.

Hildyard was ordained into Holy Orders and for many years was rector of Rowley, Yorkshire, where he died. From 1894 to 1908 was a minor canon of Windsor.

HILL, Rowland Wright Davenport

RHB; WK.
Born: Hajepur, India, 5 September 1851.

Died: Gladesville, New South Wales, Australia, 29 August 1912, aged 60.
First-class debut: 1871, Lancashire v Derbyshire, Derby.
1 match for Lancashire 1871 (amateur).
HS: 5 v Derbyshire (debut).

HILLKIRK, John Ritson
RHB; RM.
Born: Manchester, 25 June 1845.
Died: Cowes, Isle of Wight, 8 October 1921, aged 76.
Education: Ardwick School.
First-class debut: 1871, Lancashire v Derbyshire, Old Trafford.
30 matches for Lancashire 1871-77 (amateur).
HS: 56* v Yorkshire, Sheffield, 1873.

John Hillkirk was a powerful man who wielded a heavy bat to hit hard, but usually found first-class bowling too subtle for him. A superb all-round athlete who could throw a cricket ball 115 yards, he became an athletics judge and referee. Hillkirk, who was elected to the Lancashire committee in 1880, was an estate agent and surveyor at Withington Village.

HILTON, Colin
RHB; RF.
Born: Atherton, Lancashire, 26 September 1937.
First-class debut: 1957, Lancashire v Cambridge Unversity, Liverpool.
91 matches for Lancashire 1957-63 (professional). Capped 1962.
HS: 36 v Somerset, Glastonbury, 1962.
BB: 6-38 v Nottinghamshire, Liverpool, 1962.
94 wickets (26.62) 1962.
24 matches for Essex 1964.

Well-built, cheerful and really pacey, Colin Hilton's services were probably dispensed with too soon. A less than happy season with Essex followed, and then the Leagues including appearances for Ribblesdale Wanderers, Oldham and Daisy Hill.

HILTON, Jim
RHB; OB.
Born: Chadderton, Lancashire, 29 December 1930.
First-class debut: 1952, Lancashire v Worcestershire, Worcester.
8 matches for Lancashire 1952-53 (professional).
HS: Lancashire 33 v Worcestershire (debut).
BB for Lancashire: 2-27 v Northamptonshire, Northampton, 1953.
71 matches for Somerset 1954-57 (professional).

HS: 61*, Somerset v Nottinghamshire, Taunton, 1955.

BB: 7-98 Somerset v Warwickshire, Bath, 1954.

Full first-class record: 1,093 runs (10.93); 53 catches; 135 wickets (27.22).

The brother of Malcolm J.Hilton (*see next*), apart from county cricket with Lancashire and Somerset, he appeared in the Leagues with Werneth and Kelbourne. He is now Werneth CC's president.

HILTON, Malcolm Jameson
RHB; SLA.

Born: Chadderton, Oldham, Lancashire, 2 August 1928.

Died: Oldham, 8 July 1990, aged 61.

Education: Hollins School, Oldham.
First-class debut: 1946, Lancashire v Sussex, Hove.
241 matches for Lancashire 1946-61 (professional). Capped 1950. Joint benefit (with R.Tattersall, £11,655) 1960.
HS: 100* v Northamptonshire, Northampton, 1955.
BB: 8-19 v New Zealanders, Old Trafford, 1958.
100 wickets (4); 150 (14.46) 1956 best.
4 Tests for England 1950 to 1951-52. HS: 15 v India, Madras, 1951-52. BB: 5-61 (9-93 in match) v India, Kanpur, 1951-52. Test record: 37 runs (7.40); 1 catch; 14 wickets (34.07).
Full first-class record: 3,416 runs (12.11); 1 century; 202 catches; 1,006 wickets (19.42).

Malcolm Hilton, a slim, fair-haired youth, achieved the fame which knows no bounds when twice dismissing Donald Bradman in 1948. He did not gain a regular place until 1950, although 100 wickets for the Minor Counties team in 1949 suggest that he was held back a little. Indeed, any lapse in form appeared to be meted the ultimate punishment — exclusion from the team — but he gave Lancashire excellent service until losing the ability to pitch the ball.

In 1960 and 1961, Hilton captained the 2nd XI but then retired whilst still in his early 30s. Hilton's premature demise should not hide the fact that he was a brilliant natural cricketer who for several years fulfilled much of his potential. Slightly quicker than most spinners, his very sharp spin enabled him to take full advantage of helpful pitches, but he lacked the subtlety and flight needed on more plumb surfaces. As a batsman he was unorthodox with a good eye and much largely unrealised potential. He was a marvellous fieldsman anywhere — safe of hand, long of throw, sharp of anticipation.

Malcolm Hilton's clubs included Werneth, Burnley, Oldham, Radcliffe and Marsden. His brother, Jim Hilton, played for Lancashire and Somerset and is now Werneth president. Those who knew Malcolm Hilton, praised his ready smile and sense of humour, and his ability as performer of Lancashire monologues.

HIRD, Sydney Francis

RHB; OB & LB.
Born: Balmain, New South Wales, Australia, 7 January 1910.
Died: Bloemfontein, South Africa, 20 December 1980, aged 70.
Lancashire debut: 1939 v Gloucestershire, Old Trafford.
1 match for Lancashire 1939 (professional).
Did not bat or bowl due to bad weather.
Played for New South Wales 1931-32 to 1932-33;

Eastern Province 1945-46 to 1948-49; Border 1950-51.
HS: 130 Eastern Province v Griqualand West, Kimberley, 1945-46.
BB: 6-56 New South Wales v Victoria, Sydney, 1932-33.
Full first-class record: 1,453 runs (33.02); 5 centuries; 59 wickets (28.54); 8 catches.

Syd Hird came to England in 1933, signing for Ramsbottom when that club failed to persuade Don Bradman to come. After the war he emigrated to South Africa, where he eventually became coach of Eastern Province and Orange Free State, and captained the former province.

HODGSON, Geoffrey

RHB; WK.
Born: Lepton, Yorkshire, 24 July 1938.
First-class debut: 1965, Lancashire v Kent, Old Trafford.
1 match for Lancashire 1965.
HS: 1 (only innings).
1 match for Yorkshire 1964 (scored 4 in only innings).

Geoff Hodgson played Bradford League cricket for Spen Victoria.

HODGSON, Gordon

RHB; RF.
Born: Johannesburg, South Africa, 16 April 1904.
Died: Stoke-on-Trent, Staffordshire, 14 June 1951, aged 47.
First-class debut: 1928, Lancashire v Surrey, Old Trafford, 1928.
56 matches for Lancashire 1928-33 (professional).
HS: 20 v All India, Liverpool, 1932.
BB: 6-77 v Middlesex, Lord's, 1932.

Gordon Hodgson came to England to play soccer for Liverpool and scored 232 League goals for them, a club record until broken by Roger Hunt 33 years later. Hodgson, who won three England soccer caps, went on to play for Aston Villa and Leeds United. Later, he coached Leeds United and managed Port Vale, a position he held at his death. He began his cricket career in South Africa and after leaving Lancashire played for Forfarshire 1934-36.

HOGG, William

RHB; RFM.
Born: Ulverston, Lancashire, 12 July 1955.
Education: Ulverston School.
First-class debut: 1976, Lancashire v Middlesex, Lord's.
44 matches for Lancashire 1976-80.
HS for Lancashire: 19 v Middlesex, Lord's, 1978.
BB: 7-84 v Warwickshire, Old Trafford, 1978.
50 matches Warwickshire 1981-83.
HS: 31 Warwickshire v Hampshire, Edgbaston, 1981.
Full first class record: 394 runs (6.06); 222 wickets (28.99).

Willie (sometimes known as 'Hedge') Hogg could generate real pace when the mood took him but lacked the temperamental equipment necessary for a successful fast bowler. Various niggling injuries continually interrupted career which was finally terminated by a bad knee. His wife is Sharon, daughter of Sonny Ramadhin, the former Lancashire and West Indian off-spinner.

HOLDEN, Cecil

RHB; RMF.
Born: West Derby, Liverpool, 1 June 1865.
Died: Claughton, Cheshire, 22 August 1928, aged 63.

First-class debut: 1890, Lancashire v Kent, Old Trafford.
3 matches for Lancashire 1890.
HS for Lancashire: 27* v Kent (debut).
Played for Liverpool & District 1886-91.
HS: 45 Liverpool & District v Yorkshire, Liverpool, 1891.
Full first-class record: 136 runs (10.46); 6 catches.

A free-hitting batsman who failed to do himself justice against first-class opposition. For many years he played for Cheshire, and scored 109* for them against Warwickshire at Edgbaston in 1894. In a match not deemed first-class, Holden scored 172, for Liverpool & District v Cambridge University in 1897. For many years he played with great all-round success for Birkenhead Park. He skippered them from 1893 until 1912, scored more than 19,000 runs and took 650 wickets, and in 1896 scored 202 in a total of 261.

HOLDING, Michael Anthony
RHB; RF.
Born: Kingston, Jamaica, 16 February 1954.
Education: Kingston College, Jamaica.
Debut for Lancashire: 1981, v Northamptonshire, Northampton.

7 matches for Lancashire 1981.
HS for Lancashire: 32 v Gloucestershire, Old Trafford, 1981.
BB for Lancashire: 6-74 v Gloucestershire, Old Trafford, 1981.
First-class debut: 1972-73, Jamaica v Barbados, Kingston.
Played for Jamaica from 1972-73.
66 matches for Derbyshire 1983-89. Capped 1983.
60 Tests for West Indies 1975-76 to 1986-87. HS: 73 v England, St John's, Antigua, 1985-86. BB (and best in first-class cricket): 8-92 v England, The Oval, 1976. Test record: 910 runs (13.78). 22 catches. 249 wickets (23.68).
102 limited-overs matches for West Indies.
Full first-class record: 3,600 runs (15.00); 125 catches; 778 wickets (23.43).

Although Michael Holding's Lancashire career was very short, and his influence on the affairs of the county very marginal, they no doubt feel honoured to have had him as a player at all. Most appropriate was Holding's soubriquet 'Whispering Death', so quietly graceful, yet lethal, was his attack. Tall but comparatively slightly built, Holding had little of the muscular development normally associatied with a West Indian pace bowler, yet at his best he was probably as quick as any.

HOLGATE, Gideon
RHB; WK.
Born: Sawley, Barnoldswick, Yorkshire, 23 June 1839.
Died: Accrington, Lancashire, 11 July 1895, aged 56.
Lancashire debut: 1866 v Middlesex, Old Trafford.
8 matches for Lancashire 1866-67 (professional).
HS: 65 v Surrey, The Oval, 1866.
Played for Yorkshire 1865-67.
Full first-class record: 455 runs (13.78); 24 catches; 10 stumped.

Holgate split his cricket between Yorkshire and Lancashire, without ever being a regular player. An awkward, stubborn character, he was often involved in disputes whilst with Yorkshire, acting almost as the players' 'shop steward'. He became a coal agent in Accrington. His grandson, Gideon Holgate III, was secretary of the Lancashire League, 1934-49.

HOLLAND, John
RHB.
Born: Nantwich, Cheshire, 7 April 1869.
Died: Bury, Lancashire, 22 August 1914, aged 45.
Lancashire debut: 1900 v Hampshire, Old Trafford.
12 matches for Lancashire 1900-02 (professional).
HS for Lancashire: 63 v Essex, Old Trafford, 1901.
Played for Leicestershire 1894-96 (professional).
HS: 65 Leicestershire v Yorkshire, Leicester, 1895.

First-class debut: A.J.Webbe's Team v Oxford University, Oxford, 1898.
Last first-class game for MCC 1927.
Tours: West Indies with R.A.Bennett's team 1901-02; India with Oxford University Authentics 1902-03; Canada with Free Foresters 1923.
Full first-class record: 1,114 runs (21.01); 1 century; 33 catches.

Brother of A.M.Hollins (Oxford University) and J.C.H.L.Hollins (Lancashire).

HOLLINS, John Chard Humphrey Lancelott

RHB.
Born: Fulwood, Preston, Lancashire, 3 June 1890.
Died: Whittle-le-Woods, Lancashire, 13 November 1938, aged 48.
Education: Eton; Oxford.
First-class debut: 1914, Lancashire v Nottinghamshire, Old Trafford.
20 matches for Lancashire, 1914-19 (amateur).
HS: 65 v Gloucestershire, Old Trafford, 1919.

Hollins appeared in the 1911 Oxford Freshmen's Trial, but did not play a first-class match for Oxford. Brother of Sir F.H.Hollins (Lancashire) and A.M.Hollins (Oxford University). Their father was on Lancashire's committee and a well-known benefactor of the County Club.

HOLROYD, Edwin

RHB; RM.
Born: Halifax, Yorkshire, 27 October 1855.
Died: Mitchell Hay, Rochdale, Lancashire, 9 April 1914, aged 58.
Education: Summer Castle Academy.
First-class debut: 1878, Lancashire v Nottinghamshire, Trent Bridge.
1 match for Lancashire, 1878 (amateur).
HS: 4 v Nottinghamshire (debut).

Full first-class record: 1,650 runs (17.55); 25 catches.

A correct and stylish batsman, Holland scored consistently for both Leicestershire and Lancashire but was unable to become a heavy scorer. He also played for Cheshire and in 1896-97 and 1897-98 was engaged by Western Province.

HOLLINS, Sir Frank Hubert

RHB.
Born: Bowness-on-Windermere, Westmorland, 31 October 1877.
Died: Paddington, London, 31 January 1963, aged 85.
Education: Eton; Magdalen College, Oxford.
Lancashire debut: 1902 v MCC, Lord's.
12 matches for Lancashire 1902-04 (amateur).
HS: 114 v Worcestershire, Worcester, 1903.
Played for Oxford University 1900-01. Blue 1901.

HOLROYD, John

LHB; SLA.
Born: Oldham, Lancashire, 15 April 1907.
Died: Whitehaven, Cumberland, 15 September 1975, aged 68.
First-class debut: 1927, Lancashire v Derbyshire, Old Trafford.
11 matches for Lancashire 1927-33 (professional).
HS: 18* v Warwickshire, Nelson, 1929.
BB: 5-47 v Warwickshire, Nelson, 1929.

Holdroyd was a club professional, appearing for Colne, Ramsbottom and Ashton.

HOPWOOD, John Leonard

RHB; SLA.
Born: Newton Hyde, Cheshire, 30 October 1903.
Died: Denton, Lancashire, 15 June 1985, aged 81.
First-class debut: 1923, Lancashire v Kent, Gravesend.
397 matches for Lancashire, 1923-39 (professional).
HS: 220 v Gloucestershire, Bristol, 1934.
BB: 9-33 v Leicestershire, Old Trafford, 1933.
Also 9-69 v Worcestershire, Blackpool, 1934 (15-112 in match).
Match double v Leicestershire, Old Trafford, 1933 (see best bowling above) 110 & 45; 1-20 & 9-33.
1,000 runs (8); 1,972 (46.95) 1933 best.
100 wickets (2); 111 (19.29) 1934 best.

Achieved double 1934: 1,660 runs (39.52), 111 wickets (19.29); and 1935: 1,538 runs (33.43), 103 wickets (20.55). The second Lancashire player to achieve double and only one to do it twice.
2 Tests for England 1934. HS: 8 v Australia, Headingley, 1934. Test record: 12 runs (6.00); 0 wickets.
Full first-class record: 15,458 runs (29.90); 27 centuries; 673 wickets (22.45); 198 catches.

Len Hopwood, who played for the Manchester and Wallasey clubs, was a somewhat stolid all-rounder, a somewhat cramped high-order batsman and slow-medium in-slant bowler to a packed leg-side field. More of a match-saver than a match-winner, he was invaluable all the same. In 1982 he became the first professional cricketer to be elected President of Lancashire CCC.

HORNBY, Albert Henry

RHB.
Born: Nantwich, Cheshire, 29 July 1877.
Died: North Kilworth, Leicestershire, 6 September 1952, aged 75.
Education: Harrow; Trinity College, Cambridge.

Lancashire debut: 1899, Lancashire v MCC, Lord's.

283 matches for Lancashire 1899-1914 (amateur). Captain 1908-14.

HS: 129 v Surrey, The Oval, 1912.

Shared stands of 206 with Willis Cuttell v Somerset, Old Trafford, 1904, and 245 with Jack Sharp v Leicestershire, Old Trafford, 1912, both Lancashire records for the 7th wicket. 1,000 runs (1); 1,336 (28.42), 1913.

First-class debut: 1898, Cambridge University v A.J.Webbe's XI, Cambridge.

2 matches for Cambridge University 1898 (no Blue).

Toured India with Oxford Aunthentics, 1902-03.

Full first-class record: 9,784 runs (24.58); 8 centuries; 217 catches; 2 stumped.

Scored 106 v Somerset, Old Trafford, 1905, reaching a century in 43 minutes.

The son of A.N.'Monkey' Hornby, he was a brilliant aggressive batsman in his own right, as well as a brilliant field. As a captain, however, he perhaps suffered in comparison with his father, being slightly more reticent.

HORNBY, Albert Neilson

RHB; Versatile Bowler — RA or LA.

Born: Blackburn, Lancashire, 10 February 1847.

Died: Nantwich, Cheshire, 17 December 1925, aged 78.

Education: Harrow.

First-class debut: 1867, Lancashire v Yorkshire, Blackburn.

292 matches for Lancashire, 1867-99 (amateur). Captain 1880-91, and at times until 1898.

HS: 188 v Derbyshire, Old Trafford, 1881.

1,000 runs (1); 1,002 (50,10) 1881.

Carried bat for 23*/56 v Yorkshire, Old Trafford, 1876.

3 Tests for England 1878-79 to 1884. HS: 9 v Australia, The Oval, 1882. Test record: 21 runs (3.50).

Toured North America with R.A.Fitzgerald's team in 1872, and Australia with Lord Harris in 1878-79.

Full first-class record: 16,109 runs (24.07); 16 centuries; 11 wickets (23.45); 313 catches; 3 stumped.

'Monkey' Hornby was a brilliant, punishing batsman, and an all-action fieldsman whose activities probably helped earn him the soubriquet 'Monkey'. He also bowled on occasion, right-arm or left-arm according to his mood. Hornby won a place in literature in Francis Thompson's *At Lord's*, although mention of his partnership with Dick Barlow is by no means the most important point in the poem. On his Test debut at Sydney in 1878-9, he dealt with the spectator who

assaulted Lord Harris in the most effective manner possible. Hornby often appeared with his son, A.H.Hornby, in the Lancashire side, and made his last first-class appearance for an England XI in 1906, aged 59. His brother, C.L.Hornby, also played for Lancashire. In non-first-class cricket Hornby did lots of spectacular things, amongst which was a score of 201 for Cheshire v Shropshire in 1868. In 1870 he scored 213* for East Lancashire v Accrington at Blackburn and altogether made nine centuries that season. Whilst at Harrow he played against Eton, aged 17, and was so small that he allegedly weighed barely 6st and stood only 4ft 7in. Hornby, who was Lancashire's President for many years, was a good enough Rugby Union footballer to win nine England caps. He also rode to hounds very enthusiastically.

HORNBY, Cecil Lumsden

RHB.
Born: Blackburn, Lancashire, 25 July 1843.
Died: Leamington Spa, Warwickshire, 27 February 1896, aged 52.
Education: Harrow.
Debut for Lancashire: 1877, Lancashire v MCC, Lord's.
1 match for Lancashire, 1877 (amateur).
HS for Lancashire: 4 (above); also took 1-3.
Played for Gentlemen of England v Oxford & Cambridge at The Oval, 1874, scoring 23 in the only innings.

Short and stocky, like his brother A.N.Hornby, Cecil Hornby was a regular officer in the 58th Foot Regiment and was unable to play a great deal of cricket. He was a vigorous forward batsman and a fine field or wicketkeeper.

HORNBY, Edgar Christian

LHB; SLA.
Born: Wavertree, Liverpool, 14 September 1863.
Died: Claygate, Surrey, 2 April 1922, aged 58.
Education: Winchester.
First-class debut: 1885, Lancashire v MCC, Lord's (amatuer).
9 matches for Lancashire, 1885-87.
HS: 82 v Oxford University, Oxford, 1886.
Played first-class for Liverpool & District, 1886-94.
Full first-class record: 360 runs (18.94); 6 wickets (29.50); 6 catches.

A long-serving player, and then President, of Liverpool CC, Hornby was a cotton broker in that city. A cousin, although not a close one, of 'Monkey' Hornby — at 6ft 3in and 13½st, they differed physically as much as is possible.

HORRIDGE, Leonard

RHB; OB.
Born: Adlington, Lancashire, 18 August 1907.
Died: Deepdale, Preston, Lancashire, 1 September 1976, aged 69.
First-class debut: 1927, Lancashire v Northamptonshire, Northampton.
3 matches for Lancashire, 1927-29 (professional).
HS for Lancashire: 11* v Northamptonshire (debut).
BB: 2-46 v Leicestershire, Leicester, 1927.
Played for Minor Counties 1928, 1930.
HS: 15 Minor Counties v West Indians, Exeter, 1928.
Full first-class record: 57 runs (11.40); 3 wickets (26.33).

A club professional with Adlington and Little Lever.

HORROCKS, Richard

RHB.
Born: Church, Lancashire, 29 August 1857.
Died: Church, Lancashire, 19 June 1926, aged 68.
First-class debut: 1880, Lancashire v Derbyshire, Old Trafford.
6 matches for Lancashire, 1880-82 (professional).
HS: 61 v Derbyshire (debut).

A Church professional promising enough to play for 22 Colts of England v MCC at Lord's in 1880. After 1881 a knee injury at football handicapped him severely.

HORROCKS, William John

RHB.
Born: Warrington, Lancashire, 18 June 1905.
Died: Melbourne, Victoria, Australia, 15 November 1985, aged 80.
Debut for Lancashire: 1931, Lancashire v New Zealanders, Liverpool.
15 matches for Lancashire 1931-33 (professional).
HS for Lancashire: 100* v Nottinghamshire, Old Trafford, 1931.

Played for Western Australia 1926-27 to 1936-37.
HS: 148* Western Australia v Tasmania, Hobart, 1929-30.
Full first-class record: 1,255 runs (33.02); 3 centuries; 4 catches.

Having gone to Australia aged seven, Horrocks came to Lancashire in 1931, on a birth qualification after impressive form for Western Australia. Failing to fulfil the promise of a good start, he returned to Australia where he again exhibited signs of real quality.

HOULDSWORTH, William Harry

RHB.
Born: Levenshulme, Manchester, 6 April 1873.
Died: Barnfield, Flixton, Lancashire, 19 April 1909, aged 36.
First-class debut: 1893, Lancashire v Oxford University, Old Trafford.
10 matches for Lancashire, 1893-94 (amateur).
HS: 21 v Sussex, Old Trafford, 1894.

HOULTON, Gerard

RHB; LM.
Born: St Helens, Lancashire, 25 April 1939.
First-class debut: 1961, Lancashire v Derbyshire, Chesterfield.
20 matches for Lancashire, 1961-63 (professional).
HS: 86 v Kent, Folkestone, 1961.

Gerry Houlton made a most promising start with his aggressive style and, although he lacked polish, he seemed to have some possibilities. He gradually faded from the scene, however. Houlton played Middleton, St Helens Recreation and Pilkington's.

HOWARD, Barry John

RHB.
Born: Gee Cross, Hyde, Cheshire, 21 May 1926.
Education: Rossall; Manchester University.
First-class debut: 1947, Lancashire v Surrey, The Oval.
32 matches for Lancashire 1947-51 (amateur).
Capped 1947.
HS for Lancashire: 109 v Warwickshire, Blackpool, 1947.
HS: 114 MCC v Essex, Lord's, 1949.
Full first-class record: 1,232 runs (25.66); 2 centuries; 29 catches.

Barry Howard was a batsman of style and ability who sometimes seemed to suffer from nerves. The son of Rupert Howard and brother of Nigel (both Lancashire), he had a good record in non-first-class cricket, appearing for Manchester University, Stockport, Sale and Brooklands.

HOWARD, Kenneth

LHB; ROB.
Born: Manchester, 2 June 1941.
First-class debut: 1960, Lancashire v Sussex, Blackpool.
61 matches for Lancashire 1960-66 (professional).
HS 23 v Sussex, Liverpool, 1965.
BB: 7-53 v Warwickshire, Old Trafford, 1963.

Ken Howard started off most promisingly, with 4-9 in 8.3 overs in his first bowl in first-class cricket, but he was never capped and never made

the progress his ability suggested. Perhaps he was unlucky in not having a fair chance, and also in having to compete with Sonny Ramadhin.

HOWARD, Nigel David

RHB.
Born: Gee Cross, Hyde, Cheshire, 18 May 1925.
Died: Douglas, Isle of Man, 31 May 1979, aged 54.
Education. Rossall; Manchester University.
First-class debut: 1964, Lancashire v Middlesex, Old Trafford.
170 matches for Lancashire 1946-53 (amateur).
Capped 1948. Captain 1949-53.
HS: 145 v Derbyshire, Old Trafford, 1948.
1,000 runs (1); 1,174 (37.87) 1951.
4 Tests for England 1951-52 (all as captain). HS: 23 v India, Calcutta, 1951-52. Test record: 86 runs (17.20); 4 catches.
Toured India with MCC, 1951-52, as captain.

Nigel Howard was regarded as one of the most promising of batsmen when appointed Lancashire's youngest-ever captain in 1949. Stylish and cultured, he had a fine season in 1950 but the strain of captaincy took its toll and his form declined. After 1953 he retired, aged 27, to concentrate on the family textile business. Nigel Howard, whose father Rupert and brother Barry both played Lancashire, was a Cheshire county player at hockey and golf.

HOWARD, Rupert

RHB.
Born: Ashton-under-Lyne, Lancashire, 17 April 1890.
Died: Manchester, 10 September 1967, aged 77.
First-class debut: 1922, Lancashire v Worcestershire, Worcester.
8 matches for Lancashire, 1922-33 (amateur).
HS: 88* v Worcestershire (debut) in 80 minutes.

Major Howard left the Army in 1932 and was Secretary of Lancashire 1932-48. A respected administrator, Howard managed MCC in Australasia, 1936-37 and 1946-47. His sons, Nigel and Barry, played for Lancashire. He also played for Cheadle Hulme and Preston.

HOWE, Richard

RHB.
Born: Denton, Manchester, 17 February 1953.
Died: Alderley Edge, Cheshire, 21 January 1914, aged 60.
Education: Hyde Commercial School.

First-class debut: 1876, Lancashire v Yorkshire, Sheffield.
3 matches for Lancashire 1876-77 (amateur).
HS for Lancashire: 13 v Surrey, Old Trafford, 1876.
HS: 14 Gentlemen of the North v Players of the North, Huddersfield, 1877.

A free hitter, and a power in local cricket, Howe was a hat manufacturer at Denton.

HUBBACK, Theodore Rathbone

RHB; WK.
Born: Mount Pleasant, Liverpool, 17 December 1872.
Died: 1942, Malaya, aged 69.
First-class debut: 1892, Lancashire v Middlesex, Old Trafford.
4 matches for Lancashire, 1892.
HS for Lancashire: 33 v Middlesex (debut).
2 matches for Liverpool & District, 1892-93.
HS: 67 Liverpool & District v Yorkshire, Liverpool, 1892.
Full first-class record: 140 runs (15.55); 3 catches; 2 stumped.

Hubback played for Dingle CC.

HUDDLESTON, William

RHB; RMOB.
Born: Earlestown, Lancashire, 27 February 1873.
Died: Warrington, Lancashire, 21 May 1962, aged 89.
First-class debut: 1899, Lancashire v Australians, Liverpool.
183 matches for Lancashire 1899-1914 (professional). Benefit 1914 (£896).
HS: 88 v Yorkshire, Sheffield, 1914 (added 141 with James Tyldesley, second-best 9th wicket stand for Lancashire).
BB: 9-36 v Nottinghamshire, Liverpool, 1906.
100 wickets (1); 113 (19.68) 1913.

Signed for Lancashire after professional engagements with Todmorden and Church, Huddleston was supposedly devastating on false turf but ineffective in good conditions, otherwise he may have taken many more wickets.

HUDSON, Bennett

RHB; RF.
Born: Sheffield, Yorkshire, 29 June 1852.
Died: Wortley, Yorkshire, 11 November 1901, aged 49.
First-class debut: 1886, Lancashire v Sussex, Old Trafford.
5 matches for Lancashire, 1886-88 (professional).
HS: 98 v Sussex (debut).
BB: 2-14 (debut).

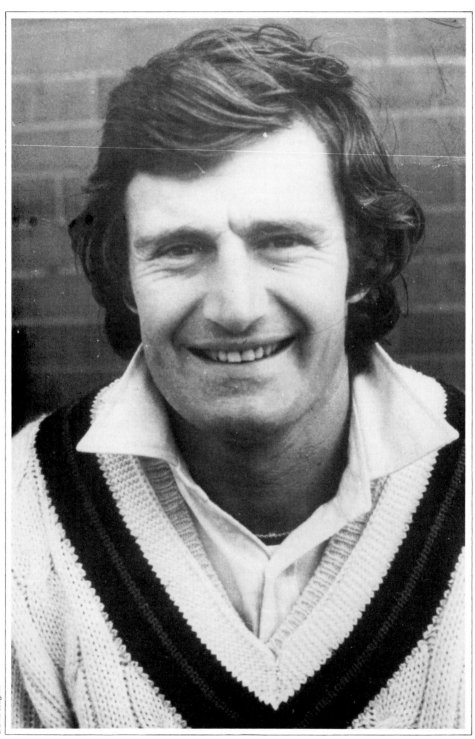

David Hughes

Played 3 matches for Yorkshire 1880.
Full first-class record: 220 runs (22.00); 3 wickets (19.66); 3 catches.

Bennett Hudson played for Lancashire whilst professional with Longsight. He made a brilliant start, with 98 and 85 in his first two matches, but soon dropped out. He had other professional engagements at Sheffield, Bacup, Batley, Grimsby and Manchester.

HUDSON, George Neville

RHB; OB.
Born: Clitheroe, Lancashire, 12 July 1905.
Died: Preston, Lancashire, 24 November 1981, aged 76.
First-class debut: 1936, Lancashire v Derbyshire, Old Trafford.
2 matches for Lancashire, 1936 (amateur).
HS: 1 v Indians, Liverpool, 1936.
Hudson also played for Bacup CC.

HUGHES, David Paul

RHB; SLA.
Born: Newton-le-Willows, Lancashire, 13 May 1947.
Education: Newton-le-Willows Grammar School.
First-class debut: 1967, Lancashire v Oxford University, Old Trafford.
428 matches for Lancashire 1967-90. Capped 1970.
Testimonial (£76,500) 1981. Captain 1987-date.
HS: 153 v Glamorgan, Old Trafford, 1983.
BB: 7-24 v Oxford University, Oxford, 1970.
1,000 runs (2); 1,303 (48.25) 1982 best.
82 wickets (28.98) 1970 best.
Tours: D.H.Robins' XI to South Africa 1972-73; English Counties to West Indies 1974-75; Lancashire to Jamaica 1986-87; Lancashire to Zimbabwe 1988-89.
Full first-class record: 10,308 runs (21.83); 8 centuries; 321 catches; 650 wickets (30.17).
David Hughes' career has had three distinct phases. Initially a left-armed spinner and late-order bat, persuaded by the exigences of the limited-overs game to compromise flight and spin for flatness and economy, he became a hitter capable of such memorable performances as the late-evening destruction of Gloucestershire in the 1971 Gillette semi-final, with poor John Mortimore hit for 24 in an over, skipper Bond a nervous spectator at the other end, and the Manchester street lamps past light-up time. As his bowling slipped away, Hughes became a high-order batsman capable of a season's average of near 50, and finally, in his 40s, when he could claim to be neither batsman nor bowler except as courtesey titles, Hughes was plucked from the shadows to lead the county's march back to respectability. His former club was Newton-le-Willows CC.

HULTON, Campbell Arthur Grey

RHB.
Born: Manchester, 16 March 1846.
Died: Marylebone, London, 23 June 1919, aged 73.
Education: Rossall, Aldenham.
First-class debut: 1869, Lancashire v Sussex, Hove.
8 matches for Lancashire, 1869-82 (amateur).
HS: 19 v Derbyshire, Old Trafford, 1873.
Hulton was a member of the MCC Committee in 1913. His sons, C.B and J.M.Hulton, played for MCC.

HULTON, Harrington Arthur Harrop

Born: Ashton-under-Lyne, Lancashire, 9 November 1846.
Died: Lansdown, Bath, 28 January 1923, aged 76.
Education: Rossall.
First-class debut: 1868, Lancashire v Surrey, The Oval.
2 matches for Lancashire 1868 (amateur).
HS: 6 v Surrey (debut)

I'ANSON, John

RHB; RFM.
Born: Scorton, Yorkshire, 26 October 1868.
Died: Eccleston, Cheshire, 14 September 1936, aged 67.
First-class debut: 1896, Lancashire v MCC, Lord's.
57 matches for Lancashire 1896-1908 (professional).
HS: 110 v Surrey, Old Trafford, 1902.
BB: 7-31 v Australians, Liverpool, 1899.
Despite some excellent performances, I'Anson was never able to establish a regular place. After retirement from cricket he became head gardener at Eton Park, Chester, the estate of the Duke of Westminster.

IDDISON, Roger

RHB; RF/lobs.
Born: Bedale, Yorkshire, 15 September 1834.
Died: York, 19 March 1890, aged 55.
Debut for Lancashire: 1865 v Middlesex, Old Trafford.
16 matches for Lancashire 1865-1870 (professional).
HS for Lancashire: 106 v Surrey, The Oval, 1866.
BB for Lancashire: 6-29 v Nottinghamshire, Old Trafford, 1868.
First-class debut: 1883, Yorkshire v United England XI, Sheffield.
Played for Yorkshire 1853-76. Captain 1863-1870.
HS: 112 Yorkshire v Cambridgeshire, Hunslet, 1869.

BB: 7-30 v Nottinghamshire, Bradford, 1863.
Full first-class record: 3,791 runs (18.76); 2
centuries; 133 catches; 211 wickets (about 17.00).

Yorkshireman Roger Iddison was one of the
great professional cricketing personalities of the
mid-19th century. A stockily-built man, he was
a batsman with a free style who used his feet
to reach the pitch of the ball and could hit very
hard. Originally a fast round-arm bowler, he
fairly soon changed to under-arm lobs depending
on flight and pitch variations. At point he was
a brilliant fielder. In 1865 and 1872, matches
were played for his benefit. He had many
professional engagements, some of which
included Stockton-on-Tees, Marlborough College, Ipswich, Thirsk, West Hartlepool, Richmond (Yorks), Broughton, Whalley, Sefton,
Uppingham School and Harrow. Once a butcher,
he opened a sports shop in Manchester with his
brother, W.H.Iddison,, but 1869 saw him
working as a commission agent in York. In 1874
he was secretary of the newly-founded Yorkshire
United XI. In 1861-62 he was in the touring team
to Australia.

IDDISON, William Holdsworth
RHB.
Born: Bedale, Yorkshire 5 February 1840.
Died: Withington, Lancashire, 6 March 1898,
aged 58.
First-class debut: 1867, Lancashire v Yorkshire,
Old Trafford.
4 matches for Lancashire 1867-68 (amateur).
HS: 19 v Yorkshire, Middlesbrough, 1867.

A brother of Roger Iddison, he had various
engagements, for Bowdon CC, Rusholme and
Enfield, before playing as an amateur for
Longsight. He became a dealer in sports
equipment with his brother in Manchester and
subsequently a paper and packing materials
dealer in Manchester.

IDDON, John
RHB; SLA.
Born: Mawdesley, near Ormskirk, Lancashire,
8 January 1902.
Died: Madeley, Staffordshire (in road traffic
accident), 17 April 1946, aged 44.
First-class debut: 1924, Lancashire v Oxford
University, Oxford.
483 matches for Lancashire 1924-25 (professional). Capped 1926. Benefit (£1,266) 1936.
HS: 222 v Leicestershire, Liverpool, 1929.
Also scored 217* v Worcestershire, Old Trafford,
1939; 204* v Warwickshire, Edgbaston, 1933; 201
v Sussex, Old Trafford, 1932; 200* v Nottingamshire, Old Trafford, 1934.

Added 230 with T.M.Halliday v Surrey, The
Oval, 1928 (Lancashire 5th-wicket record until
1939).
Added 278 with H.R.W.Butterworth v Sussex,
Old Trafford, 1932 Lancashire 6th-wicket
record).
BB: 9-42 v Yorkshire, Sheffield, 1937.
1,000 runs (13); 2,381 (52.91) 1934 best.
5 Tests for England 1934-35 to 1935. HS: 73
v West Indies, Port-of-Spain, 1934-35. Test
record: 170 runs (28.33).
Tours: Sir Julien Cahn's team in Jamaica
1928-29; MCC in West Indies 1934-35.
Full first-class record: 22,681 runs (36.76); 46
centuries; 217 catches; 551 wickets (26.90).

Iddon, who played for Adlington and Leyland
Motors before joining Lancashire, was a hard-
driving batsman and steady left-arm spinner,
especially effective on helpful wickets. He had
hoped to play as an amateur in 1946, when he
was killed in a car accident whilst going about
his business. His widow was awarded £9,810.

IKIN, John Thomas

LHB; RLBG.
Born: Bignall End, Staffordshire, 7 March 1918.
Died: Bignall End, 15 September 1984, aged 66.
Debut for Lancashire: 1938 v West Indies, Old Trafford (dismissed George Headley in first bowling spell).
288 matches for Lancashire 1939-57 (professional). Capped 1946. Benefit (£7,175) 1953.
HS: 192 v Oxford University, Oxford, 1951.
BB: 6-21 v Nottinghamshire, Old Trafford, 1947 (11-119 in match and scored 67 and 85* to complete match double).
1,000 runs (10); 1,729 (36.78) 1955 best.
Carried bat through completed innings twice: 119*/261 v Middlesex, Old Trafford, 1949; 125*/197 v Surrey, The Oval, 1951.
Hat-trick v Somerset, Taunton, 1949.
18 Tests for England 1946-55. HS: 60 v Australia, Sydney, 1946-47. Test record: 606 runs (20.89); 3 wickets; 31 catches. 12 catches v South Africa 1951 equalled record for series in England.
Tours: MCC to Australia and New Zealand 1946-47; MCC to West Indies 1947-48; Commonwealth XI to India 1950-51.

First-class debut: Minor Counties v Oxford University, Oxford, 1938 (amateur).
Represented Players v Gentlemen 1946, 1951.
Full first-class record: 17,968 runs (36.81); 27 centuries; 419 catches; 339 wickets (30.27).
Minor Counties cricket for Staffordshire (amateur), 1933-38; 1958-68 (captain). Also captained Minor Counties 1959, 1960.

Jack Ikin was an unusually graceful left-hander, with a strong top-hand producing a wide range of stylish off-side strokes to go with the normal left-hander's leg side facility. Happiest when opening, he faced the fastest and most intimidating bowling with courage and determination; he was also a gifted close fielder, usually at short leg, and a right-armed bowler of leg breaks and googlies who may have gained greater success in an overall weaker bowling side.

Dark, good-looking and of average height and build, Jack Ikin returned from war service as a 'Desert Rat' and walked straight into the England team, winning his Test cap before his county award. But, although playing in 18 Tests, and winning frequent recalls, he never established himself for England. For Lancashire, however, he was a bastion of the side for 12 seasons, despite recurring ill health which severely curtailed his activities in the 1954 and 1956 seasons. He also underwent major surgery after touring Australasia as assistant manager of MCC in 1965-66. He played club cricket for Bignall End (North Staffordshire League) and was professional coach at Denstone College 1958-63.

Jack Ikin was deservedly popular, both as a player and during retirement, when he devoted much time, and sympathy, to schools cricket. A thorough gentleman, his election as an honorary member of MCC, and as Lancashire vice-president, were no more than he deserved.

His father, A.W.Ikin, and his son, M.J.Ikin, both played for Staffordshire. M.J Ikin also played two first-class matches for Minor Counties, in 1972 and 1979.

INGLEBY, Charles Willis

RHB: Useful bowler.
Born: Sheepscar, Leeds, Yorkshire, 19 December 1870.
Died: Eccleshill, Bradford, Yorkshire, 15 November 1939, aged 68.
First-class debut: 1899, Lancashire v Derbyshire, Old Trafford.
1 match for Lancashire (professional).
HS: 29 v Derbyshire (debut).

Charles Ingleby played on occasions for Cumberland.

IRANI, Ronald

RHB; RM.
Born: Leigh, Lancashire, 26 October 1971.
Education: Smithills School, Bolton.
First-class debut: 1990, Lancashire v Zimbabwe, Old Trafford.
1 match for Lancashire 1990.
Did not bat.
BB: 1-12 (debut).

ISHERWOOD, Frederic

Middle-order batsman.

Born: Over Darwen, Lancashire, 30 August 1858.
Died: Blackley, Manchester, 20 February 1927, aged 68.
First-class debut: 1881, Lancashire v Kent, Old Trafford.
1 match for Lancashire 1881 (professional).
HS: 0 (only innings).
Did not bowl.

A local professional of whom very little is known.

JACKSON, Edward
RHB; WK.
Born: Lancaster, 12 March 1849.

Died: details unknown.
Education: Amersham Hall.
First-class debut: 1871, Lancashire v Yorkshire, Sheffield.
15 matches for Lancashire 1871-85 (amateur).
HS: 11 v Nottinghamshire, Trent Bridge, 1876.

He was a top class wicketkeeper from Huyton who was unable to play regularly due to business commitments. Eventually he disappeared from Liverpool and his death has not been traced.

JACKSON, J.

Debut for Lancashire: 1867.

This is believed to have been Frank Hardcastle playing under an assumed name.

JAQUES, Thomas Robinson
RHB; RM.
Born: Middleton, Lancashire, 9 November 1911.
Died: Denbigh, Wales 13 August 1976, aged 64.
First-class debut: 193 , Lancashire v v Oxford University, Oxford.
2 matches for Lancashire 1937 (professional).
HS: 2 v Oxford University (debut).
BB: 1-45 v Oxford University (debut).

A professional attached to the Middleton Club.

JEFFERIES, Stephen Thomas
LHB; LFM.

Born: Cape Town, South Africa, 8 December 1959.
Education: Plumstead High School.
Debut for Lancashire: 1983 v Oxford University, Oxford.
32 matches for Lancashire 1983-85.
HS: 93 v Sussex, Old Trafford, 1985.
BB for Lancashire: 8-46 v Nottinghamshire, Trent Bridge, 1983.
BB: 10-59 Western Province v Orange Free State, Cape Town, 1987-88.
Has played Western Province (Currie Cup) since 1978-79; also played Derbyshire 1982 (1 match) and Hampshire 1988-89 (Capped 1989).
Full first-class record: 3,689 runs (25.97); 53 catches; 454 wickets (27.92).

A talented left-handed all-rounder, Jefferies never quite hit it off in England.

JERVIS, William Swynfen

RHB.
Born: Stafford, 18 November 1840.
Died: Southsea, Hampshire, 3 April 1920, aged 79.
Debut for Lancashire: 1874 v Derbyshire, Old Trafford.
1 match for Lancashire 1874 (amateur).
HS for Lancashire: 6 (debut).
Other first-class match: Gentlemen of Kent v Gentlemen of MCC, Canterbury, 1865.
HS: 13 for Gentlemen of Kent.
BB: 6-30 for Gentlemen of Kent.

Captain Swynfen Jervis, a kinsman of Lord Harris, is something of a mystery man. He made a single appearance for Lancashire and, apart from playing in Kent, he appeared for Warwickshire, being involved in the present club's formation in 1882 and re-formation in 1884, and for Cheshire. Another relative, Hon W.M.Jervis, played for Derbyshire and Warwickshire.

JESTY, Trevor Edward

RHB; RM.
Born: Gosport, Hampshire, 2 June 1948.
Education: Privet County Secondary School, Gosport.
Debut for Lancashire: 1988 v Worcestershire, Old Trafford.
55 matches for Lancashire 1988-90. Capped 1989.
HS for Lancashire: 98 v Kent, Maidstone, 1990.
340 matches for Hampshire 1966-84. Capped 1971. Benefit 1982.
68 matches for Surrey 1985-87. Capped 1985.
Captain 1985.

Played Border 1973-74; Griqualand West 1974-75 to 1980-81; Canterbury 1979-80.
Tours: West Indies with Interntional XI 1982-83; Zimbabwe with Lancashire 1988-89. Also sent as replacement, England in Australia and New Zealand 1982-83, but played no first-class matches.
10 limited-overs matches for England.
HS: 248 Hampshire v Cambridge University, Cambridge, 1984.
BB: 7-75 Hampshire v Worcestershire, Southampton, 1976.
Full first-class record: 21,790 runs (32.52); 34 centuries; 265 catches; 585 wickets (27.47).

Trevor Jesty, an effective all-rounder cricketer, reached his best county form at an age usually too old for a successful Test career to be commenced.

JOHN, Henry Celestine Robert

RHB; RFM.
Born: Agra, India, 26 May 1862.
Died: Oxford, 24 June 1941, aged 79.
Education: Stonyhurst.
First-class debut: 1881, Lancashire v Middlesex, Old Trafford.
1 match for Lancashire 1881 (amateur).
HS: 15* Lancashire v Middlesex (debut).
BB: 5-53 Bombay Presidency XI v Oxford University Authentics, Bombay, 1902-03.
Full first-class record: 65 runs (16.25); 19 wickets (20.00).

JOLLEY, William Turner

RHB; RFM.
Born: Smallthorne, Stoke on Trent, Stafford-
shire, 3 August 1923.
Education: Manchester University.
First-class debut: 1947, Lancashire v Notting-
hamshire, Old Trafford.
2 matches for Lancashire 1947 (amateur).
HS: 13 v Hampshire, Old Trafford, 1947.
BB: 4-31 v Hampshire, Old Trafford, 1947.

Jolley, who played for Staffordshire from 1949-
55 and who also appeared for the Norton and
Stone clubs, was President of that county.

JONES, Charles Langton

RHB.
Born: Seaton, Liverpool, 27 November 1853.
Died: Toxteth Park, Liverpool, 2 April 1904,
aged 50.
Education: Carlton House School, Liverpool.
First-class debut: 1876, Lancashire v Notting-
hamshire, Old Trafford.
5 matches for Lancashire 1876-88 (amateur).
HS for Lancashire: 20* v Sussex, Old Trafford,
1888.
6 matches for Liverpool & District 1882-90.
HS: 36 Liverpool & District v Australians,
Liverpool, 1882.

Charles Jones played club cricket for Sefton.

JONES, James Lindley

RHB; WK.
Born: Liverpool, 1876.
Died: details unknown.
Education: Liverpool College.
First-class debut: 1910, Lancashire v Notting-
hamshire, Old Trafford.
4 matches for Lancashire 1910 (amateur).
HS: 7* v Surrey, The Oval, 1910.
James Jones, a Liverpool wicketkeeper, also
played for Cheshire.

JORDAN, John

RHB; WK.
Born: Cloughfield, Rossendale, Lancashire, 7
February 1932.
First-class debut: 1955, Lancashire v Scotland,
Old Trafford.

62 matches for Lancashire 1955-57. Capped
1956.
HS: 39 v Yorkshire, Headingley, 1956.

John Jordan, a useful wicketkeeper, retired after
breaking a finger.

JOWETT, George Edwin

RHB; RF.
Born: Roby, Prescott, Lancashire, 20 August
1863.

Died: Eccles, Lancashire, 19 May 1928, aged 64.
Education: St William's College, Isle-of-Man.
First-class debut: 1885, Lancashire v Oxford University, Old Trafford.
19 matches for Lancashire 1885-89 (amateur).
HS: 58 v Oxford University, Liverpool, 1887.

A Huyton amateur, who was in business as a broker in Liverpool, Jowett was a good aggressive batsman whose main claim to 'fame' is that in the match against Surrey at Liverpool in 1885 he was called for throwing by umpire John Platts.

KAYE, Joseph Lowther

RHB; RF.
Born: Honley, Huddersfield, Yorkshire, 21 June 1846.
Died: Whitefield, Bury, Lancashire, 12 October 1882, aged 36.
First-class debut: 1867, Lancashire v Yorkshire, Middlesbrough.
1 match for Lancashire 1867 (professional).
HS: 20 v Yorkshire (debut).
Little is known of this professional.

KELLY, Edward Arthur

RHB; RFM.
Born: Bootle, Cheshire, 26 November 1932.
Education: Christ Church School, Liverpool.
First-class debut: 1957, Lancashire v Scotland, Old Trafford.
4 matches for Lancashire 1957.
HS: 16* v Cambridge University, Cambridge, 1957.
BB: 3-77 v Glamorgan, Old Trafford, 1957.
He played for Litherland, Hightown, Chorley and the Royal Army Medical Corps.

KELLY, John Martin

RHB.
Born: Bacup, Lancashire, 19 March 1922.
Died: Rochdale, Lancashire, 13 November 1979, aged 57.
First-class debut: 1947, Lancashire v Hampshire, Old Trafford.
6 matches for Lancashire 1947-49 (professional).
HS for Lancashire: 58 v Gloucestershire, Bristol, 1949.
253 matches for Derbyshire 1950-60 (professional). Capped 1951. Benefit 1960 (£2,250).
HS: 131 Derbyshire v Middlesex, Lord's, 1956.
1,000 runs (5) for Derbyshire; 1,535 (30.70) 1957 best.
Full first-class record: 9,614 runs (23.56); 9 centuries; 122 catches.

Jack Kelly, who played club cricket for Bacup, was a stylish, graceful batsman, always attractive to watch despite a chronic inability to beat the field. After moving to Derbyshire he formed a 'Roses' opening partnership with Yorkshireman, Arnold Hamer.

KEMBLE, Arthur Twiss

RHB; WK.
Born: Sebergham, Carlisle, Cumberland, 3 February 1862.
Died: Crawley Down, Sussex, 13 March 1925, aged 63.
Education: Appleby Grammar School.
First-class debut: 1885, Lancashire v Sussex, Old Trafford.
76 matches for Lancashire 1885-94 (amateur).
HS: 50 v Surrey, The Oval, 1892.
Played first-class cricket for Liverpool & District and Gentlemen's teams.
Full first-class record: 1,347 runs (11.13); 122 catches; 54 stumped.

Player and secretary of Liverpool CC, Arthur Kemble, a solicitor, was a first-class wicket-keeper, useful batsman and occasional deputy skipper. At various times he was on the committee of both Lancashire and Surrey. At Rugby Union football, Kemble played for Lancashire and England. A member of a well-known theatrical family, Kemble entered local politics and became chairman of Garston District Council and a member of Liverpool Council.

KEMP, Sir George (knighted 1909; created 1st Baron Rochdale 1913)

RHB; RA (spin).
Born: Rochdale, Lancashire, 9 June 1866.
Died: Keswick, Cumberland, 24 March 1945, aged 78.
Education: Mill Hill and Shrewsbury Schools; Trinity College, Cambridge.
First-class debut: Lancashire v MCC, Lord's, 1885.
18 matches for Lancashire 1885-92 (amateur).
HS for Lancashire: 109 v Yorkshire, Huddersfield, 1885.
Played for Cambridge University 1885-88 (Blue 1885-86-88).
Also played for MCC. His last match was for A.J.Webbe's team in 1899.
HS: 125 Cambridge University v Yorkshire, Cambridge, 1886.
Full first-class record: 1,641 runs (18.64); 17 catches.

An excellent all-round sportsman, excelling in University lawn-tennis and athletics, George Kemp was a heavy scorer in minor cricket, once hitting 213* in 105 minutes for P.M.Thornton's XI v Manor House School in 1899. Kemp entered politics as MP for Heywood 1895-1906, in the Liberal interest, and for Manchester North West 1910-12. He served in the South African War

with great distinction and during World War One commanded a Territorial regiment in the Dardanelles.

KENNEDY, Andrew

LHB; RM.
Born: Blackburn, Lancashire, 4 November 1949.
Education: Nelson Grammar School.
First-class debut: 1970, Lancashire v Jamaica, Old Trafford.
149 matches for Lancashire 1970-82. Capped 1975.
HS: 180 v Derbyshire, Chesterfield, 1981.
BB: 3-58 v Warwickshire, Liverpool, 1980.
1,000 runs (2); 1,194 (34.11) best.
Set Lancashire 5th-wicket record, adding 249 with Barry Wood v Warwickshire, Edgbaston, 1975.
Toured South Africa with D.H.Robins' XI 1975-76.
Full first-class record: 6,298 runs (28.24); 6 centuries; 10 wickets (39.80); 85 catches.

Andrew Kennedy was voted Young Player of

the Year by the Cricket Writers' Club in 1975 but never really fulfilled early hopes as opening bat. From 1983 he played for Dorset in the Minor Counties Championship.

KENTFIELD, Richard William
LM.
Born: Bognor, Sussex, 25 May 1862.
Died: On or after 16 October 1904, his body being found in the River Ouse at Bedford, aged 42.
First-class debut: 1888, Lancashire v Oxford University, Old Trafford.
2 matches for Lancashire 1888 (amateur).
HS: 18 v Oxford University (debut).
BB for Lancashire: 2-52 v Oxford University (debut).
2 matches for Sussex 1894-96.
BB: 6-45 Sussex v Middlesex, Lord's 1894.
Full first-class record: 49 runs (6.12); 10 wickets (23.20).

An amateur who was given few opportunities.

KENYON, Myles Noel
RHB.
Born: Walshaw Hall, Bury, Lancashire, 25 December 1886.
Died: Birdham, Sussex, 21 November 1960, aged 73.
Education: Eton; Cambridge.

First-class debut: 1919, Lancashire v Derbyshire, Old Trafford.
91 matches for Lancashire 1919-25 (amateur).
Captain 1919-22.
HS: 61* v Surrey, The Oval, 1921.

After skippering the 2nd XI in 1914, Myles Kenyon became captain of the 1st XI on the resumption of cricket in 1919, when A.H.Hornby decided to retire to Ireland. Kenyon became Lancashire President and also High Sheriff, and a Deputy Lieutenant of the County.

KERMODE, Alexander
RHB; RFM.
Born: Sydney, New South Wales, Australia, 15 May 1876.
Died: Balmain, New South Wales, 17 July 1934, aged 58.
Debut for Lancashire: 1902, Lancashire v Australians, Liverpool.
76 matches for Lancashire 1902-08 (professional).
HS: 64* v Worcestershire, Liverpool, 1905.
BB: 7-44 v Essex, Old Trafford, 1905.
100 wickets (1); 113 (21.60) 1905.
Hat-trick v Leicestershire, Leicester, 1906.
Played for New South Wales 1901-02.

Kermode was brought over from Australia by A.C.MacLaren, a move which brought much criticism. Tall and strong with good variation of pace, Kermode did pretty well for a time but

faded so badly that he departed in 1908. From 1910-14 he played for Bacup and also appeared for Cheshire.

KERSHAW, John Edward
RHB; WK.

Born: Heywood, Lancashire, 12 January 1854.
Died: Burnley, Lancashire, 29 November 1903, aged 49.
Education: Eccleshall College, Newbourne Park, Sheffield.
First-class debut: 1877, Lancashire v Kent, Old Trafford.
33 matches for Lancashire 1877-85 (amateur).
HS: 66 v Sussex, Old Trafford, 1877.

John Kershaw was a capital batsman and excellent fielder who kept wicket occasionally. He captained Heywood CC from 1878 to 1898 and then moved to Burnley.

KEVAN, Joseph Henry
Born: Bolton, Lancashire, 13 September 1855.
Died: Bolton, Lancashire, 9 December 1891, aged 36.
First-class debut: 1875, Lancashire v Kent, Old Trafford.
2 matches for Lancashire 1875 (amateur).
HS: 12 v Kent, Catford, 1875.

A Bolton amateur, Kevan failed to score in his first three first-class innings.

KEWLEY, Edward
RHB.
Born: Eton, Buckinghamshire, 20 June 1852.
Died: Winchester, Hampshire, 17 April 1940, aged 87.
Education: Marlborough.
First-class debut: 1875, Lancashire v Kent, Catford.
1 match for Lancashire 1975 (amateur).
HS: 3 v Kent (debut).

Kewley, an England Rugby Union international, played cricket for Liverpool CC.

KING, Benjamin Philip
RHB; Occasional WK.
Born: Leeds, Yorkshire, 22 April 1915.
Died: Bradford, Yorkshire, 31 March 1970, aged 54.
Debut for Lancashire: 1946, Lancashire v Cambridge University, Cambridge.
37 matches for Lancashire 1946-47 (professional). Capped 1946.
HS: 145 v Gloucestershire, Gloucester, 1946.
First-class debut: 1935, Worcestershire v Northamptonshire, Northampton.
80 matches for Worcestershire 1935-39. Capped 1938.
1,000 runs (1); 1,145 (30.94) 1946.
Moved from 34 to 145 before lunch on third day v Gloucestershire, Gloucester, 1946.

Full first-class record: 4,124 runs (22.05); 54 catches; 6 stumped.

Phil King was an adventurous batsman who lacked the discipline necessary to make him a regular scorer, but he was good value for the spectators' money. Slow and awkward in the field, King tried to solve the wicketkeeper

problem in 1946 but was found wanting. An engaging personality, King became cricket and Rugby League correspondent on *The People* newspaper and was preparing for his third Australian tour with the Great Britain Rugby League team when he suffered a fatal heart attack.

KNOWLES Arthur

RHB; RM.
Born: Pendlebury, Manchester, 10 April 1858.
Died: Alvaston, Cheshire, 10 July 1929, aged 71.
Education: Rugby.
First-class debut: 1888, Lancashire v Oxford University, Oxford.
1 match for Lancashire 1888 (amateur).
HS for Lancashire: 6 v Oxford University (debut).

Played for MCC 1895-96.
HS: 16 MCC v Sussex, Lord's, 1895.

KNOX, Gerald Keith

RHB; RM.
Born: North Shields, County Durham, 22 April 1937.
Education: Newcastle-on-Tyne Grammar School.
First-class debut: 1964, Lancashire v Glamorgan, Old Trafford.
52 matches for Lancashire 1964-67.
HS: 108 v Yorkshire, Old Trafford, 1965.

Gerry Knox came from teaching in Tynemouth to try first-class cricket but, although playing some good innings, he had many failures and after three seasons returned north. He played Minor Counties cricket for Northumberland and club cricket for Tynemouth.

KRIKKEN, Brian Egbert

RHB; WK.
Born: Horwich, Lancashire, 26 August 1946.
First-class debut: 1966, Lancashire v Oxford University, Oxford, 1966.
2 matches for Lancashire 1966-67.
HS: 4 v Oxford University (debut).
1 match for Worcestershire 1969.

Brian Krikken also played for Horwich and Westhoughton. His son, Karl Krikken, also a wicketkeeper, is currently with Derbyshire and was their regular 'keeper in first-class cricket in 1990.

LANCASHIRE, Oswald Philip

RHB.
Born: Newton Heath, Manchester, 10 December 1857.
Died: West Didsbury, Manchester, 23 July 1934, aged 76.
Education: Lancing; Jesus College, Cambridge.
First-class debut: 1878, Lancashire v Nottinghamshire, Trent Bridge.
97 matches for Lancashire 1878-88 (amateur).
HS: 76* v MCC, Lord's, 1885.
Played for Cambridge University 1878-81 (Blue 1880).
Full first-class record: 2,349 runs (13.12); 45 catches.

Oswald Lancashire was a useful batsman and a capital fielder who first played for Lancing aged 15, but it would be wrong to pretend he fulfilled his early promise and his county record was moderate. An excellent soccer player, he won

his Blue at Cambridge. He was Lancashire CCC President 1923 and 1924.

LANCASTER, Thomas

LHB; SLA.
Born: Dalton, Huddersfield, Yorkshire, 11 February 1863.
Died: Blackburn, Lancashire, 12 December 1935, aged 72.
First-class debut: 1894, Lancashire v Nottinghamshire, Old Trafford.
27 matches for Lancashire 1894-99 (professional).
HS: 66 v Gloucestershire, Old Trafford, 1899.
BB: 7-25 v Middlesex, Old Trafford, 1898.

Took wicket of Charles Wright (Notts) with his first ball in first-class cricket.

Tom Lancaster was a delightful character who played a non-first-class match for Yorkshire in 1891 before coming to Lancashire. Initially a professional with Huddersfield, he became celebrated as a stalwart of Enfield CC, first as professional and, after 1902, as an amateur. He took 127 wickets for Enfield in 1892, and 112 in 1904. He is thus unique in holding the record for both paid and unpaid players.

LANDON, Charles Whittington

RHB; RM.
Born: Bromley, Kent, 30 May 1850.
Died: Ledston, Yorkshire, 5 March 1903, aged 52.
Education: Bromsgrove.
First-class debut: 1874, Lanacshire v Kent, Old Trafford.
6 matches for Lancashire 1874-75 (amateur).
HS: 47 v Kent (debut).
9 matches for Yorkshire 1878-82.

A useful amateur, Landon played for both Lancashire and Yorkshire on residential qualifications.

LATCHFORD, John Richard

RHB; RM.
Born: Delph, Yorkshire, 10 June 1909.
Died: Omagh, County Tyrone, Republic of Ireland, 30 April 1980, aged 70.
First-class debut: 1930, Lancashire v Minor Counties, Old Trafford.
7 matches for Lancashire 1930-32 (professional).
HS: 63 v Gloucestershire, Bristol, 1931.
BB: 1-6 v Gloucestershire, Bristol, 1931.

Latchford went to Consett after leaving Lancashire, and played for Durham in the Minor Counties Championship 1935-39. He is also believed to have been engaged as a professional at Bromsgrove.

LAWSON, Geoffrey Francis

RHB; RF.
Born: Wagga Wagga, New South Wales, Australia, 7 December 1957.
Education: University of New South Wales.
Debut for Lancashire: 1979 v Cambridge University.
1 match for Lancashire 1979.
HS for Lancashire: 17 v Cambridge University (debut).

BB for Lancashire: 4-81 v Cambridge University (debut).
Played for New South Wales since 1977-78.
46 Tests for Australia 1977-78 to 1989-90. HS: 74 v England, Lord's, 1989. BB: 8-112 v West Indies, Adelaide, 1984-85. Test record: 894 runs (15.96). 10 catches. 180 wickets (30.56).
Tours (all with Australia): to England 1981, 1985, 1989; to India and Pakistan 1979-80; to Sri Lanka 1980-81; to Pakistan 1982-3; to West Indies 1983-4.
Full first-class record: 2,335 runs (14.77); 618 wickets (24.34); 68 catches.

Geoff Lawson, who played once for Lancashire whilst a professional with Heywood, is one of the leading Australian pace bowlers of recent years. By profession he is an opthalmologist in Sydney.

LAWTON, Albert Edward
RHB; RM; Occasional WK.
Born: Dukinfield, Cheshire, 31 March 1879.
Died: Manchester, 25 December 1955, aged 76.
Education: Rugby.
Debut for Lancashire: 1912 v Kent, Tunbridge Wells.
12 matches for Lancashire 1912-14 (amateur).
HS for Lancashire: 52 v Nottinghamshire, Trent Bridge, 1913.

BB for Lancashire: 4-33 v Derbyshire, Old Trafford, 1914.
First-class debut: 1900, Derbyshire v Lancashire, Old Trafford.
131 matches for Derbyshire 1900-10 (amateur) Captain (with breaks) 1902-09. Also played for MCC and London County.
HS: 168 Leveson Gower's team v Oxford University, Eastbourne, 1910.
BB: 4-19 Derbyshire v Sussex, Hove, 1908.
Full first-class record: 7,509 runs (24.78); 11 centuries; 125 catches; 1 stumped; 113 wickets (31.92).

A powerfully-built batsman, Lawton hit very hard. He played for Derbyshire until his activities in the cotton industry took him to Manchester, when he began to play occasionally for Lancashire.

LAWTON, William
RHB; RM.
Born: Pitses, Ashton-under-Lyne, 4 June 1920.
First-class debut: 1948, Lancashire v Australians, Old Trafford.
2 matches for Lancashire 1948 (professional).
HS: 3 v Oxford University, Oxford, 1948.

Bill Lawton established a big reputation in League cricket and, despite unimpressive returns in his two county matches, would almost certainly have made the grade under different circumstances. Amongst his clubs were Ashton, St Anne's, Oldham, Walsall, Cleator Moor and Whitehaven. He played for Cumberland 1954-56. Lawton also played soccer for Oldham Athletic, Chester, Bacup Borough and Colwyn Bay. He married the actress Dora Bryan.

LEACH, Edward Leach Cecil
RHB.
Born: Featherstall, Lancashire, 28 November 1896.
Died: Nailsea, Somerset, 4 January 1973, aged 76.
First-class debut: 1923, Lancashire v Middlesex, Old Trafford.
12 matches for Lancashire 1923-24 (professional).
HS: 79 v Middlesex (debut).
8 matches for Somerset 1924-28; in 1924 appeared for both Lancashire and Somerset, but for the latter only in non-Championship cricket.
Full first-class record: 250 runs (8.92); 1 wicket; 6 catches.

LEACH, Harold
RHB; RA (slow).
Born: Lower Fold, Rochdale, Lancashire, 13 March 1862.

Died: Widcombe, Bath, Somerset, 15 February 1928, aged 65.
Education: Marlborough.
First-class debut: 1881, Lancashire v Surrey, Old Trafford.
1 match for Lancashire 1881 (amateur).
HS for Lancashire: 33 v Surrey (debut).
2 first-class matches for Liverpool & District 1884-91.
HS: 46 Liverpool & District v Yorkshire, Liverpool, 1891.

He was brother of John, Robert, Roger and W.E.Leach, all Lancashire players.

LEACH, John
RHB.
Born: Lower Fold, Rochdale, Lancashire, 17 October 1846.
Died: Lower Fold, Rochdale, 1 February 1893, aged 46.

Education: Marlborough.
First-class debut: 1866, Lancashire v Middlesex, Old Trafford.
5 matches for Lancashire 1866-77 (amateur).
HS: 34 v Middlesex (debut).

Brother of Harold, Robert, Roger and W.E.Leach, all Lancashire players.

LEACH, Robert
RHB.
Born: Lower Fold, Rochdale, Lancashire, 18 December 1849.

Died: Westbury, Newport Pagnall, Buckinghamshire, 10 September 1939, aged 89.
Education: Marlborough.
First-class debut: 1868, Lancashire v Yorkshire, Holbeck.
3 matches for Lancashire 1868-76 (amateur).
HS: 14 v Yorkshire, Old Trafford, 1876.

Ordained into the Church of England ministry, he was brother of Harold, John, Roger and William Leach, all Lancashire players.

LEACH, Roger Chadwick
RHB.
Born: Lower Fold, Rochdale, Lancashire, 21 September 1853.
Died: Salta, Argentina, 21 April 1889, aged 35.
Education: Marlborough.
First-class debut: 1885, Lancashire v Sussex, Hove.
1 match for Lancashire 1885 (amateur).
HS: 39 v Sussex (debut).

Brothers Harold, John, Robert and William played Lancashire; N.M.K.Smith, the present Warwickshire player, is a descendant.

LEACH, William Edmund
RHB; RM (lobs).
Born: Lower Fold, Rochdale, Lancashire, 7 November 1851.
Died: Ivinghoe, Buckinghamshire, 30 November 1932, aged 81.
Education: Marlborough.
Debut for Lancashire: 1885 v Derbyshire, Old Trafford.
5 matches for Lancashire 1885 (amateur).
HS: 56 v Sussex, Hove 1885.
Played for Canterbury v Otago, Hagley Park, 1876-77; also played cricket in Argentinian North v South series.

Brothers Harold, John, Robert and Roger all played Lancashire. W.E.Leach was one of ten brothers at Marlborough, eight of whom played in the XI there.

LEE, Peter Granville
RHB; RMF.
Born: Arthingworth, Northamptonshire, 27 August 1945.
Education: Arthingworth School.
Debut for Lancashire: 1972 v Australians, Old Trafford.
152 matches for Lancashire 1972-82. Capped 1972.
HS for Lancashire: 25 v Australians, Old Trafford, 1977.

BB: 8-34 v Oxford University, Oxford, 1980.
100 wickets (2); 112 (18.45) 1975 best.
44 matches for Northamptonshire 1967-71.
HS: 26 Northamptonshire v Gloucestershire, Northampton, 1969.
Toured South Africa with D.H.Robins' team 1973-74, 1975-76.
Full first-class record: 779 runs (8.11); 29 catches; 599 wickets (25.60).

Lee played for Durham in the 1983 Minor Counties Championship, when professional with Gateshead Fell.

LEESE, Charles Philip
RHB.
Born: Eccles, Manchester, 22 May 1889.
Died: Hope-Bagot, Shropshire, 19 January 1947, aged 57.
Education: Wellington School; Oriel College, Oxford.
Debut for Lancashire: 1911 v All-India, Old Trafford.
1 match for Lancashire 1911 (amateur).
HS: 10 v All-India (debut).
Played for Oxford University 1908-10 (no Blue).
HS: 48 Oxford University v Worcestershire, Oxford, 1910.

Full first-class record: 341 runs (12.17).

Leese's father, Ernest, and his uncle, Sir Joseph, both played for Lancashire.

LEESE, Ernest
RHB.
Born: Bowdon, Cheshire, 30 November 1854.
Died: Southport, Lancashire, 15 November 1913, aged 58.
Education: Cheltenham.
First-class debut: 1880, Lancashire v Derbyshire, Old Trafford.
8 matches for Lancashire 1880-84 (amateur).
HS: 62 v Derbyshire (debut).

He was the father of C.P.Leese and brother of Sir Joseph, both Lancashire players. His nephews, N. and W.H.Leese, played for MCC, and V.F.Leese for Cambridge University. His great nephew, Sir Oliver, was MCC President in 1965. Ernest Leese was a cotton spinner at Eccles.

LEESE, Sir Joseph Francis (Baronet)
RHB.
Born: Manchester, 28 February 1845.

Died: Sutton Park, Guildford, Surrey, 29 July 1914, aged 69.
Education: London University.
First-class debut: 1865, Lancashire v Middlesex, Old Trafford.
24 matches for Lancashire 1865-81 (amateur).
HS: 44 v Surrey, The Oval, 1868.
BB: 3-49 v Middlesex, Old Trafford, 1866.

A very fast run-getter, J.F.Leese found his technique insufficient to be able to cope well with the best bowling, but he was a useful batsman and fine fielder nonetheless. A barrister-at-law and cotton spinner, Leese was MP for Accrington from 1892 to 1908, with one small break. He was created a baronet in 1908. Leese's brother, Ernest, and nephew, C.P., played for Lancashire, whilst his sons, Sir William (MCC), V.F.(Cambridge U) and N.(MCC), all played first-class cricket. His grandson, Sir Oliver Leese, was MCC President 1965.

LEIGH, James
RHB.
Born: West Leigh, Lancashire, December 1862.
Died: Shepperton-on-Thames, Middlesex, 25 September 1925, aged 62.
Education: Uppingham.
First-class debut: 1887, Lancashire v Yorkshire, Old Trafford.
1 match for Lancashire 1887 (amateur).
HS for Lancashire: 1 v Yorkshire (debut).
Toured West Indies with A Priestley's team 1896-97.
HS: 26 Priestley's XI v West Indies XI, Port-of-Spain, 1896-97.
Full first-class record: 157 runs (9.81).

LEVENTON, Edwin Charles
RHB.
Born: Nottingham, 1845.
Died: Roby, Lancashire, 21 August 1909.
First-class debut: 1867, Lancashire v Yorkshire, Whalley.
1 match for Lancashire 1867 (amateur).
HS: 6 v Yorkshire (debut).
BB: 2-24 v Yorkshire (debut).
Little is known of this cricketer who played for Huyton CC.

LEVER, Peter
RHB; RFM.
Born: Todmorden, Yorkshire, 17 September 1940.
Education: Todmorden Grammar School.
First-class debut: 1960, Lancashire v Cambridge University, Old Trafford.

268 matches for Lancashire 1960-76 (professional). Capped 1965. Benefit (£7,000) 1972.
HS for Lancashire: 83 v Essex, Colchester, 1966.
BB: 7-70 v Glamorgan, Old Trafford, 1972.
Played for Tasmania 1971-72.
17 Tests for England 1970-71 to 1975. HS: 88* v India, Old Trafford, 1971. BB: 6-38 v Australia, Melbourne, 1974-75. Test record: 350 runs (21.87); 11 catches; 41 wickets (36.80).
Toured Australia and New Zealand with England 1970-71 and 1974-75.
Full first-class record: 3,534 runs (14.25); 106 catches; 796 wickets (25.59).

Tall and strong, Peter Lever delivered a pacey ball and when he struck a rhythm could be very good indeed. After back trouble caused his retirment he became county coach until his dismissal in 1986. His bother, Colin Lever, played for Buckinghamshire and for Minor Counties XIs.

LISTER, William Hubert Lionel
RHB.
Born: Freshfield, Lincolnshire, 11 October 1911.

Peter Lever

Education: Malvern College; Pembroke College, Cambridge.
Debut for Lancashire: 1933 v Gloucestershire, Old Trafford.
158 matches Lancashire 1933-39. Captain 1936-39.
HS: 104* v Middlesex, Lord's, 1936.
First-class debut: 1933, Cambridge University v Middlesex, Cambridge.
Played for Cambridge University 1933 (no Blue).
Full first-class record: 3,709 runs (18.45); 2 centuries; 73 catches; 2 stumped.

Lionel Lister, a slightly surprising choice as Eckersley's successor as Lancashire skipper in 1936, led the side keenly, although with no outstanding success, until the outbreak of war. His first-class career had a somewhat macabre end; he was actually padded-up, waiting to bat against Northamptonshire, when he was summoned to join his regiment, a week before war was declared. He played club cricket for Formby. He was an England amateur soccer international.

LITTLEWOOD, George Hubert

SLA.
Born: Friarmere, Yorkshire, 12 May 1882.
Died: Oldham, Lancashire, 20 December 1917, aged 35.
First-class debut: 1902, Lancashire v Leicestershire, Old Trafford.
14 matches for Lancashire 1902-04 (professional).
HS: 42 v Nottinghamshire, Trent Bridge, 1903.
BB: 7-49 v Australians, Liverpool, 1902 (12-98 in the match).

George Littlewood, whose father, George, also played for Lancashire, made a brilliant start to his career with figures of 12-98 against the 1902 Australian tourists, in only his second match, but despite continued promise he was never given a proper chance. He played for Accrington as professional, and for Crompton as an amateur.

LITTLEWOOD, George William

RHB; WK.
Born: Holmfirth, Yorkshire, 10 May 1857.
Died: Watersheddings, Oldham, Lancashire, 5 March 1928, aged 70.
First-class debut: 1885, Lancashire v Derbyshire, Old Trafford.
3 matches for Lancashire 1885 (professional).
HS: 8* v Surrey, The Oval, 1885.

His several professional engagements include Epworth, Triemere, Moorside, and from 1887 with Essex CCC at Leyton, for whom he played in non-first-class matches. In 1888 he scored 200 for Essex Club & Ground v Colchester. His son, G.H.Littlewood, also played for Lancashire.

LLOYD, Clive Hubert

LHB; RM.
Born: Queenstown, Georgetown, British Guiana, 31 August 1944.
Education: Chatham High School, Georgetown.
Debut for Lancashire: 1968 v Australians, Old Trafford.
219 matches for Lancashire 1968-86. Capped 1969. Captain 1981-83; 1986. Testimonial (£27,199) 1977.
HS for Lancashire: 217* v Warwickshire, Old Trafford, 1971.

BB: 4-48 v Leicestershire, Old Trafford, 1970.
1,000 runs (7); 1,458 (63.39) 1974 best.
110 Tests for West Indies 1966-67 to 1984-85.
Captain a record 74 times. HS 242* v India, Bombay, 1974-75. BB: 2-13 v England, Bridgetown, 1973-74. Test record: 7,515 runs (46.67); 19 centuries; 90 catches; 10 wickets (62.20).
Played for British Guiana and Guyana 1963-64 to 1983-84. Made Test tours with West Indies as follows: to England 1969, 1973, 1976, 1980 and 1984; to Australia 1968-69, 1975-76, 1979-80, 1981-82 and 1984-85; to New Zealand 1968-69, 1979-80; to India 1966-67, 1974-75 and 1983-84; to Pakistan 1974-75 and 1980-81. Also toured with World XI teams to Pakistan 1970-71 and 1973-74; to Australia 1971-72; and played for the Rest of the World against England in 1970.
Full first-class record: 31,232 runs (49.26); 79 centuries; 377 catches; 114 wickets (36.00).
Scored 200* in 2 hours for West Indians v

David Lloyd

Glamorgan, Swansea, 1976, to equal record for fastest-ever double-century in first-class cricket.

Clive Lloyd was a left-hander of tremendous power and authority, not withstanding heavy spectacles, and one of the most prehensile of all fieldsmen, at cover or slip, until knee trouble inhibited his movements. His captaincy of the West Indies was a period of almost unbroken success; he had the material to work upon, but did the job well. For Lancashire his leadership was less successful, but he gave his all for the county in every respect, and is one of the most successful of all imports to the County game. His autobiography *Living for Cricket* was published 1980.

LLOYD, David

LHB; SLA.
Born: Accrington, Lancashire, 18 March 1947.
Education: Accrington Technical School.
First-class debut: 1965, Lancashire v Middlesex, Old Trafford.
378 matches for Lancashire 1965-83. Capped 1968. Captain 1973-77. Testimonial (£40,171) 1978.

HS for Lancashire: 195 v Gloucestershire, Old Trafford, 1973.
BB: 7-38 v Gloucestershire, Lydney, 1966.
1,000 runs (10); 1,510 (47.18) 1972 best.

9 Tests for England 1974 to 1974-75. HS (and in all first-class cricket): 214* v India, Edgbaston, 1974. Test record: 552 runs (42.46); 1 century; 11 catches.
Tours: England to Australia 1974-75; D.H.Robins' XI to South Africa 1975-76.
Full first-class record: 19,269 runs (33.33); 38 centuries; 334 catches; 237 wickets (30.26).

A tall and basically sound left-hander, David Lloyd looked to have a big Test future but he found the pace of Lillee and Thomson too much for him and quietly resumed his county career, becoming a respected captain in succession to Jack Bond, although never reaching the predicted heights. As a bowler he once looked likely to reach genuine 'all-rounder' class but, again, he never developed his bowling as hoped. After a season on the first-class umpires' list, David Lloyd is now employed by the TCCB, marketing 'Kwik Cricket'. He played Minor Counties cricket for Cumberland in 1984, and League cricket for Accrington, where he was professional in 1984 and 1985. His son, Graham, now plays for Lancashire.

LLOYD, Graham David

RHB.
Born: Accrington, Lancashire, 1 July 1969.
Education: Hollins County High School.
First-class debut: 1988, Lancashire v Derbyshire, Derby.

22 matches for Lancashire 1988-1990.
HS: 117 v Nottinghamshire, Worksop, 1989.

His father, David, also played Lancashire.

LLOYD, Richard Averil

RHB.
Born: Dungannon, County Tyrone, Ireland, 4 August 1891.
Died: Belfast, Ireland, 23 December 1950, aged 59.
Education: Armagh Royal School; Portora Royal School; Dublin University.
Debut for Lancashire: 1921 v Gloucestershire, Liverpool.
3 matches for Lancashire 1921-22 (amateur).
HS: 51 v Gloucestershire (debut).
First-class debut: 1911, Ireland v Scotland, Dublin.
Full first-class record: 202 runs (20.20); 5 catches.
Richard Lloyd, who played cricket for Ireland in 1911 and 1912, was attached to the Liverpool club. He was much better known as an Irish Rugby Union international, winning 19 caps. He also played the winter game for Ulster, Liverpool and Lancashire.

LOMAX, James Geoffrey

RHB; RMF.
Born: Rochdale, Lancashire, 20 May 1925.
First-class debut: 1949, Lancashire v Oxford University, Oxford.

57 matches for Lancashire 1949-53. Capped 1952.
HS for Lancashire: 78 v Kent, Maidstone, 1952.
BB for Lancashire: 5-18 v Surrey, The Oval, 1952.

211 matches for Somerset 1954-62. Capped 1954.
HS: 104 Somerset v Sussex, Eastbourne, 1954.
BB: 6-75 Somerset v Surrey, The Oval, 1954.
Full first-class record: 8,672 runs (19.70); 2 centuries; 238 catches; 316 wickets (34.09).

Geoff Lomax showed all-round promise in 1952 with 675 runs (18.24) and 51 wickets (25.66), but a bad time in 1953 saw him leave the staff. He served Somerset well as a batsman and close fielder, although he lost his bowling. He played for Devon in 1966 and was professional for Milnrow.

LYON, John

RHB; WK.
Born: St Helen's, Lancashire, 17 May 1951.
Education: Central Secondary School, St Helens.
First-class debut: 1973, Lancashire v Oxford University, Oxford.

84 matches for Lancashire 1973-79. Capped 1975.
HS: 123 v Warwickshire, Old Trafford, 1979. (adding 158 with Bob Ratcliffe to create county record for 8th wicket).
Toured South Africa with D.H.Robins' team 1974-75.

McDONALD, Edgar Arthur

RHB; RF.
Born: Launceston, Tasmania, Australia, 6 January 1891.
Died: Blackrod, Bolton, Lancashire, 22 July 1937, aged 46 (killed in road traffic accident).

Debut for Lancashire: 1924 v Kent, Old Trafford.
217 matches for Lancashire 1924-31 (professional).
HS: 100* v Middlesex, Old Trafford, 1926.
BB for Lancashire: 8-53 v Kent, Old Trafford, 1928 (15-154 in the match).
100 wickets (6); 198 (18.55) 1925 best.
Achieved three hat-tricks: v Sussex, Hove, 1925;

v Kent, Dover, 1926; v Warwickshire, Edbaston, 1930.
Played for Tasmania 1909-10 and 1910-11; played for Victoria 1911-12 to 1921-22.
11 Tests for Australia 1920-21 to 1921-22. HS: 36 v England, The Oval, 1921. BB: 5-32 v England, Trent Bridge, 1921. Test record: 116 runs (16.57); 3 catches; 43 wickets (33-27).
Tours (all with Australia): to England 1921; to South Africa 1921-22.
BB: 8-41 Australians v Leicestershire, Leicester, 1921.
Full first-class record: 2,663 runs (10.44); 1 centuries; 98 catches; 1,395 wickets (20.76).

The signing of Ted McDonald was not universally popular, especially amongst traditionalists who felt that English Counties should use 'home' players, but there can be no doubt that it was a successful move for Lancashire. Although a bowler of execptional pace, such was his rhythm and athleticism that he seemed to put little effort into his deliveries. He was certainly a 'quiet destroyer'. After a triumphant tour of England in 1921, McDonald signed professional for Nelson. After retiring from the county game he joined Bacup. McDonald stayed in Lancashire after his playing days and died when he was knocked down by a car after escaping from his own crashed vehicle.

McFARLANE, Leslie Leopold

RHB; RFM.
Born: Portland, Jamaica, 19 August 1952.

Debut for Lancashire: 1982 v Nottinghamshire, Old Trafford.
35 matches for Lancashire 1982-84.
HS: 15* v Northamptonshire, Southport, 1984.
BB: 6-59 v Warwickshire, Southport, 1982.
First-class debut: 1979, Northamptonshire v Surrey, The Oval.
8 matches for Northamptonshire 1979.
13 matches for Glamorgan 1985.
Full first-class record: 127 runs (5.77); 13 catches; 102 wickets (40.58).

McFarlane played Minor Counties cricket for Bedfordshire.

McINTYRE, Hugh
RHB; WK.
Born: Glasgow, Scotland, 16 January 1857.
Died: Westminster, London, 25 June 1905, aged 48.
First-class debut: 1884, Lancashire v Derbyshire, Derby.
1 match for Lancashire 1884 (professional).
HS: 1* v Derbyshire (debut).

McIntyre was much better known as an outstanding soccer player. He played for Glasgow Rangers and won one cap for Scotland.

McINTYRE, William
RHB; RF (round-arm).

Born: Eastwood, Nottinghamshire, 24 May 1844.
Died: Prestwich, Lancashire, 13 September 1892, aged 48.
Debut for Lancashire: 1872 v Yorkshire, Old Trafford.
72 matches for Lancashire 1872-80 (professional). Benefit (£1,000) 1881.
HS for Lancashire: 66 v Derbyshire, Derby, 1875.
BB: 8-31 v Derbyshire, Derby, 1877 (15-47 in the match).
89 wickets (11.41) 1876; 85 wickets (11.15) 1877.
First-class debut: 1869, Nottinghamshire v Kent, Tunbridge Wells.
Played for Nottinghamshire 1869-71.
HS: 99 Nottinghamshire v Kent, Trent Bridge, 1869.
Full first-class record: 1,323 runs (10.41); 70 catches; 510 wickets (12.60).

A fast round-armed bowler, he was of very great value to Lancashire, after a not very successful spell with Nottinghamshire, his native county. He had professional engagements with Nottingham Commercial, Bolton and Castleton. His brother, Martin McIntyre, played for Nottinghamshire.

MacKINNON, Donald William
RHB.
Born: Bangalore, India, 3 March 1842.
Died: Stakes, Waterlooville, Hampshire, 19 November 1931, aged 89.
First-class debut: 1870, Lancashire v Hampshire, Old Trafford.
2 matches for Lancashire 1870-71 (amateur).
HS: 24 v Hampshire (debut).
BB: 3-13 v Derbyshire, Derby, 1871.

MacLAREN, Archibald Campbell
RHB; RFM.
Born: Whalley Range, Manchester, 1 December 1871.
Died: Warfield Park, Bracknell, Berkshire, 17 November 1944, aged 72.
Education: Harrow.
First-class debut: 1890, Lancashire v Sussex, Hove (scored 108 on debut).
307 matches for Lancashire 1890-1914 (amateur). Captain 1894-96; 1899-1907.
HS: 424 v Somerset, Taunton, 1895 (the highest-ever score in English first-class cricket).
Also scored 244 v Kent, Canterbury, 1897; 226* v Kent, Canterbury, 1896; 204 v Gloucestershire, Liverpool, 1903. 3 centuries in succession in 1895: 152 v Nottinghamshire, Old Trafford; 108 v Middlesex, Lord's; 135 v Leicestershire, Leicester.
Scored a century before lunch on first day of

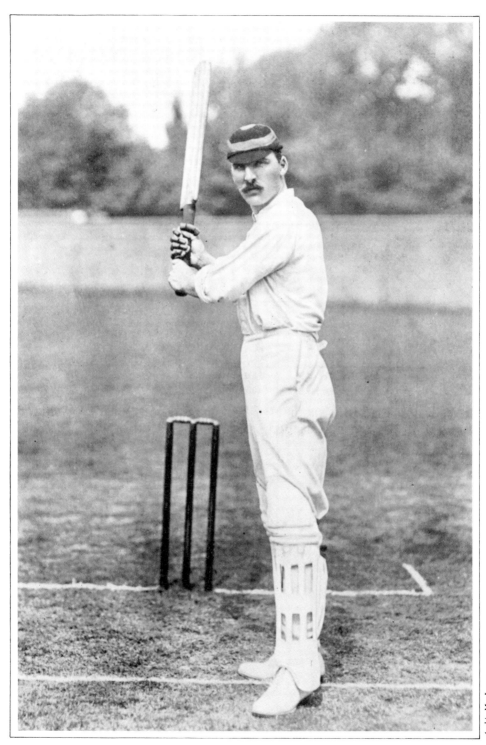

Archie MacLaren

match twice: v Leicestershire, Leicester, 1895; v Gloucestershire, Bristol, 1900.
Shares two Lancashire partnership records: 368 for 1st wicket (with R.H.Spooner v Gloucestershire, Liverpool, 1903); 324 for 4th wicket (with J.T.Tyldesley v Nottinghamshire, Trent Bridge, 1904).
1,000 runs (7); 1,647 (39.21) 1903 best.
35 Tests for England 1894-95 to 1909. Captain 22 times. HS: 140 v Australia, Trent Bridge, 1905.
Test record: 1,931 runs (31.11); 5 centuries; 29 catches.
Tours: England to Australia 1894-95, 1897-98, 1901-02; Ranjitsinhji's team to USA & Canada 1899; MCC to Argentine 1911-12; MCC to New Zealand 1922-23.
Full first-class record: 22,141 runs (34.11); 47 centuries; 451 catches; 1 wicket.

Archie MacLaren was tall and strongly built, sharp-eyed and eagle-faced, and one of the most stylish of all batsmen, with upright stance, high backlift and a wide range of strokes in front of the wicket. As a captain he was deep thinking and very original, but at Test level he was notably unsuccessful. After his retirement he acted as county coach. Brothers J.A. and G.MacLaren both played for Lancashire; their father, James, was Honorary Treasurer of Lancashire CCC.

MacLAREN, Frederic Grahame

Batsman.
Born: Worsley, Manchester, 5 November 1875.
Died: Bowdon, Cheshire, 10 May 1952, aged 76.
Education. Fettes.
First-class debut: 1903, Lancashire v Philadelphians, Old Trafford.
1 match for Lancashire 1903 (amateur).
HS: 19 v Philadelphians (debut).

An amateur who also played for Cheshire.

MacLAREN, Geoffrey

RHB.
Born: Whalley Range, Manchester, 28 February 1883.
Died: Bexhill-on-Sea, Sussex, 14 September 1966, aged 83.
Education: Harrow.
First-class debut: 1902, Lancashire v Sussex, Hove.
2 matches for Lancashire 1902 (amateur).
HS: 3 v Sussex (debut) and v Surrey, The Oval, 1902.

The younger brother of A.C. and J.A.MacLaren, like them he played for Harrow.

MacLAREN, James Alexander

RHB.
Born: Whalley Range, Manchester, 4 January 1870.
Died: Oldstock, Salisbury, Wiltshire, 8 July 1952 (after a fall), aged 82.
Education. Harrow.
First-class debut: 1891, Lancashire v Sussex, Old Trafford.
4 matches for Lancashire 1891-94.
HS: 6 v Sussex (debut).

The elder brother of A.C.MacLaren, he became a medical practioner and played for Bowden CC.

McLEOD, Kenneth Grant

RHB; RFM.
Born: Liverpool, 2 February 1888.
Died: St James, Cape Town, South Africa, 7 March 1967, aged 79.

Education: Fettes; Pembroke College, Cambridge.
Debut for Lancashire: 1908 v Warwickshire, Blackpool.
75 matches for Lancashire 1908-13 (amateur).
HS: 131 v Leicestershire, Old Trafford, 1911.
BB: 6-29 v Sussex, Eastbourne, 1909 (12-172 in the match).

When scoring 128 v Somerset, Bath, 1909, reached century in 63 minutes.
1,000 runs (1); 1,353 (30.06) 1911.
First-class debut: 1908, Cambridge University v Lancashire, Cambridge.
Played for Cambridge University 1908-09 (Blue each year).
Last match in 1914 for Free Foresters.
Full first-class record: 3,458 runs (23.86); 6 centuries; 107 catches; 103 wickets (26.67).

A brilliant all-rounder at school, being an aggressive batsman and a tearaway fast bowler, McLeod did pretty well in his limited first-class career, but was not sufficiently single-minded to fulfill his potential. There were many other strings to his sporting bow: he won a Rugby Blue (1905-06, 1906-07, 1907-08) and played ten times for Scotland as wing three-quarter (1906-08). He also represented Cambridge in the 100 yards and long jump.

McLEOD, Kenneth Walcott
RHB; LFM.
Born: St Elizabeth's, Jamaica, 18 March 1964.
Education: High school in Jamaica.
Debut for Lancashire: 1987 v Middlesex, Old Trafford.
6 matches for Lancashire 1987.
HS: 31 v Worcestershire, Old Trafford, 1987.
BB: 5-8 v Leicestershire, Leicester, 1987.
6 matches for Jamaica 1982-83 to 1987-88.
Full first-class record: 128 runs (8.00); 4 catches; 28 wickets (32.03).

MacNAIRY, Roy
RHB; Pace bowler.
Born: Barrow-in-Furness, Lancashire, 11 February 1904.
Died: Bradley, Huddersfield, Yorkshire, 5 September 1962, aged 57.
First-class debut: 1925, Lancashire v Gloucestershire, Cheltenham.
1 match for Lancashire 1925 (professional).
HS: 4* (only innings).
BB 1-23 v Gloucestershire (debut).

McNairy came from Barrow and was engaged with Manchester CC.

MAKEPEACE, Joseph William Henry
RHB, LB.
Born: Middlesbrough, Yorkshire, 22 August 1881.
Died: Spital, Bebington, Cheshire, 19 December 1952, aged 71.
First-class debut: 1906, Lancashire v Essex, Leyton.

487 matches for Lancashire 1906-30 (professional). Benefit 1922 (£2,110).
HS: 203 v Worcestershire, Worcester, 1923.
BB: 4-33 v Warwickshire, Old Trafford, 1913.
Scored 200* v Northamptonshire, Liverpool, 1923.
Carried bat throughout innings four times: 39*/208 v Nottinghamshire, Trent Bridge; 1923; 92*/159 v Nottinghamshire, Trent Bridge, 1926.
1,000 runs (13); 2,340 (48.75) 1926 best; also 2,286 (50.80) 1923.

4 Test matches for England 1920-21. HS: 117 v Australia, Melbourne, 1920-21. Test record: 279 runs (34.87) 1 century.
Tour: MCC to Australia 1920-21.
Full first-class record: 25,799 runs (36.23); 43 centuries; 194 catches; 42 wickets (46.92).

After playing for the Clubmoor and Wavertree clubs, Harry Makepeace gave great service to Lancashire, first as an obdurate opening bats-man with strong defence, who relied on pushes, nudges, and good placement for most of his runs. He was also a good cover fieldsman and occasionally a useful leg-spinner. Appointed coach to the county, in 1931, Makepeace remained in that position until 1951, when he finally retired aged 70 and was made an honorary life member of the County Club. A fine soccer half-back, he played for Everton in the FA Cup Finals of 1906 and 1907 and won four England caps between 1906 and 1912.

MAKINSON, David John

RHB; LFM.
Born: Eccleston, Lancashire, 12 January 1961.
Education: St Mary's High School, Leyland.

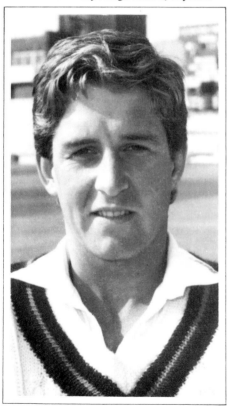

First-class debut: 1984, Lancashire v Northamp-tonshire, Northampton.
35 matches for Lancashire 1984-1988.
58* v Northamptonshire, Lytham, 1985.
BB: 5-60 v Derbyshire, Old Trafford, 1985.

Makinson, who joined Lancashire from Leyland Motors, has played for Cumberland since 1989.

MAKINSON, Joseph

RHB; RFM (round-arm).
Born: High Broughton, Manchester, 25 August 1836.
Died: Roundthorne, Sale, Cheshire, 14 March 1914, aged 77.

Education: Huddersfield College; Owen's College, Manchester; Clare College, Cambridge.
Debut for Lancashire: 1865 v Middlesex, Old Trafford.
5 matches for Lancashire 1865-73 (amateur).
HS for Lancashire: 45 v Middlesex, Old Trafford, 1865.
BB for Lancashire: 4-49 v Surrey, Old Trafford, 1867.
Cambridge Blue 1856-1857, in the 1856 Varsity game scoring 31 & 64, and taking 3-4 and 5-36, a match-winning performance. Played for Cambridgeshire 1857-58.
HS: 66 Gentlemen of the North v Gentlemen of the South, The Oval, 1860.
BB: 7-38 Cambridge University v Oxford University, Lord's, 1857.
Full first-class record: 862 runs (17.95); 46 wickets; 23 catches; 2 stumpped.

Short and slightly built, Joe Makinson was one of Lancashire's most talented amateurs, who was unfortunately unable to make many appearances for the county. A busy batsman who used his feet to get to the pitch of the ball, and a quick round-arm bowler and fine fielder, his profession as a barrister prevented his making the name in the cricket world which his talent deserved. He was a player, then honorary secretary, of Manchester Broughton CC. His brother, Charles Makinson, also played for Broughton and later went to Australia, living in Melbourne and playing for Victoria.

MALONE, Michael Francis
RHB; RFM.
Born: Scarborough, Perth, Western Australia, 9 October 1950.
Education: Scarborough High School, Perth.
Debut for Lancashire: 1979 v Nottinghamshire, Blackpool.
19 matches for Lancashire 1979-80.
HS for Lancashire: 38 (each innings) v Northamptonshire, Southport, 1980.
BB: 7-88 v Nottinghamshire (debut).
1 Test for Australia 1977: HS: 46 v England, The Oval, 1977; BB: 5-63 v England, The Oval, 1977. Test record: 46 runs (46.00); 6 wickets (12.83).
Played for Western Australia 1974-75 to 1981-82. Also played Kerry Packer cricket 1977-78 to 1978-79.
Full first-class record: 914 runs (16.03); 30 catches; 260 wickets (24.77).

Mick Malone was a talented cricketer who unfortunately seemed to lose interest easily. He did extremely well in his only Test and began his short Lancashire career with match-figures

of 7-99 v Nottinghamshire, and 11-92 v Leicestershire at Old Trafford. He also played for Haslingden in the Lancashire League.

MARCHBANK, Walter James
WK.
Born: Preston, Lancashire, 2 November 1838.
Died: Walton-le-Dale, Preston, 9 August 1893, aged 54.
First-class debut: 1869, Lancashire v Sussex, Hove.
4 matches for Lancashire 1869-70 (professional).
HS: 15 v Hampshire, Southampton, 1870.

Marchbank was a professional wicketkeeper, about whom little is known.

MARNER, Peter Thomas
RHB; RM.
Born: Greenacres, Oldham, Lancashire, 31 March 1936.
Education: Greenhill Grammar School, Oldham.
First-class debut: 1952, Lanchashire v Sussex, Hove. (16 years, 5 months, Lancashire's youngest-ever first-class player).
236 matches for Lancashire 1952-64 (professional). Capped 1958.
HS: 142 * v Leicestershire, Old Trafford, 1963.
BB for Lancashire: 5-46 v Nottinghamshire, Liverpool, 1962.
1,000 runs (7); 1,685 (38.29) 1958 best.
165 matches for Leicestershire 1965-70.

Capped 1965.

BB: 7-29 Leicestershire v Glamorgan, Coalville, 1966.

Tours: Commonwealth XI to Pakistan 1967.

Full first-class record: 17,513 runs (28.33); 18 centuries; 379 catches; 360 wickets (31.62).

Peter Marner, a fierce-hitting batsman, fine slip fielder and useful seamer, was perhaps one of Lancashire cricket's biggest disappointments. After showing fine form for Crompton when he was 15, he became the county's youngest-ever player the following season and showed great promise when only 17. His career was then

interrupted by a severe illness and a neck injury sustained at Rugby League which caused him to wear a surgical collar. Despite a fine season in 1958, and many excellent performances subsequently, he became very inconsistent as a player and gained a reputation for indiscipline which finally led to his dismissal after the 1964 season. He then enjoyed several useful seasons with Leicestershire but with increasing weight becoming a handicap, he quit the county game, aged 34, and went into the League with Todmorden.

MARRIOTT, Charles Stowell

RHB; RA; LBG.

Born: Heaton Moor, Lancashire, 14 September 1895.

Died: Dollis Hill, Middlesex, 13 October 1966, aged 71.

Education: St Columba's College, Dublin; Peterhouse, Cambridge.

First-class debut: 1919, Lancashire v Essex, Leyton.

12 matches for Lancashire 1919-21 (amateur).

HS for Lancashire: 16 v Middlesex, Lord's, 1919.

BB: 8-98 v Nottinghamshire, Trent Bridge, 1919.

Played for Cambridge University 1920-21 (Blue both years).

101 matches for Kent 1924-37.

HS: 21 Kent v Sussex, Maidstone, 1937.

1 Test for England 1933: Took 5-37 and 6-59 v West Indies, The Oval. Did note score.

Tours: S.B.Joel's team to South Africa 1924-25; MCC to India & Ceylon 1933-34.

Full first-class record: 574 runs (4.41); 47 catches; 711 wickets (20.11).

'Father' Marriott was a tall man with a high action and sharp spin, whose variations put the batsmen constantly on their guard. He was unlucky to play in only one Test. Unfortunately, an almost complete lack of physical co-ordination made him one of the worst fielders in first-class cricket and one of the few players with a 'career' to have comfortably scored fewer runs than wickets taken. Marriott did have his glory day with the bat, however. On his last appearance for Kent, against Sussex at Maidstone in 1937, he was sent in at the end of the first day to open the batting with Doug Wright, Wright failed but Marriott went on to score 21, the first time he ever ran into the 20s, and was second-highest scorer in the Kent innings. Doubtless he then retired happily to Dulwich College, where for many years he ran the cricket.

MARTIN, Peter James

RHB; RFM.
Born: Accrington, Lancashire, 15 November 1968.
Education: Danum School, Doncaster.
First-class debut: 1989, Lancashire v Australians, Old Trafford.
12 matches for Lancashire 1989-90.
HS: 21 v Nottinghamshire, Trent Bridge, 1990.
BB: 4-68 v Nottinghamshire, Trent Bridge, 1990.

Martin, a promising pace bowler, was brought up in Yorkshire but was turned down by them because he was not born in that county.

MASSEY, William Morton

RHB.
Born: Scotland, 11 April, 1846.
Died: New York City, USA, 19 April 1899, aged 53.
Debut for Lancashire: 1883 v Kent, Old Trafford.
1 match for Lancashire 1883 (amateur).
HS: 5 v Kent (debut).
1 match for Somerset 1882.
Played in non-first-class cricket for Devon 1875.

After emigrating to the United States, Massey played for Staten Island CC in 1886. He then went to Florida, where he made 264* in a very inferior game, and returned to New York.

MATTHEWS, Christopher Darrell

LHB; LFM.
Born: Cunderin, Western Australia, 22 September 1962.
Debut for Lancashire: 1988 v Worcestershire, Old Trafford.
3 matches for Lancashire 1988.
HS for Lancashire: 31 v Warwickshire, Old Trafford, 1988.
BB for Lancashire: 4-47 v Warwickshire, Old Trafford, 1988.
Has played for Western Australia since 1984-85.
HS: 65 Western Australia v Victoria, Perth, 1986-87.

BB: 8-101 Western Australia v Queensland, Perth, 1987-88.
3 Tests for Australia 1986-87 to 1988-89. HS: 32 v West Indies, Brisbane, 1988-89. BB: 3-95 v England, Brisbane, 1986-87. Test record: 56 runs (10.80). 1 catch. 6 wickets (52.16).
Full first-class record: 1,169 runs (20.15); 14 catches; 213 wickets (24.77).

MATTHEWS, Dudley Muir

LHB.
Born: Rainhill, near Liverpool, 11 September 1916.
Died: Bangkok, Thailand, 3 December 1968, aged 52.
Education: Felsted; Brasenose College, Oxford.
First-class debut: 1936, Lancashire v Nottinghamshire, Trent Bridge.
7 matches for Lancashire 1936-38 (amateur).
HS: 46 v Kent, Old Trafford, 1938.

A tall and attractive left-handed batsman from Formby CC, Dudley Matthews showed promise but his career was interrupted by World War Two. He played in trials at Oxford but failed to play a first-class match there. His brother, J.D.Matthews, played for Scotland.

MAYALL, James

WK.
Born: Oldham, Lancashire, 8 January 1856.
Died: Oldham, 13 September 1916, aged 60.
First-class debut: 1885, Lancashire v Gloucestershire, Old Trafford.
1 match for Lancashire 1885 (professional).
Scored 0 in only innings.
Mayall, one of a number of wicketkeepers tried during this period, played for Oldham.

MAYNARD, Christopher

RHB; WK.
Born: Haslemere, Surrey, 8 April 1958.
Education: Bishop Vesey's Grammar School, Sutton Coldfield.
Debut for Lancashire: 1982 v Hampshire, Southampton.
91 matches for Lancashire 1982-86. Capped 1986.
HS: 132* v Yorkshire, Headingley, 1986.
Dismissed 9 batsman (8 catches; 1 stumped) in match v Somerset, Taunton, 1982, to equal the then Lancashire record. Caught 6 in innings (and 8 in match) v Glamorgan, Swansea, 1983, which also equalled Lancashire record at the time.
First-class debut: 1978, Warwickshire v Lancashire, Edgbaston.
24 matches for Warwickshire 1978-82.
Tours: D.H.Robins' XI to New Zealand 1979-80; Lancashire to Jamaica 1987.

Full first-class record: 2,541 runs (20.65); 186 catches; 28 stumped.

Chris Maynard was a talented cricketer who somehow lacked the necessary consistency and resilience to reach quite the top grade. He was a sensitive individual who tended to take criticisms, real or imagined, too much to heart and these seemed to have a detrimental effect on both his game and his way of life. He was forced into premature retirement by a knee injury which did not seem to respond to treatment.

MELHUISH, Francis
RHB.
Born: Birkenhead, Cheshire, 17 May 1857.
Died: details unknown.
Education: Marlborough.
First-class debut: 1877, Lancashire v Derbyshire, Derby.
3 matches for Lancashire 1877 (amateur).
HS: 13 v Derbyshire (debut).

Meluish was one of several players tried at this period, whose inclusion caused criticism in the local Press.

MELLING, John
RHB; RA (fastish round-arm).
Born: Clayton-le-Moors, Lancashire, 6 April 1848.

Died: Burnley, Lancashire, 31 January 1881, aged 32.
First-class debut: 1874, Lancashire v Kent, Maidstone.
3 matches for Lancashire 1874-76 (professional).
HS: 20 v Kent (debut).

Melling was a sound batsman, whose fast bowling was given little chance, and good short slip fielder. He also played for Rishton.

MELLOR, Horace
RHB.
Born: Paddington, London, 21 February 1851.
Died: Castletown, Isle-of-Man, 27 February 1942, aged 91.
Education: Cheltenham College.
First-class debut: 1874, Lancashire v Derbyshire, Old Trafford.
2 matches for Lancashire 1874-75 (amateur).
HS: 17 v Derbyshire (debut).

Mellor was another amateur involved fleetingly with the county side.

MENDIS, Gehan Dixon
RHB; RM.
Born: Colombo, Ceylon (Sri Lanka), 24 April 1955.
Education: St Thomas College, Colombo; Brighton, Hove & Sussex Grammar School; Durham University.

First-class debut: 1986, Lancashire v Sussex, Hove.

114 matches for Lancashire 1986-1990. Capped 1986.

HS for Lancashire: 203* v Middlesex, Old Trafford, 1987.

1,000 runs (5); 1,551 (53.48) 1,990 best.

201 matches for Sussex 1974-85. Capped 1980.

HS: 209 Sussex v Somerset, Hove, 1984.

Tours: International XI to Pakistan 1981-82, to Jamaica 1982-83; Lancashire to Jamaica 1986-87.

Full first-class record: 18,798 runs (37.37); 36 centuries; 131 catches; 1 wicket.

Gehan Mendis never quite realized the high hopes held for him as a possible England batsman, but since moving to Lancashire from the more sylvan surroundings of Sussex he has confirmed the ability which places him amongst the leading openers on the county circuit.

MILLER, Frank Noble

Batsman

Born: South Africa, 8 April 1880.

Died: details unknown.

Education: Dale College, Kingwilliamstown, South Africa.

First-class debut: 1905, Lancashire v South Africa, Old Trafford.

1 match for Lancashire 1904.

HS: 37 v South Africa (debut).

Miller has been identified as the Old Dalian who played for Natal v MCC, Maritzburg, 1909-10.

MILLER, Henry

RHB; RF.

Born: Liverpool, 18 September 1859.

Died: Walton-on-Thames, Surrey, 11 April 1927, aged 67.

Education: Uppingham.

First-class debut: 1880, Lancashire v Derbyshire, Old Trafford.

5 matches for Lancashire 1880-81 (amateur).

HS: 27 v Yorkshire, Sheffield, 1881.

BB: 5-46 v Yorkshire, Sheffield, 1881.

Miller was a strongly-built amateur who bowled quickly and fielded well close to the wicket. Originally an engineer, he eventually went to India to do some tea-planting and while there played cricket in Assam.

MILLS, Josiah

RHB; WK.

Born: Oldham, Lancashire, 25 October 1862.

Died: Oldham, 23 November 1929, aged 67.

First-class debut: 1889, Lancashire v Oxford University, Old Trafford.

1 match for Lancashire 1889 (professional).

HS: 1 (in only innings).

An Oldham wicketkeeper, Mills made an impression in his only first-class match.

MILLS, Walter George

RHB; RF (round-arm).

Born: Dalston, London, 2 June 1852.

Died: Chorlton-cum-Hardy, Manchester, 6 January 1902, aged 49.

Education: Sheffield College.

First-class debut: 1871, Lancashire v Derbyshire, Old Trafford.

6 matches for Lancashire 1871-77 (amateur).

HS: 26 v Sussex, Hove, 1876.

BB: 3-52 v Kent, Gravesend, 1876.

He was a better class of player than some amateurs who appeared around this period. A round-armed bowler of considerable pace and a good batsman, he also fielded well at point or slip. Mills lived and played at Longsight, Manchester.

MILNE, Robert Oswald

Batsman.

Born: Manchester, 10 September 1852.

Died: Leamington Spa, Warwickshire, 6 September 1927, aged 75.

Education: Rugby; Oxford.

First-class debut: 1882, Lancashire v Somerset, Old Trafford.

1 match for Lancashire 1882 (amateur).

HS: 7* (in only innings).

Milne also played for Warwickshire (in non-first-class cricket) on the basis that he had a family home at Leamington Spa. He played for Oxford at both raquets and tennis, but had no proper trial at cricket.

MOLD, Arthur Webb

RHB; RF.

Born: Middleton Cheney, Northamptonshire, 27 May 1863.

Died: Middleton Cheney, 29 April 1921, aged 57.

First-class debut: 1889, Lancashire v MCC, Lord's.

260 matches for Lancashire 1889-1901 (professional). Benefit 1900.

HS: 57 v Leicestershire, Old Trafford, 1895.

BB: 9-29 v Kent, Tonbridge, 1892.

Also took 9-41 v Yorkshire, Huddersfield, 1890; 9-62 v Kent, Old Trafford, 1895 (match analysis of 16-111); 15-85 v Nottinghamshire, Trent Bridge, 1895; 15-87 v Sussex, Hove, 1894; 15-131 v Somerset, Taunton, 1891.

Arthur Mold

Took 4 wickets in 4 balls v Nottinghamshire, Trent Bridge, 1895; and hat-trick v Somerset, Old Trafford, 1894.
100 wickets (7); 192 (13.73); 1895 best. Took 189 wickets (11.84) in 1894.
In 1895, in all first-class matches, took 213 wickets (15.96) and in 1894, 207 wickets (12.31).
3 Tests for England 1893. 0 runs; BB: 3-44 v Australia, Lord's, 1893.
Full first-class record: 1,850 runs (7.14); 111 catches; 1,673 wickets (15.54).

Arthur Mold was a genuine fast bowler whose pace off the pitch made him devastating on the numerous bumpy wickets of his time. His best ball was probably the out-swinger which became a fast leg-break on pitching.

The tragedy of Arthur Mold was that throughout his career, his action, especially when bowling the leg-break, was not above suspicion. He was not 'called', however, until 1900, in his 12th season of first-class cricket, when he had bowled more than 60,000 balls without incurring the ire of the umpires, Jim Phillips called him from square-leg in the Notts match at Trent Bridge. During the following winter, the county captains voted that Mold's action was one of those which was unfair. Matters came to a head in the 1901 Somerset match at Old Trafford, when Phillips called him 16 times, both from square-leg and the bowler's end. Although Mold seemed to satisfy other umpires, Phillips' actions destroyed him and he played only three more matches before dropping out of cricket forever.

Not surprisingly, Mold became an embittered man, feeling that all his bowling triumphs now counted for naught. Apart from his native Northamptonshire, Mold played club cricket for Middleton Cheney, Banbury, St Helens Recreation and Manchester.

Mold was described as gentle and genial (except to those fielders who dropped catches off him). Back home he looked after his aged mother, ran a pub, and indulged in a little shooting. He was a civilised working man of his day, one who indulged professionally in the civilised pastime at which he excelled. Then one umpire, and the captains of the opposition counties, proceeded to destroy the dream.

MOORE, Frederick W.

RHB; RMF.
Born: Rochdale, Lancashire.
Education: Rochdale Central Technical School.
First-class debut: 1954, Lancashire v Oxford University, Oxford, 1954.
24 matches for Lancashire 1954-58 (professional).
HS: 18 v Nottinghamshire, Old Trafford, 1955.
BB: 6-45 v Essex, Chelmsford, 1956.
Achieved hat-trick during best bowling above.

Fred Moore, who played for Rochdale, Horwich, Elland and Walkden, was one of those bowlers who it was hoped would make Brian Statham a partner. However, despite some good performances he lacked devil.

MOORHOUSE, Edward

WK.
Born: Shawclough, Haslingden, Lancashire, 11 April 1851.

Died: Chorlton-cum-Hardy, Manchester, 10 March 1927, aged 75.
First-class debut: 1873, Lancashire v Kent, Gravesend.
5 matches for Lancashire 1873-75 (amateur).
HS: 34 v Derbyshire, Derby, 1873.
Moorhouse was an amateur wicketkeeper of Haslingden.

MOORSOM, Lewis Henry

Batsman.
Born: 1835.
Died: Moordown, Bournemouth, Hampshire, 10 March 1914.
First-class debut: 1865, Lancashire v Middlesex, Islington.
1 match for Lancashire 1865 (amateur).
HS for Lancashire: 7 v Middlesex (debut).
2 games for Trinidad v Demerara, Port-of-Spain, 1868-69.
HS: 15 for Trinidad (first of matches above).
Full first-class record: 41 runs (6.83).

MORTIMER, Sir Ralph George Elphinstone

RHB; RM.
Born: Newcastle upon Tyne, 7 July 1869.
Died: Melbourne, Northumberland, 3 May 1955, aged 85.
Education: Harrow; Cambridge University.
First-class debut: 1891, Lancashire v Oxford University, Oxford.
1 match for Lancashire 1891 (amateur).
HS: 22* v Oxford University (debut).
Mortimer played with great batting success for Northumberland from 1893 .

MUGLISTON, Francis Hugh

RHB; RM.
Born: Singapore, 7 June 1886.
Died: Westminster, London, 3 October 1932, aged 46.
Education: Rossall; Pembroke College, Cambridge.
Debut for Lancashire: 1906 v Somerset, Liverpool.
7 matches for Lancashire 1906-08 (amateur).
HS for Lancashire: 35 v Sussex, Old Trafford, 1906.
Played for Cambridge University 1905-08 (Blue 1907-08).
Last first-class match in 1911, for Leveson Gower's XI.
HS 109 Cambridge University v Lancashire, Cambridge, 1908.

BB; 3-32 Cambridge University v Gloucestershire, Cambridge, 1905.
Full first-class record: 874 runs (16.81); 1 century; 16 catches; 4 wickets (75.25).

Francis Mugliston was an outstanding all-round sportsman, playing cricket for Cambridge and Lancashire, soccer for Cambridge and The Corinthians, golf for Cambridge, and racquets and fives for his school. Until his death he represented Cambridge University on the FA Council and was on the Surrey CCC committee.

MURPHY, Anthony John

RHB; RMF.
Born: Manchester, 6 August 1962.
Education: Xaverian College; Swansea University.
First-class debut: 1985, Lancashire v Leicestershire, Leicester.
13 matches for Lancashire 1985-88.
HS for Lancashire: 5* v Somerset, Taunton, 1987.
BB for Lancashire: 4-115 v Somerset, Taunton, 1987.
31 matches for Surrey 1989-90.
HS: Surrey v Gloucestershire, The Oval, 1989.
BB: 6-97 Surrey v Derbyshire, Derby, 1989.
Played for Central Districts (New Zealand) 1985-86.
Full first-class record: 109 runs (3.89); 8 catches; 128 wickets (36.27).

MUSSON, Francis William, CMG, AFC

RHB; WK.
Born: Clitheroe, Lancashire, 31 May 1894.
Died: Chatham, Kent, 2 January 1962, aged 67.
Education: Tonbridge; Emmanuel College, Cambridge.
First-class debut: 1914, Lancashire v Leicestershire, Liverpool, 1914.
16 matches for Lancashire 1914-21 (amateur).
HS: 75 v Hampshire, Southampton, 1920.
Played last first-class match for Civil Service v New Zealanders, 1927.
Full first-class record: 539 runs (17.96); 13 catches; 4 stumped.

Musson was a member of the Royal Flying Corps in World War One and was injured in 1915. He was awarded the Air Force Cross in 1918, and was created CMG in 1958. His brothers, A.H. and R.G. Musson, played first-class cricket for Services teams.

NAPIER, John Russell

RHB; RF (round-arm)
Born: Preston, Lancashire, 5 January 1859.
Died: Sidley, Bexhill, Sussex, 12 March 1939, aged 80.

Education: Marlborough College; Cambridge University.
Debut for Lancashire: 1888 v Australians, Old Trafford.
2 matches for Lancashire 1888 (amateur).
HS: 37 v Australians (debut).
BB: 4-0 v Yorkshire, Sheffield, 1888.
First-class debut: 1881, Cambridge University v Gentlemen, Cambridge.
This talented cricketer suffered ill luck when in 1881, certain of his Blue at Cambridge, he injured his back. Entering the church in 1883, he became curate at Leigh but was able to play only twice for the county, in 1888, albeit with startling success. Against the Australians at Old Trafford, he achieved figures of 3-54 and 4-48, as well as top-scoring for the county with 37. A few weeks later, against Yorkshire, he achieved his best figures, 4-0 in 3.2 overs. He subsequently had church appointments at Preston and Walsden.

NASH, George
RHB; SLA.
Born: Oving, Aylesbury, Buckinghamshire, 1 April 1850.
Died: Aylesbury, Buckinghamshire, 13 November 1903, aged 53.
First-class debut: 1879, Lancashire v Nottinghamshire, Trent Bridge.
54 matches for Lancashire 1879-85 (professional). Benefit 1885.
HS: 30 v Gloucestershire, Old Trafford, 1881.
BB: 8-14 v Somerset, Old Trafford, 1882 (12-38 in the match).
Took 4 wickets in 4 balls during best bowling.
It was said that only George Nash's lack of pace ensured there was not as much fuss made about the legality of his action as that of his colleague, John Crossland. This notwithstanding, Nash was a very effective bowler for a few seasons with some fine performances to his credit. Apart from playing for Buckinghamshire, Nash had a number of professional engagements, notably Worcester County 1873 and 1874, Barrow-in-Furness, Accrington, Darwen and Leyland. He subsequently kept a pub. George Nash was known as 'Jolly Nash', after a well-known comic singer.

NAZIR ZAIDI, Syed Mohammed
RHB; LB.
Born: Karachi, Pakitan, 25 March 1961.
First-class debut: 1983, Lancashire v Oxford University, Oxford.
19 matches for Lancashire 1983-84.
HS: 51 v Somerset, Old Trafford, 1983.
BB: 3-27 v Sussex, Horsham, 1983.
Nazir Zaidi was on the MCC groundstaff before joining Lancashire.

NELSON, John
Batsman.
Born: Marton, Blackpool, 28 October 1891.
Died: France, 12 August 1917 (killed in action), aged 25.
First-class debut: 1913, Lancashire v Warwickshire, Old Trafford.
1 match for Lancashire (amateur) 1913.
HS: 5 v Warwickshire (debut).

A little-known amateur from Blackpool.

NORBURY, Duncan Victor
RHB; RA (Spin)
Born: Bartley, Hampshire, 3 August 1887.
Died: Sutton, Surrey, 23 October 1972, aged 85.
Debut for Lancashire: 1919 v Derbyshire, Old Trafford.

14 matches for Lancashire 1919-22 (professional).
HS: 100 v Surrey, The Oval, 1919.
BB: 4-28 v Derbyshire (debut).
First-class debut: 1905, Hampshire v Worcestershire, Worcester.
11 matches for Hampshire 1905-06.

Last first-class game in 1935, for Sir L.Parkinsons XI.

Full first-class record: 806 runs (19.19) 1 century; 8 catches; 30 wickets (33.20).

Norbury, who played for Northumberland in 1910, was a well-known club professional, whose engagements included East Lancashire, Church, Blackpool, Westhoughton.

NUTTER, Albert Edward

RHB; RMF.
Born: Burnley, Lancashire, 28 June 1913.
First-class debut: 1935, Lancashire v Sir Julien Cahn's XI, West Bridgford.
70 matches for Lancashire 1935-45. (professional). Capped 1938.

HS: 109* v Nottinghamshire, Old Trafford, 1939.
BB for Lancashire: 6-66 v Hampshire, Southampton, 1938.
1,000 runs (1); 1,156 (32.11) 1938. Also took 91 wickets (24.64) 1938.
145 matches for Northamptonshire 1948-53; Capped 1948. Testimonial with Norman Oldfield 1953 (£2,728).

BB: 7-52 Northamptonshire v Kent, Northampton, 1948.

Took 105 wickets (22.88) 1948. Set Northamptonshire 8th-wicket record of 155 with F.R.Brown v Glamorgan, Northampton, 1952. Full first-class record: 4,828 runs (19.54); 1 century; 161 catches; 600 wickets (26.23).

Albert Nutter had been one of those players upon whom the post-war Lancashire team expected to rely. Thus, it was a big disappointment when he decided to go into the Leagues, and subsequently to Northamptonshire. Amongst his professional engagements were contracts with Nelson, Formby, Crompton, Old Hill, Mitchell's & Butlers and Horton House.

NUTTER, Ezra

Batsman.
Born: Colne, Lancashire, 21 November 1858.
Died: Nelson, Lancashire, 17 November 1903, aged 44.
First-class debut: 1885, Lancashire v Derbyshire, Derby.
1 match for Lancashire 1885. (professional).
HS: 18 v Derbyshire (debut).

Ezra Nutter played for Rishton CC and Bingley CC.

OAKLEY, William

RHB; LM.
Born: Shrewsbury, Shropshire, 6 May 1861 (or 1868).
Died: details unknown.
First-class debut: 1893, Lancashire v MCC, Lord's.
20 matches for Lancashire 1893-94 (professional).
HS: 24 v Nottinghamshire, Old Trafford, 1893.
BB: 6-50 v Yorkshire, Scarborough, 1894.
Played Liverpool & District 1892-95.
First-class record: 144 runs (4.96); 21 catches; 60 wickets (18.28).

Medium-paced with an easy action, Bill Oakley was professional for Sefton and did very well in his only full season with the county in 1893. Possibly he was older than was thought, but he soon disappeared from the county team. Oakley, who played for Shropshire before Lancashire, was of average height and slightly built. Despite considerable searching of the death registers, no trace of his death has been found.

OLDFIELD, Norman

RHB.
Born: Dukinfield, Cheshire, 5 May 1911.
First-class debut: 1935, Lancashire v Middlesex, Lord's.

151 matches for Lancashire 1935-39 (professional). Capped 1935.
HS for Lancashire: 147* v Nottinghamshire, Old Trafford, 1939.
1,000 runs (5); 1,823 (44.46) 1939 best.
159 matches for Northamptonshire 1948-54. Capped 1948.
Joint testimonial with Bert Nutter (£2,728) 1953.
HS: 168 Northamptonshire v Worcestershire, Worcester, 1949.
Scored 2,192 runs (49.81) in all matches 1949.
Northamptonshire 1st-wicket record with Vince Broderick, 361 v Scotland, Peterborough, 1953.
Held Lancashire 3rd-wicket record with Eddie Paynter, 306 v Hampshire, Southampton, 1938. (beaten by Atherton and Fairbrother in 1990).
First-class record: 17,811 runs (37.89); 38 centuries; 96 catches.
1 Test for England 1939: v West Indies, The Oval. Scored 80 and 19.
Tours: Sir Julien Cahn's XI to New Zealand 1938-39; Commonwealth XI to India and Pakistan 1949-50.

'Buddy' Oldfield was small and quick-footed and a delightful stroke-maker whose blossoming career was interrupted by World War Two, and whose Lancashire days were ended in 1946 when he decided that League cricket offered better pay and security. He later joined Northamptonshire and for seven further seasons gave Lancashire supporters ample evidence of what they had missed. When he left Northamptonshire, Oldfield became an umpire and subsequently returned to Old Trafford as coach. He should never have left.

OLLIVANT, Alfred

Batsman.
Born: Stretford, Lancashire, 14 January 1839.
Died: Bowdon, Cheshire, 26 May 1906, aged 67.
First-class debut: 1873, Lancashire v Derbyshire, Derby.
2 matches for Lancashire 1873-74 (amateur).
HS: 24* v Derbyshire, Old Trafford, 1874.

Ollivant played for Sale.

OPENSHAW, William Edward

RHB.
Born: 5 February 1852.
Died: Haydock, Newton-le-Willows, Lancashire, 7 February 1915, aged 63.
Education: Harrow.
First-class debut: 1879, Lancashire v Nottinghamshire, Trent Bridge.
4 matches for Lancashire 1879-83 (amateur).
HS: 16 v Nottinghamshire (debut).

W.E.Openshaw was a member of the Lancashire Committee in 1880 and later played for the Gentlemen of Cheshire. He played football for Harrow and in 1879 won an England Rugby Union cap against Ireland.

ORMROD, Joseph Alan

RHB; OB.
Born: Ramsbottom, Lancashire, 22 December 1942.
Education: Kirkcaldy High School, Fife, Scotland.
Debut for Lancashire: 1984 v Oxford University, Oxford.
27 matches for Lancashire 1984-85. Capped 1984.
HS for Lancashire: 139* v Hampshire, Portsmouth, 1984.
1,000 runs (1); 1,199 (32.40) 1984.
First-class debut: 1962, Worcestershire v Lancashire, Stourbridge.
465 matches for Worcestershire 1962-83. Capped 1966. Benefit (£19,000) 1977.
HS: 204* Worcestershire v Kent, Dartford, 1973.
BB: 5-27 Worcestershire v Gloucestershire, Bristol, 1972.
Scored 1,000 runs in all first-class matches 13 times in all; 1,535 (45.14) in 1978 best.
Holds Worcestershire 4th-wicket record of 281 with Younis Ahmed, v Nottinghamshire, Trent Bridge, 1979.
Tours: Worcestershire to Jamaica 1965-66; MCC Under-25s to Pakistan 1966-67.
Full first-class record: 23,205 runs (30.89); 32 centuries; 399 catches; 25 wickets (43.76).

After an excellent career with Worcestershire,

Ormerod was signed by Lancashire to provide experience. It was too late for him to make a great deal of impact on the field but since his appointment as manager in 1986, Lancashire cricket has made great progress again.

O'SHAUGHNESSY, Steven Joseph
RHB; RM.
Born: Bury, Lancashire, 9 September 1961.
Education: Harper Green Secondary School, Farnworth.
First-class debut: 1980, Lancashire v Oxford University, Oxford.
100 matches for Lancashire 1980-87. Capped 1985.
HS: 159* v Somerset, Bath, 1984.
BB: 4-66 v Nottinghamshire, Trent Bridge, 1982.
1,000 runs (1); 1,167 (34.32) 1984.
11 matches for Worcestershire 1988-89.
Full first-class record: 3,720 runs (24.31); 5 centuries; 57 catches; 114 wickets (36.03).

Steve O'Shaughnessy was a talented all-rounder whose career was perhaps blighted when, against Leicestershire at Old Trafford in 1983, he was fed easy bowling to encourage a third-afternoon declaration, and he proceeded to score 105, reaching his century in 35 minutes to equal the all-time record of P.G.H.Fender (Surrey). He and Graeme Fowler added 201 in 43 minutes, the fastest-ever double-century stand, and O'Shaughnessy's century came off 25 scoring strokes, which was also a record. Sad it was that, after the 1987 season, it was decided he should seek pastures new; equally sad was his final departure from first-class cricket in 1989, and his undistinguished play for Northumberland in 1990.

PALMER, Septimus
Batsman.
Born: in Australia, 23 August 1858.
Died: London, 14 December 1935, aged 77.
Education: Stonyhurst.
First-class debut: 1879, Lancashire v Derbyshire, Derby.
6 matches for Lancashire 1879-80 (amateur).
HS: 8 v Kent, Canterbury, 1879.

A little-known amateur, who played occasionally for two seasons with little impact.

PARKER, Wilfred
Batsman
First-class debut: 1904, South Africans, Old Trafford.

2 matches for Lancashire 1904 (amateur).
HS: 40 v South Africans (debut).
BB: 2-47 v South Africans (debut).

Nothing is known of this amateur, who showed promise in his two games in 1904.

PARKIN, Cecil Harry

RHB; OB & LB.
Born: Egglescliffe, County Durham, 18 February 1886.
Died: Cheetham Hill, Manchester, 15 June 1943, aged 57.
Debut for Lancashire: 1914 v Leicestershire, Liverpool.

157 matches for Lancashire 1914-26 (professional). Benefit 1925 (£1,880).
HS: 57 v Kent, Old Trafford, 1922.
BB: 9-32 v Leicestershire, Ashby-de-la-Zouch, 1924.
Match analysis of 15-95 v Glamorgan, Blackpool, 1923.
100 wickets (4); 194 (13.38) 1924 best.
In all first-class amtches in 1923 took 209 wickets (16.95) and in 1924 took 200 wickets (13.27).
10 Tests for England 1920-21 to 1924. HS: 36 v Australia, Sydney, 1920-21; BB: 5-38 v Australia, Old Trafford, 1921. Test record: 160 runs (12.30); 3 catches; 32 wickets(35.25).
1 match for Yorkshire (v Gloucestershire, Headingley, 1906) but was found not be qualified.
Tours: MCC to Australia 1920-21.
Full first-class record: 2,425 runs (11.77); 126 catches; 1,048 wickets (17.58).

Cec Parkin, tall, dark and good-looking, got off to a false start with Yorkshire (above) but by the time he started with Lancashire he had honed his skills in the Leagues, with his native Durham (and allegedly against his wife) and was one of the most versatile of all bowlers. If he had a stock ball it was the off-break, but delivered with so many variations of flight and pace as to defy any 'stock' label. He could also turn it the other way (although not bowled as a googly), could bowl a straight, quick one, a looping slow one, one that seemed to gather speed as a top-spinner, and probably the master ball, a combination of the lot which put bowler, batsman and wicketkeeper in the charge of the men in white coats (not umpires!).
In League cricket he had many engagements, the main ones being for Tunstall and Church before World War One, then Rochdale and Blackpool.
A clown, an inveterate chatterbox and a genuine eccentric, Parkin was always in trouble with authority. An article under his name, criticising the captaincy of A.E.R.Gilligan in 1924, cost him his Test career; a couple of years later, a dispute with Lancashire saw him leave the county game. It was a sad but appropriate end to a career that was very good, but could have been marvellous. Parkin was his own worst enemy, but he was also born under an unlucky star.
His son, R.H.Parkin, also played for Lancashire.

PARKIN, Reginald Henry

RHB; ROB.
Born: Tunstall, Stoke-on-Trent, Staffordshire, 25 July 1909.
First-class debut: 1931, Lancashire v Somerset, Taunton.

20 matches for Lancashire 1931-39 (professional).
HS: 60 v Gloucestershire, Old Trafford, 1938.
BB: 3-52 v Hampshire, Old Trafford, 1937.

Reg Parkin, son of Cecil, was a competent all-round cricketer and superb fieldsman who was never able to establish a place in the county side. He also played for his native Staffordshire, for clubs in the North Staffs Leagues, and for Castleton in Lancashire.

PARKINSON, Herbert Black

RHB; WK.
Born: Barrow-in-Furness, Lancashire, 11 September 1892.
Died: Barrow-in-Furness, 27 April 1947, aged 54.
First-class debut: 1922, Lancashire v Nottinghamshire, Old Trafford.

15 matches for Lancashire 1922-23.
HS: 8 v Worcestershire, Old Trafford, 1922.

A wicketkeeper from Barrow-in-Furness, Parkinson was given a good trial but was negligible with the bat and not in the same class as George Duckworth, his successor.

PARKINSON, Leonard Wright

RHB; LB.
Born: Salford, Manchester, 15 September 1908.
Died: Manchester, 16 March 1969, aged 60.
First-class debut: 1932, Lancashire v Yorkshire, Bradford.
88 matches for Lancashire 1932-36 (professional).
HS: 93 v Nottinghamshire, Old Trafford, 1934.
BB: 6-112 v Essex, Leyton, 1933.

Len Parkinson was a most useful all-rounder whose leg-breaks seemed to be getting progressively more penetrative when, after the 1936 season, he retired to join Lowerhouse in the Lancashire League.

PARR, Francis David

LHB; WK.
Born: Wallasey, Cheshire, 1 June 1928.
Education: Wallasey Grammar School.
First-class debut: 1951, Lancashire v Cambridge University, Cambridge, 1951.
48 matches for Lancashire 1951-54 (professional). Capped 1952.
HS: 42 v Sussex, Hove, 1952.

Frank Parr sometimes looked the best of the numerous wicketkeepers tried during the 1950s, but a weakness against spin gradually showed itself and he was finally superceded. Parr then made his mark in the world of music; he was for some time a professional jazz trombonist. He became founder-member of the Merseyssippi Jazz Band and played with the Mick Mulligan Band, backing George Melly. He subsequently went into management and for a number of years looked after the affairs of Acker Bilk.

PARR, Henry Bingham

RHB.
Born: Grappenhall Hayes, near Warrington, Lancashire, 6 June 1845.
Died: Liverpool, 24 March 1930, aged 84.
Education: Cheltenham College.

First-class debut: 1872, Lancashire v Yorkshire, Sheffield.
10 matches for Lancashire 1872-76 (amateur).
HS: 61 v Derbyshire, Old Trafford, 1873.

H.B.Parr, who played very successfully for Liverpool, was a batsman who could hit hard but usually played a patient game. In 1874 he made 202 for Liverpool against Dingle and, apart from Lancashire, appeared for The North and for Cheshire.

PATTERSON, Balfour Patrick

RHB; RF.
Born: Portland, Jamaica, 15 September 1961.
Education: Happy Grove High School; Wolmers School, Jamaica.
Debut for Lancashire: 1984 v Northamptonshire, Southport.
70 matches for Lancashire 1984-90. Capped 1987.
BB for Lancashire: 7-49 v Oxford University, Oxford, 1985.

18 Test for West Indies 1985-86 to 1989-90. HS: 21* v India, Bombay, 1987-88; BB: 5-24 v India, Delhi, 1987-88. Test record: 90 runs (7.50); 3 catches; 60 wickets (30.73).

31 one-day internationals for West Indies.

Played for Jamaica 1982-83 to date.

Tours: West Indies to England 1988; to Australia 1988-89; to New Zealand 1986-87; to India 1987-88; to Pakistan 1986-87.

Full first-class record: 505 runs (6.02); 403 wickets (27.39).

PATTERSON, William Seeds

RHB; SRA.

Born: Mossley Hill, Liverpool, 19 March 1854.

Died: Hook Heath, Woking, Surrey, 20 October 1939, aged 85.

Education: Uppingham; Trinity College, Cambridge.

Debut for Lancashire: 1874 v Kent, Old Trafford.

7 matches for Lancashire 1874-82 (amateur).

HS for Lancashire: 50 v Gloucestershire, Old Trafford, 1878.

BB: 7-30 v Nottinghamshire, Trent Bridge, 1877 (14-102 in the match).

First-class debut: 1874, Cambridge University v England XI, Cambridge.

Played for Cambridge University 1874-77 (Blue 1875-76-77). Captain 1877.

HS: 105* Cambridge University v Oxford University, Lord's, 1876 (when he also had first-innings figures of 5-42 and played a big part in his side's nine-wicket victory.

Full first-class record: 1,059 runs (18.25); 1 century; 18 catches; 157 wickets.

An excellent all-round cricketer, Patterson was a steady batsman who usually waited for the bad ball, a sound fielder and a slow round-arm bowler who tended to beat the batsmen by flight and sublety rather than power of spin.

PAUL, Arthur George

RHB; Occasional WK

Born: Belfast, Ireland, 24 July 1864.

Died: Didsbury, Lancashire, 14 January 1947, aged 72.

Education: Victoria College, Douglas, Isle-of-Man.

First-class debut: 1889, Lancashire v Oxford University, Old Trafford.

95 matches for Lancashire 1889-1900 (professional). Benefit 1913.

HS: 177 v Somerset, Taunton, 1895 (when he added 363 for 2nd wicket with A.C.MacLaren, then a Lancashire record).

Tall and strongly built, Arthur Paul had a good defence and drove well, but ill health proved

to be a handicap. In 1900 he retired and became county coach, a position which he held with a high degree of success and respect for nearly 30 years. The son of an Army officer who became Chief Constable of the Isle of Man, Arthur Paul was a considerable all-round sportsman. In addition to cricket he played Rugby football for Swinton, touring Australia in 1888, and he played in goal at soccer for Blackburn Rovers. Trained to be an architect, Arthur Paul became a professional cricketer for Leeds Clarence in 1882, and subsequently had engagements with Notts Castle and Nelson.

PAYNE, James

Bowler.

First-class debut: 1898, Lancashire v Sussex, Hove.

1 match for Lancashire 1898 (professional).

Scored 0 and 0 and took no wickets.

Nothing has been traced about this player, originally recorded by this writer as 'W.Payne'.

PAYNE, John Henry

RHB; WK.

Born: Broughton, Lancashire, 19 March 1858.

Died: Victoria Park, Manchester, 24 January 1942, aged 83.

Education: Cheltenham College; Cambridge University.

Debut for Lancashire: 1883 v Derbyshire, Derby.

9 matches for Lancashire 1883 (amateur).

HS: 33 v Surrey, Old Trafford, 1883.

First-class debut: 1880, Cambridge University v England XI, Cambridge.

2 matches for Cambridge University 1880 (no Blue).

Full first-class record: 166 runs (10.37); 7 catches; 4 stumped.

Payne played for Manchester Broughton CC. His father, J.B.Payne, was a well-known cricketer in the North.

PAYNTER, Edward

LHB; RM.

Born: Oswaldtwistle, Lancashire, 5 November 1901.

Died: Keighley, Yorkshire, 5 February 1979, aged 77.

Education: Clayton-le-Moors Secondary School.

First-class debut: 1926, Lancashire v Somerset, Old Trafford.

293 matches for Lancashire 1926-45 (professional). Capped 1931. Grant in lieu of benefit (£1,078) 1945.

HS: 322 v Sussex, Hove, 1937.

Full first-class record: 20,075 runs (42.26); 45 centuries; 160 catches; 30 wickets (45.70).

Despite his small size, Eddie Paynter packed a remarkably powerful punch and was one of the bravest and most admired left-handed batsmen ever to play in English cricket. Paynter, who started off with Enfield CC and later played for Keighley, did not make his debut for Lancashire until he was 24; and he had reached his 30th year before being assured of a regular place.

He scored all 322 runs of his best score in one day in 1937 — the Lancashire record and at the time the second-best ever in the County Championship. That epitomised his aggressive nature; his bravery was proved when he rose from his sick-bed for a match-winning 83 for England at Brisbane in 1932-33.

Also scored 291 v Hampshire, Southampton, 1938; 266 v Essex, Old Trafford, 1937; 222 v Derbyshire, Old Trafford, 1939; 208* v Northamptonshire, Northampton, 1935.
BB: 3-13 v Sussex, Hove, 1933.
1,000 runs (9); 2,626 (58.35) 1937 best.
Also scored 2,020 runs (57.71) 1938; 2,016 runs (45.81) 1936.
Scored 2,904 runs (53.77) in all first-class matches 1937; 2,691 runs (58.50) in all matches 1938.
Scored 125 and 113* in match v Warwickshire, Edgbaston, 1938.
Scored three consecutive centuries 1936: 123* v Nottinghamshire, Trent Bridge; 177 v Glamorgan, Old Trafford; 119 v Northamptonshire, Old Trafford.
During highest score 322 (above) scored century before lunch on first day. Also scored century before lunch during innings of 260* on second morning, Lancashire v Essex, Old Trafford, 1937.
Added 306 with Buddy Oldfield v Hampshire, Southampton, 1938 (Lancashire 3rd-wicket record until 1990).
20 Tests for England 1931-39. HS: 243 v South Africa, Durban, 1937-39. Test record: 1,540 runs (59.23) 4 centuries; 7 catches.
Tours: MCC to Australia and New Zealand 1932-33; to South Africa 1938-39. Commonwealth XI to India 1950-51.

Life was not too kind for Paynter in later years. He was a club professional for a time, and in 1951 joined the first-class umpires list. Not too long afterwards, he was discovered labouring on a construction site in the north of England. He perked up in later years, however, and enjoyed the Centenary Test trip to Australia in 1977. His autobiography *Cricket All The Way* appeared in 1962.

PENNINGTON, Harry

WK.
Born: Salford, Manchester, 21 April 1880.
Died: Moston, Manchester, 17 March 1861, aged 80.
First-class debut: 1900, Lancashire v Derbyshire, Glossop.
4 matches for Lancashire 1900 (professional).
HS: 29* v Derbyshire (debut).

Harry Pennington was one of three wicketkeepers tried in 1900. According to *Wisden'* '. . .he possesses some mannerisms which are hardly likely to strengthen his position in County Cricket'. What can the writer possibly have meant? Pennington — mannerisms or not — was a successful soccer player for Notts County.

PERRY, William

Born: Oxford, 12 August 1830.
Died: Thatcham, Berkshire, 15 March 1913, aged 82.
Debut for Lancashire: 1865 v Middlesex, Old Trafford.
1 match for Lancashire 1865 (professional).
HS: 16 v Middlesex (debut). No wickets.

William Perry was first noted as early as May 1849, playing for '16 of Oxfordshire' against Kent on The Prince of Wales' ground at Oxford. He also played for Berkshire teams and made his first-class debut for The North against The South on the Manchester Broughton ground, where he was engaged, in 1856.

PEWTRESS, Alfred William

RHB.
Born: Rawtenstall, Lancashire, 27 August 1891.
Died: Brighton, Sussex, 21 September 1960, aged 69.
Education: Christ's Hospital; Manchester Grammar School.
First-class debut: 1919, Lancashire v Australian Imperial Forces, Old Trafford.
50 matches for Lancashire 1919-25 (amateur).
HS: 89 v Nottinghamshire, Old Trafford, 1925.
BB: 1-10 (his only wicket) v Yorkshire, Old Trafford, 1925..

Alf Pewtress, who played for Rawtenstall, was deputy captain in 1925 and was chosen for the same job in 1926 — but never played.

PHILLIPS, William

RHB; WK.
Born: details unknown.

Died: believed in January 1952.
First-class debut: 1904, Lancashire v Surrey, The Oval.
10 matches for Lancashire 1904-08 (professional).
HS: 18 v Kent, Old Trafford, 1908.

William Phillips played for Blackley CC and Longsight CC.

PHILLIPSON, William Edward

RHB; RFM.
Born: North Reddish, Cheshire, 3 December 1910.
First-class debut: 1933, Lancashire v Sussex, Old Trafford.

158 matches for Lancashire 1933-48 (professional).
Grant in lieu of benefit 1948 (£1,750).
HS: 113 v Glamorgan, Preston, 1939.
BB: 8-100 v Kent, Dover, 1934.
100 wickets (2); 133 (22.33) 1939 best.
Tour: Sir Julien Cahn's XI to New Zealand 1938-39.
Full first-class record: 4,096 runs (25.76); 2 centuries; 555 wickets (24.72); 82 catches.

Eddie Phillipson was another of those unfortunates whose cricket career was neatly severed by World War Two. In 1937 and 1939 he had approached the double and there seems little doubt that his peak would have been reached in the first half of the 1940s. Alas, as Corporal Philipson he then had more important matters to hand. His figures for the first post-war season were still reasonable but he had begun to struggle and his form then collapsed.

Phillipson played as a professional for Littleborough and after retirement became a well known umpire. He was on the list from 1956 to 1978 and stood in 12 Tests from 1958 to 1965.

This must have been some recompense of the ill luck of his playing career.

PILKINGTON, Charles Carlisle

RHB; RM.
Born: Woolton, Liverpool, 13 December 1876.
Died: South Warnborough, Hampshire, 8 January 1950, aged 73.
Education: Eton; Magdalene College, Oxford.
First-class debut: 1895, Lancashire v Derbyshire, Old Trafford.
2 matches for Lancashire 1895 (amateur).
HS for Lancashire: 18 v Derbyshire (debut).
BB: 3-70 v Derbyshire (debut).
Played for Oxford University 1896 (Blue).

Charles Pilkington

Harry Pilling

2 matches for Middlesex 1902. Last first-class match in 1919, for the Gentlemen.
HS: 86 Oxford University v A.J.Webbe's team, Oxford, 1896.

Pilkington was a gifted all-rounder who gave up first-class cricket when he went on the Stock Exchange. His brother, H.C.Pilkington, played for Oxford University and Middlesex.

PILLING, Harry
RHB; OB.
Born: Ashton-under-Lyne, Lancashire, 23 February 1943.
Education: Ashton Technical School.
First-class debut: 1962, Lancashire v Sussex, Old Trafford.
323 matches for Lancashire 1962-80 (profes-

Tours: Commonwealth XI to Pakistan 1970-71; World XI to Pakistan 1973-74; D.H.Robins' XI to Sri Lanka 1977-78.
Full first-class record: 15,279 runs (32.23); 25 centuries; 89 catches; 1 wicket.

At 5ft 2ins, Harry Pilling was one of the smallest of all first-class cricketers, but he was a brave and remarkably consistent number-three batsman who, with better luck, may have played for England. He played League cricket for Oldham and Radcliffe.

PILLING, Richard
RHB; WK.
Born: Bedford, 5 July 1855.

sional). Capped 1965. Testimonial (£9,500) 1974.
HS: 149* v Glamorgan, Liverpool, 1976.
1,000 runs (8); 1606 (36.50) 1967 best.
Scored: 109* and 104* v Warwickshire, Old Trafford, 1970.

Four stalwart nineteenth-century Lancashire cricketers. From left to right: Dick Pilling, Alec Watson, A.N.'Monkey' Hornby and Dick Barlow.

Died: Old Trafford, Manchester, 28 March 1891, aged 35.

First-class debut: 1877, Lancashire v Sussex, Old Trafford.

177 matches for Lancashire 1877-89 (professional). Benefit 1889.

HS: 78 v Somerset, Old Trafford, 1882.

486 dismissals (333 catches; 153 stumped) puts him second to George Duckworth amongst Lancashire wicketkeepers.

8 Tests for England 1881-82 to 1888; HS: 23 v Australia, Sydney, 1881-82. Test record: 91 runs (7.58); 10 catches; 4 stumped.

Tours: MCC to Australia 1881-82; 1887-88.

Full first-class record: 2,572 runs (9.85); 461 catches; 206 stumped.

Dick Pilling, known as 'The Prince of Wicket-keepers' was economical of movement yet agile, brave, yet unobtrusive. A description which would qualify him for top place in any age of cricket. Sadly, Dick, whose brother William also played for Lancashire, suffered deteriorating health for the last three years of his life. This undoubtedly affected his cricket and although the Lancashire club sent him on a sea voyage to Australia in the winter of 1890-91, he died of consumption a few weeks after his return to England.

By trade a stonemason, Pilling qualified for Lancashire by residence, but he subsequently opened a cricket warehouse with Alec Watson, his Lancashire colleague. From 1879 to 1883 he was engaged at Lord's but then signed for Manchester Broughton, where he remained until his death.

PILLING, William

RHB; WK.

Born: Church, Lancashire, circa 1858.

Died: Trafford Park, Stetchford, Manchester, 27 March 1924, aged 66.

First-class debut: 1891, Lancashire v Gloucestershire, Old Trafford.

1 match for Lancashire 1891 (professional).

HS: 9* v Gloucestershire (debut).

Richard Pilling's younger brother was likewise a wicketkeeper engaged at Manchester.

PLACE, Winston

RHB.

Born: Rawtenstall, Lancashire, 7 December 1914.

First-class debut: 1937, Lancashire v Derbyshire, Old Trafford.

298 matches for Lancashire 1937-55 (professional). Capped 1939. Benefit (£6,297) 1952.

HS: 266* v Oxford University, Oxford, 1947.

3 Tests for England 1947-48. HS: 107 v West Indies, Kingston, 1947-48. Test record: 144 runs (28.80).

Tours: MCC to West Indies 1947-48; Commonwealth XI to India, Pakistan and Ceylon 1949-50.

Full first-class record: 15,609 runs (35.63); 36 centuries; 190 catches; 1 wicket.

Winston Place — no-one with that sort of name could have been anything but a sound, reliable Lancashire opening batsman. The writer's childhood memories suggest he even looked the part and, despite missing what may have been his best years to World War Two, his record suggests that he played the part. A good basic technique enabled him to play spin bowling very well and when runs were needed quickly, he brought a hefty pull and lofted straight drive into play. His Test record suggests he should perhaps have been afforded more chances.

POIDEVIN, Leslie Oswald Sheridan
RHB; LBG.
Born: Merrila, New South Wales, Australia, 5 November 1876.

Also 226* v Nottinghamshire, Trent Bridge, 1949; 200 v Somerset, Taunton, 1948.
Scored 105 and 132* in match, Lancashire v Nottinghamshire, Old Trafford, 1947. (Scored 171 v Essex, Clacton, in previous innings, therefore three successive centuries.)
Carried bat v Warwickshire, Old Trafford, 1950 (101*/244).
Added 350* with Cyril Washbrook for 1st-wicket v Sussex, Old Trafford, 1947.
1,000 runs (8); 2,408 (68.80) 1947 best.
Scored 2,501 runs (62.52) in all first-class cricket 1947.

Died: Bondi, New South Wales, 18 November 1931, aged 55.
Debut for Lancashire: 1904 v Surrey, Old Trafford.
105 matches for Lancashire 1904-08 (amateur).
HS for Lancashire: 168* v Worcestershire, Worcester, 1905.
BB: 8-66 v Worcestershire, Worcester, 1905.
(Above 2 performances in same match; scored 76 in first innings.)
1,000 runs (1); 1,407 (40.20) 1905.
Played for New South Wales 1895-96 to 1904-05.
HS: 179 New South Wales v Queensland, Brisbane, 1904-05.
Tour: New South Wales to New Zealand 1895-96.
Full first-class record: 7,022 runs (32.96); 14 centuries; 163 catches; 46 wickets (41.69).

Leslie Poidevin came to England from Australia to qualify as a doctor. As a batsman he was more workmanlike than attractive but he scored consistently.

POLLARD, Richard

RHB; RFM.
Born: Westhoughton, Lancashire, 19 June 1912.
Died: Westhoughton, 16 December 1985, aged 73.
First-class debut: 1933, Lancashire v Notting-hamshire, Old Trafford.
266 matches for Lancashire 1933-50 (professional). Capped 1935. Benefit (£8,000) 1949.
HS: 63 v Derbyshire, Old Trafford, 1947.
BB: 8-33 v Northamptonshire, Old Trafford, 1947.
Two hat-tricks: v Glamorgan, Preston, 1939; v Warwickshire, Blackpool, 1947.
100 wickets (6); 140 (21.75) 1938 best.
4 Tests for England 1946-48. HS: 10* v India, Old Trafford, 1946 (debut); BB: 5-24 v India, Old Trafford, 1946 (debut). Test record: 13 runs (13.00). 3 catches. 15 wickets (25.20).
Tour: MCC to Australia and New Zealand 1946-47.
Full first-class record: 3,522 runs (13.29); 225 catches; 1,122 wickets (22.56).

It is surely a compliment to Dick Pollard, the fact that he only took five wickets against Australia, and the victim on two occasions was Bradman. What is more — who remembers that? Pollard was a whole-hearted new-ball bowler, whose heavy build and lumbering run-up inspired thoughts of an equine nature. He was also spot-on with length and direction and at his best the stock inswing sometimes went the other way on pitching. Pollard loved bowling (or just trying to take wickets) and was sometimes rather upset when his skipper decided on a change.

Pollard missed some good years due to World War Two but his impressive figures are tribute indeed to his ability. After leaving the county scene (with the minimum of fuss; retirement was apparently his own idea), he played in the Leagues for Aston Unity and Preston. His ability to extemporise on the piano made him a popular social animal.

PORTER, Edward Horatio

RHB; RM (round-arm).
Born: Liverpool, 13 October 1846.
Died: Hooton, Cheshire, 31 October 1918, aged 72.
Education: Privately.
First-class debut: 1874, Lancashire v Yorkshire, Bradford.
17 matches for Lancashire 1874-1882 (amateur).
HS: 61 v Yorkshire (on debut).
BB: 3-48 Gentlemen v Cambridge University, Cambridge, 1875.
Last first-class appearance in 1883, for a combined Nottinghamshire/Lancashire team.
Full first-class record: 374 runs (11.33); 3 wickets (16.00); 13 catches.

George Potter of Oldham was tried out in 1902 and *Wisden* states: 'He started with great success, but scarcely sustained his early form.' He disappeared from the Lancashire team as suddenly as he had arrived. In 1910 he was in the Cheshire side and having some success on his few appearances, but this writer can trace nothing subsequently.

POTTER, Thomas Owen
Batsman.
Born: Calcutta, India, 19 September 1844.
Died: Hoylake, Cheshire, 27 April 1909, aged 64.
First-class debut: 1866, Lancashire v Surrey, Liverpool.
1 match for Lancashire 1866 (amateur).
HS: 39 v Surrey (debut).

Thomas Potter, who played for Liverpool, was brother of William, also of Lancashire.

POTTER, William Henry
Batsman.
Born: Gufsey, India, 20 August 1847.
Died: Boreham Wood, Hertfordshire, 10 April 1920, aged 72.
First-class debut: 1870, Lancashire v Surrey, The Oval.

Edward Porter of Liverpool was usually a free hitter and bowled fast round-arm. A good local reputation was never transferred onto the first-class scene.

POTTER, George
RHB.
Born: Oldham, Lancashire, 3 October 1878.
Died: details unknown.
First-class debut: 1902, Lancashire v Warwickshire, Old Trafford.
10 matches for Lancashire 1902 (amateur).
HS: 86 v Sussex, Hove, 1902.

1 match for Lancashire 1866 (amateur).
HS: 12 v Surrey (debut).

Like his brother, Thomas, he played only once for Lancashire, preferring club cricket with Liverpool. William Potter also appeared for Hertfordshire.

PRESTON, Stephen

RHB; RM.
Born: Heywood, Lancashire, 11 August 1905.
First-class debut: 1928, Lancashire v Leicestershire, Liverpool.
5 matches for Lancashire 1928-30 (professional).
HS: 33 v Worcestershire, Old Trafford, 1930.
BB: 2-42 v Leicestershire (debut).

After a short county career, Preston returned to League cricket with Middleton.

PRICE, Alfred

RHB.
Born: Ruddington, Nottinghamshire, 5 January 1862.
Died: Oldham, Lancashire, 21 March 1942, aged 80.
Debut for Lancashire: 1885 v Oxford University, Oxford.
1 match for Lancashire 1885.
HS for Lancashire: 8 v Oxford University (debut).
First-class debut: North v South, Lord's, 1884.
3 matches for Nottinghamshire 1887.
HS: 37 Liverpool & District v Australians, Liverpool, 1884.
Full first-class record: 110 runs (9.16).

His father, Walter Price, played for Nottinghamshire, and his brother, Frederick, appeared for The North. Alfred was engaged for several years with Liverpool CC and also at Bedford County Modern School.

PRICE, Eric James

LHB; SLA.
Born: Middleton, Lancashire, 27 October 1918.
Education: St Leonard's Church of England School, Middleton.
First-class debut: 1946, Lancashire v Glamorgan, Old Trafford.
35 matches for Lancashire 1946-47 (professional). Capped 1946.
HS: 54 v Middlesex, Old Trafford, 1946.
BB for Lancashire: 6-34 v Surrey, Old Trafford, 1946.
43 matches for Essex 1948-49.

BB: 8-125 Essex v Worcestershire, Worcester, 1949.
Full first-class record: 558 runs (8.71); 40 catches; 215 wickets (26.61).

Eric Price began so well that after a handful of games he was chosen for The Rest v England in the Canterbury Test trial of 1946. He took only two wickets (including his county colleague Jack Ikin) and was reasonably economical but never again seems to have been considered for the Test side. He had two mixed seasons with Essex before returning to the Leagues, in which he played for Middleton, St Anne's and Kearsley.

PULLAR, Geoffrey

LHB; RALB.
Born: Swinton, Lancashire, 1 August 1935.
First-class debut: 1954, Lancashire v Surrey, Old Trafford.
312 matches for Lancashire 1954-68 (professional). Capped 1958. Benefit (£4,600) 1967.
HS for Lancashire: 167* v West Indies, Old Trafford, 1966.
BB: 3-91 v Pakistan, Old Trafford, 1962.
1,000 runs (9); 2,197 (54.92) 1959 best.
Scored 2,047 runs in 1961.
25 matches for Gloucestershire 1969-70.

28 Tests for England 1959 to 1962-63. HS: 175 v South Africa, The Oval, 1960. Test record: 1,974 runs (43.86); 4 centuries; 2 catches; 1 wicket.
Tours: MCC to West Indies 1959-60; to India, Sri Lanka and Pakistan 1961-62; to Australia and New Zealand 1962-63. Cavaliers to South Africa 1960-61.
Full first-class record: 21,538 runs (35.34); 41 centuries; 125 catches; 10 wickets (38.70).

A tall left-hander, 'Noddy' Pullar showed a great deal of style and grace in his early years but seemed to 'solidify' with the increased responsibilities associated with his promotion to opener in 1959. Of easy going temperament, his career seemed to lose its way and he was well past his best when he moved to Gloucestershire, with little success, aged 33. An arthritic knee finally persuaded him to retire, aged 35, and go into the restaurant business.

RADCLIFFE, George

RHB.
Born: Ormskirk, Lancashire, 25 September 1877.
Died: Dukinfield, Cheshire, 27 October 1951, aged 74.
First-class debut: 1903, Lancashire v Philadelphians, Old Trafford.
7 matches for Lancashire 1903-06 (professional).
HS: 60 v Sussex, Hove, 1905.

George Radcliffe had a tremendous record for Stalybridge and in 1915 became the only amateur to score 1,000 runs in the Central Lancashire League. He had been a Cheshire player aged 17 but appeared mainly for Stalybridge, which club he captained and later became President.

RADCLIFFE, Lees

RHB; WK.
Born: Smithy Bridge, Rochdale, Lancashire, 23 November 1865.

Died: Crumpstall, Manchester, 22 January 1928, aged 62.
First-class debut: 1897, Lancashire v Sussex, Hove.
50 matches for Lancashire 1897-1905 (professional).
HS: 25 v Warwickshire, Liverpool, 1900.

A quiet and competent wicketkeeper, Lees Radcliffe's poor batting told against him. In 1911, whilst playing for South Moor CC, he turned out for Durham County.

RADFORD, Neal Victor

RHB; RFM.
Born: Luanshya, Northern Rhodesia (now Zambia), 7 June 1957.
Education: Athlone Boys High School, Johannesburg, South Africa.
Debut for Lancashire: 1980 v Oxford University, Oxford.
24 matches for Lancashire 1980-84.
HS: 76* v Derbyshire, Blackpool, 1981.
BB for Lancashire 5-95 v Derbyshire, Buxton, 1984.
113 matches for Worcestershire 1985-1990. Capped 1985.
Played for Transvaal 1978-79 to 1988-89.
3 Tests for England 1986 to 1987-88. HS: 12* v New Zealand, Lord's, 1986. BB: 2-131 v India, Edgbaston, 1986. Test record: 21 runs (7.00); 4 wickets (87.75).
Full first-class record: 2,722 runs (16.10); 113 catches; 793 wickets (26.92).

Neal Radford, whose father Victor was a professional soccer player and whose brother Wayne has played for Orange Free State, spent five rather frustrating, and certainly disappointing, seasons with Lancashire. Bothered with nagging injuries and seemingly uncertain as to his role, his record was impressive only for its mediocrity. Yet within just over a year of joining

Worcestershire he was chosen for England. Radford is a busy, bustling sort of bowler, allegedly well below top pace, but one who can produce something pretty rapid when necessary. His Test appearances were apparently spoiled due to his 'tightening up' and with injury problems now uppermost in his mind, it seems unlikely he will get another chance in the Test arena. Neal Radford is a very sociable character, an attribute which has made him a popular member of the county circuit.

RAE, Robert Burns

RHB; RFM.
Born: Littleborough, Lancashire, 4 July 1912.

Lancashire's Bobby Rae, pictured in a wartime Bradford League XI. Back row (left to right): F.Dennis (Yorkshire), J.E.Timms (Northants), A.Dyson (Glamorgan), Jim Smith (Middlesex), W.Keeton (Notts), R.B.Rae (Lancashire). Front row: J.Appleyard, K.Fiddling (Yorkshire), G.Brooks (Worcestershire), W.Barber (Yorkshire), G.A.Wilson (Yorkshire), J.D.Robertson (Middlesex).

First-class debut: 1945, Lancashire v Yorkshire, Bradford.
1 match for Lancashire 1945 (professional).
HS: 74 v Yorkshire (debut and only innings).

Bobby Rae, who had professional engagements with Bradshaw, Bingley, Stockport, Huddersfield and Rishton, may be considered unlucky to have made only one first-class appearance, in the Hedley Verity Memorial game, since he batted very effectively and had a good reputation as a seam bowler. Strenuous efforts have been made to trace Rae, but without success, but rumours of his death have not been confirmed.

RAMADHIN, Sonny

RHB; OB and LB.
Born: Esperance Village, Trinidad, West Indies, 1 May 1929.
Education: Canadian Mission School, Duncan Village, Trinidad.
Debut for Lancashire: 1964 v Worcestershire, Old Trafford.

33 matches for Lancashire 1964-65. Capped 1964.
HS for Lancashire 13 v Worcestershire (debut).
BB for Lancashire: 8-121 v Yorkshire, Headingley, 1964.
Played for Trinidad 1949-50 to 1952-53.
43 Tests for West Indies 1950 to 1960-61. HS: 44 v New Zealand, Dunedin, 1955-56. BB: 7-49 v England, Edgbaston, 1957. Test record: 361 runs (8.20). 9 catches. 158 wickets (29.98).
BB: 8-15 West Indies v Gloucestershire, Cheltenham, 1950 (13-51 in the match).
Tours: West Indies to England 1950, 1957; to Australia and New Zealand 1951-52; 1960-61, to New Zealand 1955-56; to India and Pakistan 1958-59. Commonwealth XI to India 1950-51, 1953-54. International team to Rhodesia, India, New Zealand, Pakistan 1961-62; E.W.Swanton's team to India 1963-64.
Full first-class record: 1,092 runs (8.66); 38 catches; 758 wickets (20.24).

Sonny Ramadhin, who knows no other first name, bowled slowly, with immaculate length and control, and at his peak seemed able to turn the ball either way, or not at all, with no change in action. At his best in his 20s, as are many top-class spin bowlers, with Alf Valentine he formed the renowned 'spin twins' attack for West Indies. He was, though, destroyed in the Edgbaston Test of 1957, by Peter May and, especially, Colin Cowdrey, making as much use of their pads as bats. Ramadhin was never again the same bowler, although 92 wickets (22.23) in his first Lancashire season showed he was still to be respected, even if the old magic had gone. Sonny Ramadhin played for Lincolnshire in 1968-70 and his clubs include Crompton (in 1951), Ashcombe Park, Radcliffe, Liversage, Wakefield, Mansfield, Delph, Nantwich, Little Lever, Daisy Hill.
 Ramadhin still lives in Lancashire. His daughter, Sharon, as charming and typical a Lancashire lass as ever was, became wife of Willie Hogg (Lancashire and Warwickshire) and shares her father's love of cricket.

RAMSBOTTOM, Henry John

RHB; RM.
Born: Enfield, Lancashire, 21 October 1846.
Died: Clayton-le-Moors, Lancashire, 9 April 1905, aged 58.
First-class debut: 1868, Lancashire v Nottinghamshire, Trent Bridge.
1 match for Lancashire 1868 (professional).
HS: 1 v Nottinghamshire (debut).
Enfield player given only one opportunity, which seems less than fair.

RATCLIFFE, Edgar

Born: Liverpool, 19 January 1863.
Died: Aston, Birmingham, 29 July 1915, aged 52.
First-class debut: 1884, Lancashire v Kent, Old Trafford.
1 match for Lancashire 1884 (amateur).
HS: 7 v Kent (debut).
3 matches for Liverpool & District 1886-89.
HS: 28 Liverpool & District v Australians, 1886.

Edgar Ratcliffe played for Sefton in the Liverpool Competition.

RATCLIFFE, Robert Malcolm

RHB; RM.
Born: Accrington, Lancashire, 29 November 1951.
Education: Hollins County School, Accrington.
First-class debut: 1972, Lancashire v Nottinghamshire, Trent Bridge.
82 matches for Lancashire 1972-80. Capped 1976.

HS: 101* v Warwickshire, Old Trafford, 1979. (adding Lancashire record 8th-wicket stand of 158 with J.Lyon).
BB: 7-58 v Hampshire, Bournemouth, 1978.

Bob Ratcliffe often showed all-round potential but an injury-strewn career was finally terminated prematurely. Subsequently he appeared for Cumberland.

RAWLINSON, Elisha Barker

RHB; RFM.
Born: Yeadon, Yorkshire, 10 April 1837.
Died: Sydney, Australia, 17 February 1892, aged 54.
First-class debut: 1867, Lancashire v Yorkshire, Whalley.
1 match for Lancashire 1867 (professional).
HS: Lancashire 14 v Yorkshire (debut).
37 matches for Yorkshire 1867-75.
HS: 55 Yorkshire v Nottinghamshire, Trent Bridge, 1869.
BB: 4-41 Yorkshire v Gloucestershire, Sheffield, 1873.
Full first-class record: 1,120 runs (15.34); 8 wickets (9.87); 23 catches.

Elisha Rawlinson had several engagements, notably with Folkestone CC, at Christchurch College (Oxford), Savile Club, Dewsbury and Leeds Clarence CC. In 1876 he emigrated to Australia and became a publican in Sydney.

RAWLINSON, William

RHB; RF (round-arm).
Born: Burnley, Lancashire, 5 September 1850.
Died: details unknown.
First-class debut: 1870, Lancashire v Surrey, The Oval.
3 matches for Lancashire 1870-71 (professional).
HS: 10 v Kent, Gravesend, 1871.

William Rawlinson lived at Burnley.

RAWSTORNE, George Streynsham

Batsman.
Born: Croston, Lancashire, 22 January 1895.
Died: Rovie, Rogart, Sutherland, 15 July 1962, aged 67.
Education: Eton.
First-class debut: 1919, Lancashire v Derbyshire, Old Trafford.
1 match for Lancashire 1919 (amateur).
HS: 2 v Derbyshire (debut).

The 1914 Eton captain, Rawstorne went out to India after his only appearance.

REIDY, Bernard Wilfrid

LHB; LM and SLA.
Born: Whalley, Lancashire, 18 September 1953.
Education: St Mary's College, Blackburn.
First-class debut: 1973, Lancashire v Nottinghamshire, Trent Bridge.
107 matches for Lancashire 1973-82. Capped 1980.
HS: 131* v Derbyshire, Chesterfield, 1979.

BB: 5-61 v Worcestershire, Worcester, 1979.

Bernard Reidy was a rugged all-rounder whose failure to establish himself was a big disappointment. Perhaps he should have had greater opportunity. He has been attached to St Anne's, Blackpool, Kearsley and Walkden and has played successfully for Cumberland since 1983.

REYNOLDS, Frederick Reginald

RHB; RF (round-arm).
Born: Bottisham, Cambridgeshire, 7 August 1834.
Died: Chorlton-cum-Hardy, Manchester, 18 April 1918, aged 83.
Debut for Lancashire: 1865 v Middlesex, Old Trafford.
38 matches for Lancashire 1865-74 (professional). Benefit 1870.
HS: 34* v Kent, Gravesend, 1871.
BB for Lancashire: 6-92 v Middlesex, Islington, 1865.
First-class debut: 1854, Town v Gown, Cambridge.
Played for Cambridge Town 1854-60 and Cambridgeshire 1857-67.
BB: 6-58 Cambridgeshire v Yorkshire, Ashton-under-Lyne, 1865.
Full first-class record: 444 runs (5.55); 52 catches; 208 wickets.

Fred Reynolds was a keen, but usually ineffective, slogger with the bat, and an excellent fast round-armed bowler with a pronounced break-back. In earlier years he was engaged at Charterhouse School, MCC at Lord's, and at Botesdale, Suffolk. In 1858 he was with the United England XI, and in 1859-60 played for the All-England XI. In 1861 he began an engagement with Manchester CC and in 1870 became assistant secretary and then general manager of the Old Trafford ground, a position from which he retired in 1908, on a pension of £100 per annum. In addition to his work at Old Trafford, Reynolds produced three volumes of a work entitled *Lancashire County Cricket* which recorded complete scores of all matches from 1864-83. He was, in fact, the first historian of the County Club.

RHODES, Albert

RHB; RM.
Born: Saddleworth, Yorkshire, 9 April 1889.
Died: Blackpool, Lancashire, 10 March 1970, aged 80.
First-class debut: 1922, Lancashire v Warwickshire, Edgbaston.
17 matches for Lancashire 1922-24 (amateur).
HS: 70 v West Indians, Old Trafford, 1923.
BB: 2-24 v Derbyshire, Derby, 1923.

Albert Rhodes was connected with the Haslingden and Glossop clubs.

RHODES, Cecil A

LHB; SLA.
Born: 1906.
First-class debut: 1937, Lancashire v New Zealanders, Preston.
8 matches for Lancashire 1937-38 (amateur).
HS: 6 v Hampshire, Old Trafford, 1938.
BB: 4-37 v New Zealanders (debut).

Cecil Rhodes played for Lancaster CC.

RICHMOND, William

RHB; WK.
Born: Burnley, Lancashire, 1 December 1843.
Died: Burnley, 11 November 1912, aged 68.
First-class debut: 1868, Lancashire v Nottinghamshire, Trent Bridge.
1 match for Lancashire 1868. (professional).
HS: 1 v Nottinghamshire (debut).

Bill Richmond from Burnley played only once.

RICKETTS, James

RHB; RSM; Occasional WK.
Born: Manchester, 9 February 1842.
Died: Altrincham, Cheshire, 3 June 1894, aged 52.

First-class debut: 1867, Lancashire v Surrey, The Oval.
34 matches for Lancashire 1867-77 (professional).
HS: 195* v Surrey (debut).

Jim Ricketts made the best start of any Lancashire batsman, but never again approached such form. A tinsmith and ironmonger in Manchester, his trade sometimes prevented him from playing.

RICKMAN, William
RHB; RF.
Born: South Yarra, Victoria, Australia, 1849.
Died: Frankston, Victoria, Australia, 6 June 1911.
First-class debut: 1876, Lancashire v Derbyshire, Old Trafford.
1 match for Lancashire 1876 (amateur).
HS: 5 v Derbyshire (debut).
Played for Victoria v South Australia, Adelaide, 1880-81.
HS: 19 Victoria v South Australia (above).
Full first-class record: 29 runs (9.66); 1 catch.

RITCHIE, David Mawdsley
RHB; RF.
Born: Toxteth Park, Liverpool, 12 August 1892.
Died: Stevenage, Hertfordshire, 10 September 1974, aged 82.
Education: Loretto.
Debut for Lancashire: 1924 v Northamptonshire, Liverpool.
1 match for Lancashire 1924 (amateur).
HS for Lancashire: 3 v Northamptonshire (debut).
3 matches for Free Foresters 1922-25-26.
HS: 12 Free Foresters v Oxford University, Oxford, 1922.
BB: 3-44 Free Foresters v Oxford University, Oxford, 1922.

A Regular Army officer who reached the rank of lieutenant-colonel, Ritchie played for the Liverpool Club.

ROBERTS, John Francis Esdale
RHB; RMF.
Born: Kearsley, Bolton, Lancashire, 4 March 1933.
Education: Loweburn School, Manchester.
First-class debut: 1957, Lancashire v Surrey, Old Trafford, 1957.
2 matches for Lancashire 1957 (professional).
HS: 5 v Cambridge University, Liverpool, 1957.

Jack Roberts had no luck during his two matches, but enjoyed a good career as a professional, being engaged with Kearsley,

Radcliffe, Preston, Lascelles Hall, Kidderminster, Padiham, Bradshaw.

ROBERTS, R.
WK.
First-class debut: 1872, Lancashire v Yorkshire, Old Trafford.
10 matches for Lancashire 1872-74 (professional).
HS: 20 v Yorkshire (debut) and v Derbyshire, Old Trafford, 1872.

Nothing is known of this wicketkeeper.

ROBERTS, William Braithwaite
RHB; SLA.
Born: Kirkham, Lancashire 27 September 1914.
Died: Caernarfon & Anglesey Hospital, Bangor, North Wales, 24 August 1951, aged 36.
First-class debut: 1939, Lancashire v West Indians, Old Trafford.
114 matches for Lancashire 1939-49 (professional). Capped 1939. Testimonial (£2,623) 1950.
HS: 51 v Glamorgan, Old Trafford, 1948.
BB: 8-50 v Oxford University, Oxford, 1949.
100 wickets (1); 123 (19.34) 1946. Took 99 wickets (20.05) 1948.
3 'Victory' Tests for England against Australia 1945.
Full first-class record: 865 runs (10.67); 61 catches; 392 wickets (21.16).

Bill Roberts was another for whom World War Two meant a massive slice out of what could have been a burgeoning career, although he did make something of a name as a cricketing serviceman. A left-armed spinner whose main attributes were steadiness and control, but who possibly lacked 'devil', he was marked down in 1945 as a Test possiblity and chosen for three 'Victory' Tests. Unfortunately these were his last representative games and although he continued to bowl excellently, he was forced to withstand increasing challenges from younger spinners and, not chosen at all in 1950, he left the staff. What should have been the start of a lucrative League career suffered a quick and tragic end. After a brilliant start for Birmingham League club, West Bromwich Dartmouth, he was forced to undergo a major operation for cancer and after appearing to be on the road to recovery, he was readmitted to hospital where he died.

ROBINSON, Paul Andrew
RHB; RFM.
Born: Boksburg, South Africa, 16 July 1956.
Education: Brakpan High School.
Debut for Lancashire: 1979 v Kent, Maidstone.

Left-arm spinner Bill Roberts, chosen for three 'Victory' Tests.

The 1979 Lancashire squad. Back row (left to right): John Lyons, Christopher John Scott, Graeme Fowler, Ian Cockbain. Middle row: Geoffrey Edward Trim, Bob Arrowsmith, Paul Andrew Robinson, Paul John Walter Allott, Andrew Kennedy (glasses), Willie Hogg, Bob Ratcliffe, Bernard Wilfrid Reidy, John Abrahams, John Savage (coach). Front row: David Paul Hughes, Barry Wood, David Lloyd, Frank Hayes (captain), Jack Simmons, Harry Pilling, Peter Granville Lee.

1 match for Lancashire 1979.
HS: 15 v Kent (debut).
BB: 2-57 v Kent (debut).
Played for Northern Transvaal 1977-78 until 1987-88.
HS: 49 Northern Transvaal v Western Province 'B', Pretoria, 1977-78 and v Transvaal, Johannesburg, 1983-84.

'Long John' Robinson, at 6ft 8ins probably Lancashire's tallest-ever player, came to play for Cleckheaton and after appearing for Cheshire in 1978 was registered by Lancashire, but made only the one appearance.

ROBINSON, Walter

RHB; RM (round-arm)
Born: Greetland, Yorkshire, 29 November 1851.
Died: 14 August 1919, aged 67.
Debut for Lancashire: 1880 v Surrey, Old Trafford.

115 matches for Lancashire 1880-88 (professional).
HS: 154 v Oxford University, Old Trafford, 1883.
First-class debut: 1876, Yorkshire v Middlesex, Sheffield.
7 matches for Yorkshire 1876-77 (professional).
Full first-class record: 3,902 runs (19.31); 4 centuries; 52 catches.

Walter Robinson was slightly-built but a hard and often effective hitter, who played for his native Yorkshire somewhat irregularly and so threw in his lot for the 'enemy'. Robinson had a number of professional engagements, including Haslingden, Longwood, Bacup. Littleborough and Colne, and generally served cricket well. Although a date of death has been supplied, the writer knows nothing of his later life.

ROGERSON, George Henry

RHB.
Born: Monks Coppenhall, Nantwich, Cheshire, 13 March 1896.
Died: Crewe, Cheshire, 29 May 1961, aged 65.
First-class debut: 1923, Lancashire v Oxford University, Oxford.
12 matches for Lancashire 1923 (amateur).
HS: 47* v Surrey, Old Trafford, 1923.
Played for Julien Cahn's team 1929-30.
Full first-class record: 353 runs (16.04).

George Rogerson was a stylish batsman who showed promise in 1923 but never played again.

He was connected at various times with the Heston, Formby, Astley Bridge and Liverpool clubs.

ROPER, Edward
RHB.
Born: Richmond, Yorkshire, 8 April 1851.
Died: South Liverpool, 27 April 1921, aged 70.
Education: Clifton School, York.
First-class debut: 1876, Lancashire v Derbyshire, Old Trafford.
28 matches for Lancashire 1876-86 (amateur).
HS: 65 v Kent, Old Trafford, 1884.

5 matches for Yorkshire 1878-80. Played for Liverpool & District 1891-93.
HS: 68 Yorkshire v Middlesex, Lord's, 1878.

A player for Sefton and Liverpool, Edward Roper eventually became secretary of Liverpool CC and a Lancashire vice-president. He wrote *A Sportsman's Memories* published after his death in 1921.

ROWLAND, Daniel
RHB.
Born: 1826.
Died: Bury, Lancashire, 1 October 1891.
First-class debut: 1868, Lancashire v Yorkshire, Holbeck.
1 match for Lancashire 1868 (amateur).
Scored 0 both innings.

Played one other 'first-class' match, in 1849 for a Lancashire XI against a Yorkshire team. Since this was well before the foundation of the present club, the match is not included in any Lancashire records. Rowland scored 9 and 0 in this match.

ROWLANDS, Leslie Samuel
RHB; RM.
Born: Birmingham, 29 August 1880.
Died: Clapham Common, London, 1 October 1947, aged 65.
First-class debut: 1903, Lancashire v Leicestershire, Old Trafford.
6 matches for Lancashire 1903-10 (professional).
HS: 9 v South Africans, Old Trafford, 1904.
BB: 4-29 v Leicestershire (debut).

A local professional at Blackpool, he did pretty well on his occasional appearances.

ROWLEY, Alexander Butler
RHB; LSM (round-arm).
Born: Manchester, 3 October 1837.
Died: Dover, Kent, 9 January 1911, aged 73.
Education: Rossall.
Debut for Lancashire: 1865 v Middlesex, Old Trafford.
12 matches for Lancashire 1865-71 (amateur).
HS: 63* v Middlesex, Islington, 1866.
BB for Lancashire: 5-71 v Yorkshire, Old Trafford, 1867.
Rowley's first important match, aged 16, was for Manchester against Sheffield in 1854. His best first-class bowling was 6-21 for Gentlemen of North v Gentlemen of South, Old Trafford, 1860.

Alexander Rowley was one of those closely involved with the formation of the present

Lancashire County Cricket Club in 1864, and was one of the Honorary Secretaries. He was President from 1874 to 1879. His brother, E.B.Rowley snr, and nephew, E.B.Rowley jnr, both played for Lancashire.

ROWLEY, Edmund Butler

RHB.
Born: Manchester, 4 May 1842.
Died: Chorlton-on-Medlock, Lancashire, 8 February 1905, aged 62.
Education: Rossall.
Debut for Lancashire: 1865 v Middlesex, Islington.
81 matches for Lancashire 1865-80 (amateur).
Captain 1866-79.
HS: 78 v Surrey, The Oval, 1867.
First-class debut: 1860, Gentlemen of North v Gentlemen of South, Manchester Broughton ground.

Lancashire's first regular captain was a dashing batsman who rarely came off at first-class level but had some good performances in other cricket, and in 1867 scored 219 for Gentlemen

of Lancashire v Gentlemen of Yorkshire at Old Trafford. Edmund Rowley, whose brother, A.B., and son, Ernest, were also Lancashire amateurs, and who was on the County Committee for many years until his death, was a solicitor in Manchester.

ROWLEY, Ernest Butler

RHB.
Born: Kersal, Manchester, 15 January 1870.
Died: Manchester, 4 October 1962, aged 92.

Education: Clifton; Oxford University.
First-class debut: 1893, Lancashire v Oxford University, Old Trafford.
16 matches for Lancashire 1893-98 (amateur).
HS: 65 v Warwickshire, Edgbaston, 1896.

Ernest Rowley, son of Edmund and nephew of Alex, led the side on a few occasions, but was never officially appointed captain.

ROYLE, Vernon Peter Fanshawe Archer
RHB; SRA (round-arm).
Born: Vernon Lodge, Brooklands, Cheshire, 29 January 1854.
Died: Stanmore Park, Middlesex, 21 May 1929, aged 75.
Education: Rossall; Brasenose College, Oxford.

First-class debut: 1873, Lancashire v Yorkshire, Sheffield.
74 matches for Lancashire, 1873-91 (amateur).
HS: 81 v Kent, Town Malling, 1878.
BB for Lancashire: 1-22 v Yorkshire, Huddersfield, 1878.
Played for Oxford University 1875-76 (Blue both years).
BB: 4-51 Oxford University v Cambridge University, Lord's, 1875.
1 Test for England 1878-79. HS: 18 v Australia, Melbourne, 1878-79. Test record: 21 runs (10.50); 2 catches; 0 wickets.
Tour: Australia 1878-79 with Lord Harris.
Full first-class record: 2,322 runs (15.48); 15 wickets (25.06).

Vernon Royle was a useful batsman with a good style who drove well, and a sometimes valuable slow round-arm bowler. He was also a cover point of legendary status whose main value to any side was in the field. Royle was ordained in 1881 and became curate at Aldenham, near Watford. He subsequently taught at Stanmore Park School and at the time of this death was headmaster there.

RUSHTON, Frank
RHB; RFM.
Born: Bolton, Lancashire, 21 April 1906.
Died: Queen's Park, Bolton, 15 October 1975, aged 69.
First-class debut: 1928, Lancashire v Hampshire, Old Trafford.
6 matches for Lancashire 1928-29 (professional).
HS: 28 v Leicestershire, Liverpool, 1929.
BB: 4-30 v Gloucestershire, Old Trafford, 1929.

Frank Rushton, a swing bowler, was a well-known professional at Royton, Kearsley and, for 17 years, Eagley.

RUSHTON, Thomas Henry
RHB.
Born: Horwich, Lancashire, 14 May 1845.
Died: Barnacre, Garstang, Lancashire, 1 July 1903, aged 58.
First-class debut: 1870, Lancashire v Hampshire, Old Trafford.
1 match for Lancashire 1870 (amateur).
HS: 7 v Hampshire (debut).

Little is known of this local amateur.

RUTTER, Frederick John
Batsman.
Born: Hillingdon, Middlesex, 12 September 1840.

Died: Abbey Wood, Kent, 19 January 1907, aged 66.
Education: Rugby.
First-class debut: 1868, Lancashire v Surrey, The Oval.
2 matches for Lancashire 1868 (amateur).
HS: 8 v Surrey (debut).

Frederick Rutter's brother, Edward, played for Middlesex.

SANDERSON, Sir Lancelot

RHB; RA (Spin).
Born: Ellel, Lancashire, 24 October 1863.
Died: Ward House, Ellel, 9 March 1944, aged 80.
Education: Elstree School, Harrow; Cambridge University.
First-class debut: 1884, Lancashire v Somerset, Old Trafford.
1 match for Lancashire 1884 (amateur).
Scored 0 in only innings.
1 match for MCC in 1888, scoring 61 against Cambridge University, Cambridge.

Sir Lancelot was a useful batsman but an even better fielder in the slips. He also bowled slow round-arm on occasion. A barrister, he was MP for Appleby from 1910-15 and became Chief Justice of Bengal. He was eventually knighted. His brother, John Sanderson, played many years for Lancaster CC.

SANDERSON, Richard Withington Bromley

RHB.
Born: Cheetham Hill, Manchester, 15 January 1847.
Died: Tynemouth, Northumberland, 1934, aged 87.
First-class debut: 1870, Lancashire v Hampshire, Southampton.
1 match for Lancashire 1870 (amateur).
HS: 6 v Hampshire (debut).

Richard Sanderson's son, G.B.Sanderson, played for both Warwickshire and Worcestershire.

SAVAGE, John Scholes

RHB; OB.
Born: Ramsbottom, Lancashire, 3 March 1929.
Debut for Lancashire: 1967 v Warwickshire, Edgbaston.
58 matches for Lancashire 1967-69. Capped 1967.
HS for Lancashire: 19 v Yorkshire, Old Trafford, 1968.
BB for Lancashire: 5-1 v Hampshire, Blackpool, 1967.

First-class debut: 1953, Leicestershire v Oxford University, Oxford.
281 matches for Leicestershire 1953-66 (professional). Capped 1958. Testimonial (£2,500) 1966.
HS: 33 Leicestershire v Yorkshire, Leicester, 1957.
BB: 8-50 Leicestershire v Gloucestershire, Gloucester, 1957.
Match figures of 14-99, Leicestershire v Northamptonshire 1958.
Took 100 wickets in season three times whilst with Leicestershire. 122 (18.93) 1961 best.

John Savage made his name with Leicestershire, but returned to his native county, first as player and then, from 1970, as a respected member of the county's coaching staff.

SAWYER, Charles Montague

Batsman; Fastish bowler.
Born: Broughton, Lancashire, 1856.
Died: Ormskirk, Lancashire, 30 March 1921.
First-class debut: 1884, Lancashire v Surrey, The Oval.
2 matches for Lancashire 1884 (amateur).
HS: 11* v Surrey (debut).

A long-standing member of Manchester Broughton CC, Sawyer was much better known as a Rugby three-quarter, who played for Broughton, Lancashire and twice for England, against Scotland in 1880 and Ireland in 1881.

SCHOFIELD, J.

RHB; WK.
First-class debut: 1876, Lancashire v Derbyshire, Old Trafford.
4 matches for Lancashire 1876 (amateur).
HS: 11 v Derbyshire, Derby, 1876.

A wicketkeeper with the Castleton CC, nothing further is known of this player.

SCHOLFIELD, Frank Beaumont

Batsman.
Born: Bury, Lancashire, 16 November 1886.
Died: Chelsea, London, 1 March 1950, aged 63.
Education: Sedbergh.
First-class debut: 1911, Lancashire v All-India, Old Trafford.
1 match for Lancashire 1911 (amateur).
HS: 17 v All-India (debut).

After a single trial for Lancashire, Frank Scholfield was seen in the Cheshire side the following season.

SCHULTZ, Sandford Spence (later S.S.STOREY)

RHB; RF (round-arm).
Born: Birkenhead, 29 August 1857.
Died: South Kensington, London, 18 December 1937, aged 80.
Education: Uppingham; Jesus College, Cambridge.
Debut for Lancashire: 1877 v Sussex, Old Trafford.
9 matches for Lancashire 1877-82 (amateur).
HS for Lancashire: 42* v Nottinghamshire, Trent Bridge, 1878.
Played for Cambridge University 1876-77 (Blue 1877).
1 Test for England v Australia 1878-79. Scored 0* and 20; took 1 wicket for 26.
Full first-class record: 1,046 runs (17.14); 29 catches; 28 wickets (40.82).

Schultz, who sadly felt obliged to change his name because of the German connections of his original name, was a good club cricketer with many outstanding performances to his credit. For Uppingham Rovers against United Services at Portsmouth in 1887 he put together an innings of 286, whilst for Orleans v Bexley in 1882, he took all nine wickets to fall to a bowler. Finally, playing for the Gentlemen against Oxford University, at Oxford, Schultz achieved the unique feat of being out first ball twice in the same innings! The game was started on the Christchurch ground but the wicket was so bad that after Schultz was dismissed first ball, the game was moved over to The Parks, and started again. Schultz, the unfortunate, again fell to the first ball he received. Alas, this latest failure could not be scrubbed from the record.

SCOTT, Christopher John

LHB; WK.
Born: Swinton, Lancashire, 16 September 1959.
Education: Eccles Grammar School.
First-class debut: 1977, Lancashire v Oxford University, Oxford.

46 matches for Lancashire 1977-82.
HS: 27* v Nottinghamshire, Trent Bridge, 1981.

He played League cricket for Egerton.

SCOTT, William Ainslie

Born: 1845.
Died: Bolton, Lancashire, 17 June 1899.
First-class debut: 1874, Lancashire v Kent, Old Trafford.
1 match for Lancashire 1874 (amateur).

Little is known of this player.

SEYMOUR, Alfred

Born: 16 February 1843.

Died: Folkestone, Kent, 31 January 1897, aged
53.
Education: Rugby.
First-class debut: 1869, Lancashire v Sussex, Hove.
1 match for Lancashire 1869 (amateur).
HS: 25 v Sussex (debut).
Played for Hampshire v Lancashire, Old
Trafford, 1870, scoring 2 and 0.
Full first-class record: 47 runs (11.75); 1 catch.

SHARP, John

RHB; LFM.
Born: Hereford, 15 February 1878.
Died: Wavertree, Liverpool, 28 January 1938,
aged 59.
First-class debut: 1899, Lancashire v Surrey, Old
Trafford.
518 matches for Lancashire 1899-1925 (professional 1899-1914; amateur 1919-25). Benefit
(£1,679) 1913. Captain 1923-25.
HS: 211 v Leicestershire, Old Trafford, 1912.
BB: 9-77 Worcestershire, Worcester, 1901.
Scored 103 before lunch on second day of
Lancashire v Soamerset, Old Trafford, 1910. Also,
moved from 10* to 120 before lunch on third
day of Lancashire v Sussex, Old Trafford, 1903.
1,000 runs (10); 1,959 (41.68) 1911 best.
100 wickets (1); 113 (22.66) 1901 best.
3 Tests for England 1909. HS: 105 v Australia,
The Oval. BB: 3-67 v Australia, The Oval. Test
record: 188 runs (47.00); 1 century; 1 catch; 3
wickets (37.00).
Full first-class record: 22,715 runs (31.11); 38
centuries; 236 catches; 441 wickets (27.41).

Jack Sharp was one of the most enthusiastic and
valuable of all Lancashire cricketers. Starting out
as a left-armed fast-medium bowler who could
bat, he lost much of his bowling early, but instead
became a batsman good enough to score a Test
century. Sound and brave, he was essentially of
the contemporary orthodox school, strong on
the offside with good cuts and drives. After
World War One he reverted to amateur status
and in 1923 was appointed county captain, which
position he retained until 1925 when, after
suffering abuse from the crowd because of his
allegedly poor fielding, he decided to retire. In
1924, Sharp became the first Test selector who
was formerly a professional cricketer.

On the soccer field, Jack Sharp played for
Aston Villa and Everton and won two England
caps (and was therefore a 'double' international).
He played 342 League and Cup matches for
Everton and appeared for them in the 1906 and
1907 FA Cup Finals. J.T.Howcroft, a Football
League referee for 30 years, nominated Jack
Sharp a better outside-right than either Billy
Meredith or Stanley Matthews. He later became

a director of the Goodison Park club, as did
his son, Bert. Jack Sharp was a sports shop owner
in Liverpool.

SHELMERDINE, George Owen

RHB; RMF.
Born: Pendleton, Manchester, 7 September 1899.
Died: Roedean, Brighton, Sussex, 31 July 1967, aged 67.
Education: Cheltenham College; Christ's College, Cambridge.
First-class debut: 1919, Lancashire v Warwickshire, Old Trafford.
31 matches for Lancashire 1919-25 (amateur).

HS: 105 v Kent, Maidstone, 1921.
Played for Cambridge University 1920-22 (Blue 1922).
Full first-class record: 1,614 runs (23.39); 1 century; 19 catches; 3 wickets (68.33).

Joe Shelmerdine, who played for Leyland, became a member of the Lancashire committee, and when he died was President of the County Club.

SHORE, Charles

LHB; SLA.
Born: Sutton-in-Ashfield, Nottinghamshire, 21 November 1858.
Died: Sutton-in-Ashfield, 5 June 1912, aged 53.
Debut for Lancashire: 1886 v Gloucestershire, Old Trafford.
1 match for Lancashire 1886.
HS: 3 v Gloucestershire (debut).
First-class debut: 1881, Nottinghamshire v Lancashire, Old Trafford.
10 matches for Nottinghamshire 1881-85. Played for Liverpool & District 1886-87.
HS: 42* Liverpool & District v Australians, 1886.
BB: 5-36 Nottinghamshire v Middlesex, Lord's, 1881.
Full first-class record: 159 runs (13.25); 9 catches; 41 wickets (22.87).

Charles Shore, who played for Herefordshire and Norfolk as well as Nottinghamshire and Lancashire, was engaged as professional by Huyton (1877) and Sefton (1878 to 1888).

SHUTTLEWORTH, Kenneth

RHB; RFM.
Born: St Helens, Lancashire, 13 November 1944.

First-class debut: 1964, Lancashire v Yorkshire, Old Trafford.

Ken Shuttleworth (front row, far right), pictured in his last season with Lancashire (1976). Players are, back row (left to right): Jack Simmons, Barry Wood, Andrew Kennedy, Frank Hayes. Middle row: David Hughes, Peter Lever, John Lyon, John Sullivan. Front row: Peter Lee, Harry Pilling, David Lloyd, Farokh Engineer, Ken Shuttleworth.

177 matches for Lancashire 1964-75. Capped 1968. Joint Testimonial with John Sullivan 1975 (£12,500).
HS: 71 v Gloucestershire, Cheltenham, 1967.
BB: 7-41 v Essex, Leyton, 1968.
41 matches for Leicestershire 1977-80. Capped 1977.
5 Tests for England 1970-71 to 1971. HS: 21 v Pakistan, Edgbaston, 1971. BB: 5-47 v

Australia, Brisbane, 1970-71. Test Record: 46 runs (7.66); 1 catch; 12 wickets (35.58).
Tours: England to Australia and New Zealand 1970-71. Commonwealth XI to Pakistan 1967-68.
Full first-class record: 2,589 runs (16.59); 128 catches; 623 wickets (24.51).

Ken Shuttleworth, strongly built and tall, and with a superb action, seemed to have all in his favour as a fast bowler, except the vital spark wherein pace through the air is not deadened on impact with pitch, and the best batsman may be surprised by something special. Injuries did Shuttleworth no favours and, after leaving Lancashire to join Leicestershire, he was a shadow of his old self.

SIBBLES, Frank Marshall
RHB; RM and OB.
Born: Oldham, Lancashire, 15 March 1904.

Died: Wilmslow, Cheshire, 20 July 1973, aged 69.
First-class debut: 1925, Lancashire v Somerset, Weston-super-Mare.
308 matches for Lancashire 1925-37 (professional). Benefit 1937.
HS: 71* v Middlesex, Old Trafford, 1933.

BB: 8-24 v Somerset, Weston-super-Mare, 1927.
100 wickets (2); 131 (18.25); 1932 best.
Full first-class record: 3,478 runs (14.67); 181 catches; 940 wickets (22.43).

Frank Sibbles could open the bowling at medium pace and his stock ball was in-swing — and off-spin when the situation demanded. Perhaps some life was lacking, but he worked very hard for his team and was deservedly popular and respected. His career was cut short by what was probably 'tennis elbow', but he retained his enthusiasm and in 1950 was elected to the County Committee. He played for Werneth in the Central Lancashire League.

SILCOCK, William
All-rounder.
Born: Chorley, Lancashire, 22 February 1868.
Died: Leyland, Lancashire, 30 July 1933, aged 65.
First-class debut: 1899, Lancashire v Warwickshire, Edgbaston.
6 matches for Lancashire 1899-1902 (professional).
HS: 43 v Middlesex, Liverpool, 1902.
BB: 2-62 v Middlesex, Liverpool, 1902.

A professional from Chorley, Silcock is believed to have been a sports outfitter.

SIMMONS, Jack
RHB; OB.
Born: Clayton-le-Moors, Lancashire, 28 March 1941.
Education: Accrington Technical School; Blackburn Technical College.
First-class debut: 1968, Lancashire v Northamptonshire, Blackpool.
429 matches for Lancashire 1968-89. Capped 1971. Benefit (£128,000) 1980.
HS: 112 v Sussex, Hove, 1970.
BB for Lancashire: 7-64 v Hampshire, Southport, 1973.
Hat-trick v Nottinghamshire, Liverpool 1977.
Played for Tasmania 1972-73 to 1978-79.
Toured India with Overseas XI 1980-81.
BB: 7-59 Tasmania v Queensland, Brisbane, 1978-79.
Full first-class record: 9,417 runs (22.52); 6 centuries; 341 catches; 1,033 wickets (27.18).

'Flat Jack' was a burly and outwardly easy-going character, whose love of cricket and family was almost matched by his partiality for fish and chips! He was offered a place by Lancashire aged 19, but preferred to complete his draughtsman apprenticeship. He then played for Enfield, but was soon to join Blackpool as professional, and

Jack Simmons

Jack Simmons' appeal for lbw against Warwickshire's Mike Smith in the 1972 Gillette Cup Final is upheld by umpire Charlie Elliott. The wicketkeeper is Farokh Engineer.

here he stayed until being 're-discovered' in 1968. Simmons went on to become one of the most popular of all Lancashire cricketers, and perhaps an underrated performer as well. Never quite good enough to get a Test chance, he was still the ideal county cricketer for the 1970s and '80s, when his flat-trajectory spin bowling proved so economical in limited-overs cricket.

SLADEN, Arthur Redman

SLA.
Born: Manningham, Bradford, Yorkshire, 22 July 1877.
Died: Lake Side, Lancashire, 25 July 1934, aged 57.
Debut for Lancashire: 1903 v Somerset, Old Trafford.
2 matches for Lancashire 1903-04 (professional).
HS: 5 v Middlesex, Lord's, 1904.
BB for Lancashire: 3-77 v Middlesex, Lord's, 1904.
Played for London County 1901-02.
BB: 5-50 London County v Derbyshire, Derby, 1900.
Full first-class record: 10 runs (2.50); 19 wickets (23.68).

A Lancashire group of 1904. From left to right: J.S Heap, W.R.Cuttell, A.Kermode, J.T.Tyldesley, J.Hallows, A.R.Sladen and J.Sharp.

SLATER, R.

RHB; RF (round-arm).
First-class debut: 1865, Lancashire v Middlesex, Islington.
1 match for Lancashire 1865 (amateur).
Scored 0 in both innings.

Nothing is known of this unidentified amateur.

SMALLEY, J.

RHB.
First-class debut: 1869, Lancashire v Surrey, Old Trafford.
2 matches for Lancashire 1869 (professional).
HS: 17 v Sussex, Hove, 1869.
First name 'James' cannot be confirmed for this little-known professional.

SMITH, Alfort

RHB; WK.
Born: Bank Lane, Bury, Lancashire, 7 July 1846.
Died: Glossop, Derbyshire, 21 December 1908, aged 62.
First-class debut: 1867, Lancashire v Yorkshire, Middlesbrough.
4 matches for Lancashire 1867-71.
HS: 30 v Kent, Gravesend, 1871.
Played for Derbyshire 1873-80 under residential qualification.
Full first-class record: 305 runs (4.76); 70 catches; 12 stumped.

Alfort Smith was a talented wicketkeeper, one of first to dispense completely with a long-stop, but his poor batting handicapped him.

SMITH, Arthur Price

RHB; RM.
Born: Ruddington, Nottinghamshire, 3 December 1857.
Died: Tottenham, London, 3 June 1937, aged 79.
Debut for Lancashire: 1886 v Derbyshire, Old Trafford.
48 matches for Lancashire 1886-94 (professional).
HS: 124 v Gloucestershire, Bristol, 1891.
BB: 5-49 v Oxford University, Old Trafford, 1891.
First-class debut: 1883, Nottinghamshire v Surrey, Trent Bridge.
Played for Nottinghamshire 1883.
Full first-class record: 1,475 runs (19.93); 2 centuries; 29 wickets (17.92).

Arthur Smith played for Lancashire first, when he was professional with Rochdale, and he subsequently became associated with Oldham for many years. He was a solid batsman and good medium-pacer who should perhaps have been a regular player for longer. He became a publican in later life.

SMITH, Charles

RHB; WK.
Born: Calverley, Yorkshire, 24 August 1861.
Died: Calverley, 2 May 1925, aged 63.
First-class debut: 1893, Lancashire v Nottinghamshire, Trent Bridge.
167 matches for Lancashire 1893-1902 (professional). Benefit 1903.
HS: 81 v Sussex, Old Trafford, 1895.

Engaged at Little Lever CC, Smith qualified for Lancashire by residence and was one of the best of the early professional 'keepers, with a good pair of hands and seemingly limitless stamina. A Yorkshireman who played once for his native county in a non-first-class match in 1885, he returned to his native place, going into business as a newsagent.

SMITH, Colin Stansfield

RHB; RFM.
Born: Didsbury, Manchester, 1 October 1932.
Education: William Hulme's Grammar School, Manchester; Christ's College, Cambridge.

First-class debut: 1951, Lancashire v Hampshire, Liverpool.
45 matches for Lancashire 1951-57 (amateur).
Capped 1956.
HS for Lancashire: 67 v Middlesex, Old Trafford, 1951.
BB for Lancashire: 5-39 v Combined Services, Old Trafford, 1955.

Charles Smith

Played for Combined Services 1952-53.
Played for Cambridge University 1954-57 (Blue each year).
HS: 103* Cambridge University v Warwickshire, Edgbaston, 1957.
BB: 6-35 Cambridge University v Free Foresters, Cambridge, 1955.
Full first-class record: 2,339 runs (18.71); 1 century; 48 catches; 293 wickets (24.51).

Professor Stansfield Smith is one of the world's leading architects but had he been able to devote himself to cricket, he seems to have had the potential to reach the top in that career instead. He was also a possible county captain had he not chosen architecture. Smith played for Cheshire in his youth, and has appeared for Stockport, Dulwich and Esher. From 1977-81 he was on the MCC committee. Whilst at Cambridge he played lacrosse for the University.

SMITH, Donald James
RHB; LFM.
Born: Accrington, Lancashire, 1 May 1929.
First-class debut: 1951, Lancashire v South Africans, Old Trafford.
3 matches for Lancashire 1951-52 (professional).
HS: 14 v Hampshire, Portsmouth, 1951.

He was professional with David Brown Tractors CC.

SMITH, John
LHB; LF (round-arm).
Born: Yeadon, Yorkshire, 23 March 1833.
Died: Worcester, 12 February 1909, aged 75.
First-class debut: 1865, Lancashire v Middlesex, Islington.
6 matches for Lancashire 1865-69 (professional).
HS: 40* v Surrey, The Oval, 1866.
BB: 4-46 v Sussex, Hove, 1869.
2 matches for Yorkshire 1865.
First-class record: 181 runs (12.92); 18 wickets (20.11); 7 catches.

From 1855 to 1874, John Smith was a professional with many different engagements. His clubs included Hawick, Melrose, Langham, Glasgow Caledonian, Blackburn, Todmorden, Batley, Leeds Clarence and Marlborough. His son, Douglas Smith, played for Somerset and Worcestershire, whilst another son, William, appeared for Somerset and Wiltshire.

SMITH, Reginald
Batsman.
Born: Warrington, Lancashire, 1 May 1868.
Died: Scarborough, Yorkshire, 5 October 1943, aged 75.

Education: Royal Institute, Liverpool.
First-class debut: 1893, Lancashire v Oxford University, Old Trafford.
1 match for Lancashire 1893 (amateur).
HS: 6 v Oxford University (debut).

A medical doctor who later became known as Starkey-Smith, from 1897 he played for Norfolk.

SMITH, Sidney
RHB.
Born: Heywood, Lancashire, 14 January 1929.
Died: Heywood, 25 April 1985, aged 56.
Debut for Lancashire: 1952, v Cambridge University, Fenner's.
38 matches for Lancashire 1952-56 (professional).
HS for Lancashire: 72* v Cambridge University, Fenner's 1954.
First-class debut: 1950, Combined Services v Glamorgan, Cardiff.

6 matches for Combined Services 1950-51.
HS: 101* Combined Services v Essex, Chelmsford, 1950 (adding 238 for first wicket, unbroken, with A.C.Shirreff).
Full first-class record: 1,117 runs (18.31).

Sid Smith, a gritty batsman suited to opening, showed great promise on National Service but never quite made the county grade. Smith played League cricket for Rochdale, Kendal and, most notably, Idle in the Bradford League. Interestingly, Smith was long referred as 'Stanley' Smith in the reference books; only after his death was this found to be incorrect.

SMITH, Thomas

RHB; RM (round-arm).
Born: Glossop, Derbyshire, 26 August 1848.
Died: details unknown.
First-class debut: 1867, Lancashire v Surrey, The Oval.
2 matches for Lancashire 1867 (professional).
HS: 12 v Surrey (debut).

By trade a flannel weaver, Tom Smith had professional engagements at Cheetham Hill, St Helens, Saddleworth, Pendleton and Stayley Mill.

SNELLGROVE, Kenneth Leslie

RHB.
Born: Shepton Mallett, Somerset, 12 November 1941.
Education: Bootle Grammar School.
First-class debut: 1965, Lancashire v Glamorgan, Old Trafford.
105 matches for Lancashire 1965-74. Capped 1971.
HS: 138 v Middlesex, Old Trafford, 1970.
991 runs (31.96) 1971 best season.

Ken Snellgrove was a valuable cricketer without ever being quite able to win an assured position. He also played for Whalley CC.

SPEAK, Gary John

RHB; RFM.

Born: Chorley, Lancashire, 26 April 1962.
Education: Rivington and Blackrod High School.
First-class debut: 1981, Lancashire v Sri Lankans, Old Trafford.
5 matches for Lancashire 1981-82.
HS: 15* v Cambridge University, Cambridge, 1982.
BB: 1-78 v Surrey, Old Trafford, 1982.

SPEAK, Nicholas Jason

RHB; RM or OB.
Born: Manchester, 21 November 1966.
Education: Parrs Wood High School, Manchester.
First-class debut: 1986-87, Lancashire v Jamaica, Kingston.
13 matches for Lancashire 1986-87 to 1990.
HS: 138 v Zimbabwe, Old Trafford, 1990.
A promising batsman from Didsbury.

SPENCER, Helm

RHB; RF.
Born: Padiham, Lancashire, 31 December 1891.
Died: Burnley Lane Head, Burnley, 7 December 1974, aged 82.
First-class debut: 1914, Lancashire v Gloucestershire, Old Trafford.
2 matches for Lancashire 1914 (professional).
HS for Lancashire: 4 v Gloucestershire (debut).
BB for Lancashire: 1-0 v Gloucestershire (debut).
39 matches for Glamorgan 1923-25.
HS: 56 Glamorgan v Nottinghamshire, Cardiff, 1924.
BB: 7-33 Glamorgan v Northamptonshire, Swansea, 1925.

Helm Spencer was regarded as a promising pace bowler before World War One, but subsequently he became professional with Llanelli and qualified for Glamorgan. He later played for Colne and Lowerhouse. An eccentric-looking figure, who took to wearing a stetson and flamboyant clothing, he perhaps lost vital years in his development during the war. He is thought to have been related to Harry Spencer (Derbyshire).

SPOONER, Archibald Franklin

RHB.
Born: Litherland, near Bootle, Lancashire, 21 May 1886.
Died: Dartmouth, Devon, 11 January 1965, aged 78.
Education: Haileybury.
First-class debut: 1906, Lancashire v Somerset, Liverpool.
18 matches for Lancashire 1906-09 (amateur).

HS: 83 v Essex, Leyton, 1908.

The brother of Reggie Spooner, he was reported to have much of his brother's style. He was never as successful in first-class cricket, however.

SPOONER, Reginald Herbert

RHB; RA (spin).
Born: Litherland, near Bootle, Lancashire, 21 October 1880.
Died: Lincoln, 2 October 1961, aged 80.
Education: Marlborough.
First-class debut: 1899, Lancashire v Middlesex, Lord's.
170 matches for Lancashire 1899-1921 (amateur).
HS: 247 v Nottinghamshire, Trent Bridge, 1903.
Also scored 240 v Somerset, Bath, 1906; 224 v Surrey, The Oval, 1911; 215 v Essex, Leyton, 1904; 200* v Yorkshire, Old Trafford, 1910.
1,000 runs (5); 1,743 (56.22) 1911 best.
Centuries before lunch: First morning — during 164, Lancashire v Nottinghamshire, Trent Bridge 1905; during 240 v Somerset, Bath, 1906; 100*/186 v Hampshire, Old Trafford, 1911. Third morning — 102* v Sussex, Old Trafford 1904. Also moved from 84*; 215, second morning v Essex, Leyton, 1904.
10 Tests for England 1905-12. HS: 119 v South Africa, Lord's, 1912. Test record: 481 runs (32.06); 1 century; 4 catches.

The amateurs in Lancashire's 1904 Championship-winning team. From left to right: W.Findlay, L.O.S.Poidevin, A.C.MacLaren, A.H.Hornby and R.H.Spooner.

Last first-class match in 1923, for MCC.
Full first-class record: 13,681 runs (36.28); 31 centuries; 142 catches; 6 wickets.

Reg Spooner was regarded by many as the most graceful batsman of his time, and some also stated he was the best. As with many of the best batsmen he was of seemingly delicate build, but his graceful 'wafts' masked an unexpected power and a degree of timing which often saw the ball hit the boundary fence almost before the fieldsmen had moved. His early promise was interrupted by three years fighting in the Boer War, and possibly he may have played regularly during the years of World War One, but despite these hindrances his record is impressive. Undoubtedly, he was a leading product of 'The Golden Age'. Reg Spooner, was asked to skipper MCC in Australia in 1920-21. Lack of fitness decided his refusal and his career and reputation would probably have gained nothing from this tour. Spooner remained very concerned with Lancashire cricket and in 1945-46 was he was President. In Rugby Union he played three-quarter for Liverpool and won an England cap.

STANDRING, Kenneth Brooks

LHB; RM.
Born: Clitheroe, Lancashire, 17 February 1935.
Education: Clitheroe Grammar School; Leeds University.
First-class debut: 1955, Lancashire v Yorkshire, Old Trafford.
8 matches for Lancashire 1955-59 (amateur).
HS: 41 v Leicestershire, Leicester, 1959.

BB for Lancashire: 3-44 v Kent, Maidstone, 1955.
Played for Combined Services 1957-58.
BB: 4-61 Combined Services v Warwickshire,
Edgbaston, 1958.

Ken Standring made a wonderful start when he
dismissed Len Hutton as his first victim in first-
class cricket, but he subsequently found little time
for the game at that level. At various times he
played for Clitheroe, Bingley, Southport,
Birkdale and Ribblesdale Wanderers.

STANNING, Henry Duncan
RHB.
Born: Leyland, Lancashire, 14 November 1881.
Died: Kampi-ya-Motor, Kenya, 5 March 1946,
aged 64.
Education: Rugby; Trinity College, Cambridge.
First-class debut: 1906, Lancashire v Oxford
University, Oxford.
33 matches for Lancashire 1906-08 (amateur).
HS: 86 v Somerset, Old Trafford, 1907.

Harry Stanning enjoyed one promising season
in 1907 but rarely played subsequently. His
father, John Stanning, was on the Lancashire
committee, and his brother, John jnr, played for
Lancashire and Cambridge University.

STANNING, John
RHB.
Born: Leyland, Lancashire, 10 October 1877.
Died: Nakwin, Kenya, 19 May 1929 (in motor
accident), aged 51.
Education: Rugby; Trinity College, Cambridge.
Debut for Lancashire: 1900 v Derbyshire,
Glossop.
4 matches for Lancashire 1900-03 (amateur).
HS for Lancashire: 33 v Leicestershire, Old
Trafford, 1902.
Played for Cambridge University 1900-02 (Blue
1900).
First-class debut: 1899, MCC v Cambridge
University, Lord's.
Tour: Lord Hawke's team to New Zealand
1902-03.
HS: 120 Cambridge University v MCC, Cam-
bridge, 1900.
Full first-class record: 964 runs (24.10); 1 century;
19 catches.

John Stanning was a stylish batsman who, like
his brother Harry, showed promise before
emigrating to the colonies. Apart from Harry,
father John was a Lancashire committee member
and son John played for Worcestershire.

STANWORTH, John
RHB; WK.
Born: Oldham, Lancashire, 30 September 1960.
Education: Chadderton Grammar School;
Padgate College.
First-class debut: 1983, Lancashire v Derbyshire,
Blackpool.
37 matches for Lancashire 1983-90. Capped 1989.
HS: 50* v Gloucestershire, Bristol, 1985.

John Stanworth, who came to Lancashire from
Crompton CC, is an excellent wicketkeeper
unlucky to have come up against the exceptional
talent of Warren Hegg.

STATHAM, John Brian
LHB; RF.
Born: Gorton, Manchester, 17 June 1930.
Education: Manchester Central High School.
First-class debut: 1950, Lancashire v Kent, Old
Trafford.
430 matches for Lancashire 1950-68 (profes-
sional). Capped 1950. Benefit (£13,047) 1961.
Testimonial (£1,850) 1969. Captain 1965-67.
HS: 62 v Leicestershire, Old Trafford, 1955.
BB: 8-34 v Warwickshire, Coventry, 1957 (took
15-89 in the match); also took 8-37 v Leices-
tershire, Leicester, 1964 (took 15-108 in the
match).
Hat-tricks: v Sussex, Old Trafford, 1956; v
Leicestershire, Old Trafford, 1958.
100 wickets (9); 130 (12.08) 1965 best.

Brian Statham

70 Tests for England 1950-51 to 1965. HS: 38 v India, Lord's, 1959; BB: 7-39 v South Africa, Lord's, 1955. Test record: 675 runs (11.44); 28 catches; 242 wickets (24.84).

Tours: MCC to Australia 1950-51 (later addition), 1954-55, 1958-59, 1962-63; MCC to South Africa 1956-57; MCC to West Indies 1953-54, 1959-60; MCC to New Zealand 1950-51, 1954-55; MCC to India, Pakistan and Ceylon 1951-52; Cavaliers to South Africa 1960-61; President's XI in India 1967-68.

Full first-class record: 5,424 runs (10.80); 230 catches; 2,260 wickets (16.36).

'George' Statham, with 1,816 wickets for Lancashire (15.12) took more wickets for the county than any other bowler. Fairly tall, wiry and lithe, Statham bowled with a rhythmic run up and his superb high, loose-limbed action, fast in his early days, fast-medium in his maturity, with

a consistent, persistent and nagging accuracy unbeaten, perhaps unequalled, by any bowler of similar pace in cricket history. A measure of that accuracy can be gauged by the fact that over half his victims were either bowled or lbw.

Statham was also a useful left-handed tail-end batsman, who would have been even more valuable had he concentrated on this facet of the game, and a deep fielder with a long and unerringly accurate (naturally!) throw. He seemed almost too gentlemanly for a fast bowler, but his studied, quiet aggression was no less effective in its way than the more volatile antics of some of his contemporaries.

As Lancashire captain for three seasons he was quietly conscientious in difficult circumstances. At the end of his career, Statham was awarded the CBE for services to cricket. Never was such an award more deserved.

STAZIKER, Michael William
RHB; RMF.
Born: Croston, Lancashire, 7 November 1947.
Education: Hutton Grammar School, Preston.
First-class debut: 1970, Lancashire v Hampshire, Southampton.
2 matches for Lancashire 1970.
HS: 1* v Hampshire, Southampton, 1970.

Mike Staziker played for Cumberland in 1976. His club engagements included spells with Lancaster, Morecambe, Preston and Leyland Motors.

STEEL, Allan Gibson
RHB; RSM or RFM.
Born: West Derby, Liverpool, 24 September 1858.

Died: Hyde Park, London, 15 June 1914.
Education: Marlborough; Trinity Hall, Cambridge.
First-class debut: 1877, Lancashire v Sussex, Old Trafford, 1877.
47 matches for Lancashire 1877-93 (amateur).
HS for Lancashire: 105 v Surrey, Old Trafford, 1887.
BB: 9-63 v Yorkshire, Old Trafford, 1878.
Played for Cambridge University 1978-81 (Blue each year. Captain 1880).
13 Tests for England 1880-1888. HS: 148 v Australia, Lord's, 1884. BB: 3-27 v Australia, Sydney, 1882-83. Captain 4 times.
Test record: 600 runs (35.39); 2 centuries; 5 catches; 29 wickets (20.86).
Tour: Australia with Ivo Bligh's team 1882-83.
HS: 171 Gentlemen of England v Cambridge University, Cambridge, 1882.
Full first-class record: 7,000 runs (29.41); 1 century; 137 cathces; 789 wickets (14.78).

Allan Steel was a magnificent all-rounder, a free but scientific hitter, crafty slow-medium bowler with lots of spin, or a medium-pacer with a good break. He was also a good fielder, usually at point. Steel first came to the fore with his efforts for Cambridge University. In 1878 he took no fewer than 75 wickets (7.42) for Cambridge; in four matches against Oxford he took 38 wickets for 342 runs and scored 184 runs (30.66). In the 1879 match he performed the hat-trick.

Because of his work as a barrister — he became QC whe he was 27 — Steel had little time for cricket. However, he was on the Lancashire committee from 1881, and in 1902 was MCC President.

A.G.Steel was the best of a large cricketing family. His brothers, H.B., D.G and E.E., all played for Lancashire, whilst his son, A.I., played for Middlesex.

STEEL, Douglas Quinton

RHB; RSM (round arm).
Born: West Derby, Liverpool, 19 June 1856.
Died: Upton, Cheshire, 2 December 1933, aged 77.
Education: Uppingham; Trinity Hall, Cambridge.
Debut for Lancashire: 1876 v Nottinghamshire, Old Trafford.
22 matches for Lancashire 1876-87 (amateur).
HS for Lancashire 82 v Nottinghamshire (debut).
Played for Cambridge University 1876-79 (Blue each year).
Also played first-class games for Liverpool & District.
HS: 158 Cambridge University v England XI, Cambridge, 1877.

BB: 5-65 Cambridge University v England XI, Cambridge, 1876.
Full first-class record: 1,674 runs (19.46); 1 century; 7 wickets §24.71); 28 catches; 4 stumped.

D.Q.Steel was one of the famous Lancashire family; apart from cricket he won Blues for soccer and was also a noted University athlete. Steel was a prolific scorer in minor cricket; in 1884, for Liverpool v Sefton, he scored 226 in one innings.

STEEL, Ernest Eden

RHB; RAS.
Born: West Derby, Liverpool, 25 June 1864.
Died: Southport, Lancashire, 14 July 1941, aged 77.
Education: Marlborough.

Debut for Lancashire: 1884 v Derbyshire, Old Trafford.

40 matches for Lancashire 1884-1903 (amateur).

HS for Lancashire: 69* v South Africans, Old Trafford, 1901.

BB: 8-32 v Worcestershire, Worcester, 1902.

Played for Europeans in India 1892-93. Lived in India for several years from 1890, limiting his cricket in England. Last first-class match in 1904, for I.Zingari.

HS: 111 I.Zingari v Gentlemen, Lord's, 1904.

Full first-class record: 1,133 runs (17.43); 1 century; 131 wickets; 42 catches.

E.E.Steel, another of the brotherhood, had a very good record during a county career spread, with long gaps, over 20 seasons.

STEEL, Harold Banner
RHB; RM.
Born: South Hill, Liverpool, 9 April 1862.

Died: Burnham, Somerset, 29 June 1911, aged 49.

Education: Repton and Uppingham Schools; Trinity Hall, Cambridge.

First-class debut: 1883 v Oxford University, Oxford.

22 matches for Lancashire 1883-96 (amateur).

HS: 100 v Surrey, The Oval, 1884.

Played 12 matches for Liverpool & District 1884-94.

Full first-class record: 244 runs (10.60); 12 catches.

One of the well-known brotherhood, Harold Steel was a hard-hitting batsman, whose first-class record did him no justice, and a fine fielder who could keep wicket. H.B.Steel played a lot of club cricket at a high level, mainly for Liverpool, The Quidnuncs, Uppingham Rovers and Hoi Pepneumonoi. He was also an excellent racquets player.

STEPHENSON, Frederick
LHB; LF (round-arm).
Born: Todmorden, Lancashire, 24 April 1853.
Died: July 1927, aged 74.
First-class debut: 1875, Lancashire v Kent, Catford.
2 matches for Lancashire 1875-77 (professional).
Scored 0 runs.
BB: 1-17 v Derbyshire, Derby, 1877.

At a reported 5ft 2ins, Fred Stephenson was amongst the smallest of all cricketers. He was engaged at Castleton when he played for Lancashire.

STODDART, Wilfred Bowring
RHB; LB.
Born: West Derby, Liverpool, 27 April 1871.
Died: Wood End Park, Grassendale, Liverpool, 8 January 1935, aged 63.
First-class debut: 1898, Lancashire v Warwickshire, Liverpool.
15 matches for Lancashire 1898-99 (amateur).
HS: 43* v Warwickshire, Edgbaston, 1898.
BB: 6-121 v Kent, Canterbury, 1898.
Also played for Gentlemen's and MCC teams.
Full first-class record: 410 runs (15.18); 48 wickets (23.37); 7 catches.

Stoddart was captain of the Liverpool cricket and Rugby Union teams. At Rugby he played for Lancashire and England. He was on the Lancashire committee.

STONE, Donald Harry
LHB; RFM.
Born: Clayton, Lancashire, 9 January 1927.

Education: Droylsden School.
First-class debut: 1949, Lancashire v New Zealanders, Liverpool.
6 matches for Lancashire 1949-50 (professional).
HS: 46 v Kent, Folkestone, 1949.
BB: 4-30 v Oxford University, Oxford, 1950.

Donald Stone was a well-built pace bowler who had little real opportunity at county level. He played for Barton Hall and Flixton.

STORER, Enoch

LHB; RF (round-arm).
Born: Clay Cross, Ashover, Derbyshire, 18 May 1838.
Died: Hulme, Manchester, 1 July 1880, aged 42.
First-class debut: 1865, Lancashire v Middlesex, Islington.
6 matches for Lancashire 1865-78 (professional).
HS: 23 v Middlesex, Islington, 1865.
BB: 5-12 v Derbyshire, Old Trafford, 1878.

His several professional engagements included Ashton-under-Lyne, Manchester, Exeter College (Oxford), Longsight, Bury and Manchester Broughton.

SUGG, Frank Howe

RHB.
Born: Ilkeston, Derbyshire, 11 January 1862.
Died: Waterloo, Liverpool, 29 May 1933, aged 71.

Debut for Lancashire: 1887 v MCC, Lord's.
235 matches for Lancashire 1887-99 (professional).
HS: 220 v Gloucestershire, Bristol, 1896 (moved from 60* to 204* before lunch on second day).
First-class debut: 1883, Yorkshire v Cambridge University, Cambridge.
8 matches for Yorkshire 1883.
33 matches for Derbyshire 1886-88.
2 Tests for England 1888. HS: 31 v Australia, The Oval, 1888. Test record: 55 runs (27.50).
Full first-class record: 11,859 runs (24.45); 16 centuries; 167 catches; 10 wickets (27.30).

Frank Sugg, tall and strongly built, was, at his best, a splendid hard-hitting batsman with an eagle's eye and a wide variety of orthodox and unorthodox attacking strokes. His first county was Yorkshire and he then moved on to his native Derbyshire, but subsequently threw in his lot with Lancashire, to whom a gave wonderful service. Apart from cricket, Frank Sugg was a well-known soccer player with Sheffield Wednesday, Derby County, Burnley and Bolton Wanderers. He as also an excellent competition swimmer and, indeed, shone at almost every sport to which he put his mind. He was also a sports outfitter.

SULLIVAN, John

RHB; RM.
Born: Stalybridge, Lancashire, 5 February 1945.
First-class debut: 1963, Lancashire v Cambridge University.

John Sullivan, pictured with his teammates in 1968.
Back row (left to right): B.Wood, J.Sullivan, D.Hughes,
F.M.Engineer, K.Shuttleworth, G.Atkinson, J.Savage.
Front   row: G.Dullar,   H.Pilling,   J.D.Bond,
J.B.Statham, K.Higgs.

154 matches for Lancashire 1963-76 (professional). Capped 1969.
HS: 81* v Hampshire, Bournemouth, 1972.
BB: 4-19 v Yorkshire, Sheffield, 1973.

John Sullivan, a former ABA boxing champion, was an excellent 'bits and pieces' cricketer, particularly suited to limited-overs cricket. He had played for Holmfirth.

SUTCLIFFE, Richard John
RHB; RMF.
Born: Rochdale, Lancashire, 18 September 1954.
Education: King Edward VII School, Lytham St Anne's.
First-class debut: 1978, Lancashire v Essex, Southport.
1 match for Lancashire 1978.
HS: 10* v Essex (debut).
BB: 1-37 v Essex (debut).

Sutcliffe played for Milnrow.

SWIRE, Samuel Henry
RHB.
Born: Ashton-under-Lyne, 3 January 1839.

Died: 29 December 1905, aged 66.
First-class debut: 1865, Lancashire v Middlesex, Old Trafford.

5 matches for Lancashire 1865-68 (amateur).
HS: 18* v Middlesex (debut).

Sam Swire was Honorary Secretary of the County Club from its foundation until his death.

TATTERSALL, Roy

LHB; RMF and OB.
Born: Bolton, Lancashire, 17 August 1922.

First-class debut: 1948, Lancashire v Glamorgan, Old Trafford.
277 matches for Lancashire 1948-60 (professional). Capped 1950. Joint benefit with Malcolm Hilton (£11,655) 1960.
HS: 58 v Leicestershire, Old Trafford, 1958.
BB: 9-40 v Nottinghamshire, Old Trafford, 1953.
100 wickets (7); 171 (13.29) 1950.
Hat-trick: v Nottinghamshire, Old Trafford, 1953, during best bowling.
16 Tests for England 1950-51 to 1954. HS: 10* v India, Bombay, 1951-52; BB: 7-52 v South Africa, Lord's, 1951 (took 12-101 in the match). Test record: 50 runs (5.00). 8 catches. 58 wickets (26.08).
Tours: MCC to Australia and New Zealand 1950-51 (later addition); MCC to India and Pakistan 1951-52.
Full first-class record: 2,040 runs (9.35); 146 catches; 1,369 wickets (18.03).
'Tatters' started off as a useful seam bowler but really came into his own when reverting to off-spin. He was tall and slim, varied his flight and pace and gave the ball a tremendous 'tweak'.

Despite maintaining his form, he was pushed in and out of the side in the late 1950s, in most mystifying circumstances and the result was loss of confidence. After leaving the club in 1960, he played Birmingham League cricket for Kidderminster and since his retirement has remained in the area.

TATTERSALL, Roger Hartley

LHB; LM.
Born: Nelson, Lancashire, 12 March 1952.
Education: The Leys School.
First-class debut: 1971, Lancashire v Warwickshire, Old Trafford.
2 matches for Lancashire 1971.
Did not bat.
BB: 1-44 (v Warwickshire (debut).

TAYLOR, Frank

RHB.
Born: Rochdale, Lancashire, 4 May 1855.
Died: Heald Green, Cheadle, Cheshire, 14

August 1936, aged 81.
Education: Clifton College.
Debut for Lancashire: 1874 v Yorkshire, Old Trafford.
52 matches for Lancashire 1874-88 (amateur).
HS: 96 v Oxford University, Old Trafford, 1883.
BB: 1-4 v Nottinghamshire, Old Trafford, 1880.
3 matches for Gloucestershire 1873.

A tall and strong batsman, Frank Taylor was very successful at school, first playing for Gloucestershire whilst there.

TAYLOR, Fred
LM.
Born: Oldham, 1891.
Died: Clitheroe, 4 July 1968.
First-class debut: 1920, Lancashire v Derbyshire, Chesterfield.
15 matches for Lancashire 1920-22 (professional).

HS: 29* v Nottinghamshire, Trent Bridge, 1921.
BB: 6-65 v Middlesex, Lord's, 1921.

Fred Taylor played several matches without establishing himself. He was on Manchester CC's staff and later with Whalley.

TAYLOR, James
RHB; RF (round arm).
Born: Littleborough, Lancashire, 25 May 1846.

Died: Smallbridge, Rochdale, Lancashire, 16 August 1915, aged 69.
First-class debut: 1871, Lancashire v Kent, Gravesend.
3 matches for Lancashire 1871-73.
HS: 33 v Kent (debut).

In 1872 he was with Castleton CC, and in 1874 was coach at Windermere College.

TAYLOR, Malcolm Lees
LHB.
Born: Heywood, Lancashire, 16 July 1904.
Died: Wimborne Minster, Dorset, 14 March 1978, aged 73.

First-class debut: 1924, Lancashire v Worcestershire, Stourbridge.
95 matches for Lancashire 1924-31 (professional).
HS: 107* v Oxford University, Oxford, 1930.

Malcolm Taylor was a very stylish left-hander in whom Lancashire originally had high hopes, but he never succeeded in becoming a regular run scorer, there being an apparent fragility about his cricket which precluded his ever winning a regular place. On leaving the county in 1931, he went as coach to Canford, where he stayed until 1969. From 1934 to 1948 he played for Dorset. Alan Wharton was a cousin.

TAYLOR, Robert Joseph

RHB; RM.
Born: Liverpool, 1 November 1873.
Died: details unknown.
First-class debut: 1898, Lancashire v Surrey, Old Trafford.
2 matches for Lancashire 1898 (professional).
HS: 6 v Middlesex, Old Trafford, 1898.
BB: 1-25 v Middlesex, Old Trafford, 1898.
1 match for Worcestershire 1900.
Full first-class record: 7 runs (1.40); 2 wickets (68.50).

TAYLOR, Timothy John

RHB; SLA.
Born: Romiley, Cheshire, 28 March 1961.
Education: Stockport Grammar School; Magdalen College, Oxford.
Debut for Lancashire: 1981 v Sri Lankans, Old Trafford.
4 matches for Lancashire 1981-82.
HS for Lancashire: 2 v Sri Lankans (debut).
BB for Lancashire: 2-63 v Leicestershire, Old Trafford, 1981.
First-class debut: 1981, Oxford University v Leicestershire, Oxford.
Played for Oxford University 1981-82 (Blue both years).
HS: 28* Oxford University v Kent, Oxford, 1981.
BB: 5-81 Oxford University v Middlesex, Oxford, 1981.
Full first-class record: 115 runs (11.50); 2 catches; 37 wickets (34.37).

Tim Taylor, who played for Cheshire 1980-84, showed promise but was released after 1982. His club cricket was for Romiley.

TEBAY, Kevin

RHB.
Born: Bolton, Lancashire, 2 February 1936.
Education: Thornleigh College, Bolton.
First-class debut: 1961, Lancashire v Gloucestershire, Cheltenham.
15 matches for Lancashire 1961-63 (professional).
HS: 106 v Hampshire, Old Trafford, 1962.

A very sound batsman from Egerton CC, Tebay showed some early promise but was released after disappointing form.

TEGGIN, Alfred

RHB; LB.
Born: Broughton, Manchester, 22 October 1860.
Died: Cleveleys, Blackpool, 23 July 1941, aged 80.
First-class debut: 1886, Lancashire v Derbyshire, Old Trafford.

6 matches for Lancashire 1886 (amateur).
HS: 9 v Kent, Old Trafford, 1886.
BB: 6-53 (10-87 in the match) v Kent, Old Trafford, 1886.

Alfred Teggin, from Salford CC, was better known as a Rugby Union player who represented England, but also showed promise in his only season as a leg-spinner.

TENNENT, Hector Norman

RHB.
Born: Hobart, Tasmania, 6 April 1842.
Died: Hanover Square, London, 19 April 1904, aged 62.
Education: Merchiston Castle School; Loretto.
First-class debut: 1865, Lancashire v Middlesex, Islington.
2 matches for Lancashire 1865 and 1870.
HS for Lancashire: 21 v Middlesex (debut).
Played for various MCC and Gentlemen's teams 1866-76, and in 1878 appeared in an emergency for the Australian tourists.
HS: 45* North of Thames v South of Thames, Canterbury, 1868.
Full first-class record: 344 runs (12.28).

Hector Tennent, whose brothers J.P. (Victoria) and W.N. (Lancashire) were first-class cricketers, was better known as a theatrical agent. The firm bearing his name was later to be run by 'Binky' Beaumont, one of the Noel Coward 'set' either side of World War Two.

TENNENT, William Middleton

RHB.
Born: Hobart, Tasmania, 6 October 1845.
Died: Hastings, Sussex, 5 July 1883, aged 37.
Education: Merchiston Castle School.
First-class debut: 1867, Lancashire v Yorkshire, Old Trafford.
1 match for Lancashire 1867 (amateur).
HS: 3 v Yorkshire (debut).

Brother of H.N. (Lancashire) and J.P. (Victoria).

THOMAS, Alan

RHB; OB.
Born: Bolton, Lancashire, 7 January 1947.
Education: Canon Slade Secondary School, Bolton.
First-class debut: 1966, Lancashire v Oxford University, Oxford.
1 match for Lancashire 1966.
HS: 4 v Oxford University (debut).

Alan Thomas' various clubs included Farnworth Social Circle, Farnworth, Clifton and Horwich RMI.

THOMAS, Richard

WK.
Born: Wales, 15 July 1867.
Died: Werneth, Lancashire, 18 December 1918, aged 51.
First-class debut: 1894, Lancashire v Derbyshire, Derby.
20 matches for Lancashire 1894-1902 (professional).
HS: 17 v MCC, Lord's, 1901.

A useful wicketkeeper, Thomas found his very poor batting was a handicap.

THORNBER, Harry

RHB.
Born: Manchester, 9 November 1851.
Died: St Pancras, London, 28 July 1913, aged 62.
First-class debut: 1874, Lancashire v Kent, Maidstone.
1 match for Lancashire 1874 (amateur).
Did not score in either innings.

As captain of Cheshire, Harry Thornber was asked for his views on the 1889 reforms for the 1890 *Wisden*.

TINDALL, Sydney Maguire

RHB.
Born: Margate, Kent, 18 February 1867.
Died: Sydney, Australia, 19 September 1922, aged 55.
Education: Dane House School, Margate.
First-class debut: 1894, Lancashire v Derbyshire, Old Trafford.
42 matches for Lancashire 1894-98 (amateur).
HS: 86 v Sussex, Hove, 1897.
Played for London County 1900-01.

Tindall emigrated to Melbourne in 1911 and became secretary of Melbourne CC. A well-known hockey player, he died after a fall from a tram near the Hotel Australia. His brother, Rev H.C.L.Tindall, played for Kent.

TINSLEY, Alfred

RHB.
Born: Welham, Malton, Yorkshire, 12 March 1867.
Died: Musselburgh, Midlothian, Scotland, 25 September 1933, aged 66.
First-class debut: 1890, Lancashire v Kent, Old Trafford.
58 matches for Lancashire 1890-95 (professional).
HS: 65 v Nottinghamshire, Trent Bridge, 1895.

Alf Tinsley, who played once for Yorkshire in

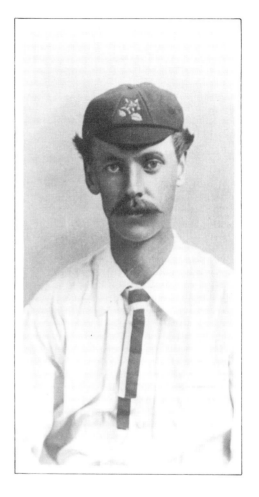

a non-first-class match in 1887, was a plucky, hard-hitting batsman. After an engagement with Leyland CC, he played for Staffordshire from 1905.

TINSLEY, Henry James

RHB; RF.
Born: Welham, Malton, Yorkshire, 20 February 1865.
Died: Haworth, Keighley, Yorkshire, 10 December 1938, aged 73.
Debut for Lancashire: 1894, Lancashire v Leicestershire, Leicester.
4 matches for Lancashire 1894-96 (professional).
HS: 18 v Middlesex, Old Trafford.
First-class debut: 1890, Yorkshire v Lancashire, Old Trafford.
9 matches for Yorkshire 1890-91 (professional).

BB: 3-15 Yorkshire v Lancashire, Old Trafford, 1890.

Full first-class record: 122 runs (5.80); 4 wickets (14.25).

Alf Tinsley's brother was a useful batsman and quick round-arm bowler, and a good fielder. He was engaged by the Warrington CC, and then by John Stanning at Leyland.

TITCHARD, Stephen Paul

RHB; OB.

Born: Warrington, Lancashire, 17 December 1967.

First-class debut: 1990, Lancashire v Zimbabwe, Old Trafford.

3 matches for Lancashire 1990.

HS: 80 v Zimbabwe (debut).

TRANTER, Enoch

LHB; LF (round-arm).

Born: Old Park, Shropshire, 27 April 1842.

Died: Donnington Wood, Lilleshall, Shropshire, 23 September 1910, aged 68.

First-class debut: 1875, Lancashire v MCC, Lord's.

3 matches for Lancashire 1875-76 (professional).

HS: 5 v Kent, Castleton, 1876.

BB: 2-11 v Derbyshire, Old Trafford, 1875.

Enoch Tranter's engagements included spells

with Wolverhampton CC, Sefton CC and at Cambridge.

TRIM, Geoffrey Edward

RHB Occasionally LB.

Born: Openshaw, Manchester, 6 April 1956.

First-class debut: 1976, Lancashire v Nottinghamshire, Trent Bridge, 1976.

15 matches for Lancashire 1976-80.

HS: 91 v Derbyshire, Chesterfield, 1979.

The slightly-built Geoff Trim was a neat batsman with sound defence who seemed to lack the confidence to play his strokes. He is currently Clerk of Works at Old Trafford.

TYLDESLEY, George Ernest

RHB.

Born: Roe Green, Worsley, Lancashire, 5 February 1889.

Died: Rhos-on-Sea, Denbighshire, 5 May 1962, aged 73.

First-class debut: 1909, Lancashire v Warwickshire, Liverpool.

573 matches for Lancashire 1909-36 (professional). Benefit (£2,458) 1924.

HS: 256* v Warwickshire, Old Trafford, 1930.

Also scored 244 v Warwickshire, Edgbaston

1920; 242 v Leicestershire, Leicester, 1928; 239 v Glamorgan, Cardiff, 1934; 236 v Surrey, The Oval, 1923; 226 v Sussex, Old Trafford, 1926; 225* v Worcestershire, Worcester, 1932.

Scored 165 and 123* v Essex, Leyton, 1921; 109 and 108* v Glamorgan, Cardiff, 1930.

Thrice scored three consecutive centuries: (1926) 131 v Surrey, The Oval; 106 v Essex, Nelson; 126 v Somerset, Taunton. (1928) 159 v Kent, Old Trafford; 242 v Leicestershire, Leicester; 118 v Sussex, Hove. (1934) 239 v Glamorgan, Cardiff; 107 v Australians, Old Trafford; 134 v Gloucestershire, Bristol.

1,000 runs (18); 2,487 (57.83) 1934 best.
Also 2,467 (77.09) in 1928; 2,432 (62.35) in 1926; 2,420 (59.02) in 1932; 2,070 (46.00) in 1922.
Scored 3,024 runs (79.57) in all first-class matches 1928.
14 Tests for England 1921 to 1928-29. HS: 122 v West Indies, Lord's, 1928; and v South Africa, Johannesburg, 1927-28. Test record: 990 runs (55.00); 3 centuries; 2 catches.
Tours: S.B.Joel's team to South Africa 1924-25; Tennyson's team to Jamaica 1926-27; MCC to

South Africa 1927-28; MCC to Australia 1928-29. Full first-class record: 38,874 runs (45.46); 102 centuries; 293 catches; 6 wickets.

Johnnie Tyldesley's young brother was less of a 'killer', essentially elegant and patient, a quiet 'killer' perhaps. He had a fine hook, an excellent drive, occasionally a fine cut. He scored more runs for Lancashire than anyone else, yet played few Tests and Johnnie was regarded as the better batsman. Most counties would have accepted Ernie with few grumbles! After 1935, Tyldesley was considered for the captaincy, but Lionel Lister got the vote. Early in 1936 he retired and soon became the first professional cricketer on the Lancashire committee.

TYLDESLEY, Harry
RHB; RA (spin).
Born: Kearsley, Bolton, Lancashire, 4 July 1892.

Died: Sandylands, Morecambe, Lancashire, 30 August 1935, aged 43.
First-class debut: 1914, Lancashire v Derbyshire, Derby.
4 matches for Lancashire 1914-22 (professional).
HS: 33* v Oxford University, Oxford, 1922.
BB for Lancashire: 2-37 v Oxford University, Oxford, 1922.
Tour: A.C.MacLaren's team to New Zealand and Australia 1922-23.
BB: 5-100 MacLaren's MCC team v South Australia, Adelaide, 1922-23.
Full first-class record: 102 runs (8.50); 7 catches; 18 wickets (27.77).

Harry Tyldesley was one of four brothers — James, Dick and William — were the others, who played for Lancashire, but his best years were in the Leagues. He took 822 wickets for Oxton CC.

TYLDESLEY, James Darbyshire

RHB; RF.
Born: Ashton-in-Makerfield, Lancashire, 10 August 1889.

Died: Queen's Park, Bolton, Lancashire, 31 January 1923, aged 33.
First-class debut: 1910, Lancashire v Northamptonshire, Northampton.
116 matches for Lancashire 1910-22 (professional).
HS: 112* v Leicestershire, Old Trafford, 1922.
BB: 7-34 v Worcestershire, Stourbridge, 1919.
Achieved two hat-tricks: Lancashire v Derbyshire, Old Trafford, 1920; Lancashire v Worcestershire, Old Trafford, 1922.

Jimmy Tyldesley, well-built and strong, was probably the most gifted of the 'Westhoughton Tyldesleys'. As with all of them, he died prematurely, under the anaesthetic whilst undergoing surgery.

TYLDESLEY, John Thomas

RHB.
Born: Roe Green, Worsley, Lancashire, 22 November 1873.
Died: Moston, Lancashire, 27 November 1930, aged 57.
First-class debut: 1895, Lancashire v Gloucestershire, Old Trafford.
507 matches for Lancashire 1895-1923 (professional). Benefit (£3,015) 1906.
HS: 295* v Kent, Old Trafford, 1906.
Also scored 272 v Derbyshire, Chesterfield, 1919; 253 v Kent, Canterbury, 1914; 250 v Nottinghamshire, Trent Bridge, 1905; 249 v Leicestershire, Leicester, 1899; 248 v Worcestershire, Liverpool, 1903; 243 v Leicestershire, Leicester, 1908; 225 v Nottinghamshire, Trent Bridge, 1904; 221 v Nottinghamshire, Trent Bridge, 1901; 210 v Somerset, Bath, 1904; 210 v Surrey, The Oval, 1913; 209 v Warwickshire, Edgbaston, 1907; 200 v Derbyshire, Old Trafford, 1898.
1,000 runs (19); 2,633 (56.02) 1901 best (and still Lancashire record). Also 2,335 runs (66.71) 1904.
Two centuries in match twice: 106 and 100* v Warwickshire, Edgbaston, 1897; 136 and 101 v Hampshire, Old Trafford, 1910.
Three successive centuries twice: (1897) 106 and 100* v Warwickshire, Edgbaston, 174 v Sussex, Old Trafford; (1904) 103 v Somerset, Old Trafford, 225 v Nottinghamshire, Trent Bridge, 196 v Worcestershire, Worcester.
Century before lunch on first day, 100*/104 v Derbyshire, Old Trafford, 1904.
Four times scored 100 plus runs before lunch, having started innings previous day: During 210, second day v Somerset, Bath 1904; 22*-128, second day v Gloucestershire, Old Trafford, 1906; during 209, second day v Warwickshire, Edgbaston, 1907; 158*-272, second day v Derbyshire, Chesterfield, 1919.
31 Tests for England 1898-1909. HS: 138 v Australia, Edgbaston, 1902. Test record: 1,661 runs (30.75); 4 centuries; 16 catches.

John Tyldesley

Full first-class record: 37,897 runs (40.66); 86 centuries; 355 catches; 3 wickets.
Tours: Lord Hawke's team to South Africa 1898-99; A.C.MacLaren's team to Australia 1901-02; MCC to Australia 1903-04.

Johnnie Tyldesley was shorter and slighter but more aggressive than brother Ernest. Very quick on his feet, Tyldesley would dictate to the bowler from the first ball, and if leg theory was tried, he would dance backwards towards square-leg and cut through the vacant off-side. Against normal attacks the off-side, with drives and cuts, was his main area of aggression. Johnnie Tyldesley was a religious man, a non-smoker and tee-totaller. He was the Lancashire coach as well as a sports outfitter in Manchester. He died suddenly whilst preparing to go to work.

TYLDESLEY, Richard Knowles

RHB; RA (spin).
Born: Westhoughton, Lancashire, 11 March 1897.
Died: Over Hulton, Bolton, Lancashire, 17 September 1943, aged 46.
First-class debut: 1919, Lancashire v Northamptonshire, Northampton.
374 matches for Lancashire 1919-31 (professional). Benefit (£2,027) 1930.
HS: 105 v Nottinghamshire, Old Trafford, 1922.

BB: 8-15 v Northamptonshire, Kettering, 1926.
Took 4 wickets in 4 balls v Derbyshire, Derby, 1929.
100 wickets (10); 167 (13.32) 1924 best.
In 1924 took 184 wickets (13.98) in all first-class matches.
7 Tests for England 1924-30. HS: 29 v South Africa, Headingley, 1924. BB: 3-50 v South Africa, Lord's, 1924. Test record: 47 runs (7.83); 1 catch; 19 wickets (32.57).
Toured Australia with MCC 1924-25.
Full first-class record: 6,419 runs (15.65); 1 century; 337 catches; 1,509 wickets (17.21).

Dick Tyldesley was the youngest, and most successful, of the four sons of a Westhoughton CC professional. He was also the last to die, aged 46. A very bulky, red-faced man, he nevertheless bowled his leg-breaks and top-spinners with remarkable stamina, great persistence and invariable success. A useful batsman, with delicate cuts and hefty cow shots in his armoury, and a valiant fielder, like many large men he was usually cheerful, but could dig in his heels. This was the reason for his leaving Lancashire, after a disagreement over terms in 1931. He then began a League career, first with Accrington, and latterly with Nantwich.

TYLDESLEY, William Knowles

LHB; LMF.
Born: Aspull, Wigan, Lancashire, 10 August 1887.

Died: Kemmel, Belgium, 26 April 1918 (killed in action), aged 30.
First-class debut: 1908, Lancashire v Kent, Old Trafford.
87 matches for Lancashire 1908-14 (professional).
HS: 152 v Derbyshire, Derby, 1911.
BB: 2-0 v Australians, Liverpool, 1909 (in 4 balls).
Scored 991 runs (34.17) in 1911.

William Tyldesley was the eldest of the Westhoughton brothers and the only one for whom batting was his strong suit. He had begun to struggle to hold his place when war was declared, and died a hero's death in Belgium. None can say what cricket may have had in store.

UNSWORTH, James

RHB; RF (round-arm).
Born: Everton, Liverpool, 4 March 1844.
Died: Warrington, Lancashire, 1 January 1893, aged 48.
First-class debut: 1871, Lancashire v Kent, Gravesend.
2 matches for Lancashire 1871 (professional).
HS: 23 v Kent, Gravesend, 1871.
BB: 3-52 v Kent, Gravesend, 1871.

Originally with Everton CC, he enjoyed several professional engagements, with New Brighton, Anfield and Huyton. In 1875 he was publican at the Rose & Crown, Huyton.

VAN DER KNAPP, David Saunders

RHB; OB.
Born: Sandton, Johannesburg, South Africa, 7 September 1948.
Education: Parktown High School, Transvaal.
First-class debut: 1967, Lancashire v Oxford University.
1 match for Lancashire 1967.
Did not bat.
BB for Lancashire: 2-24 v Oxford University (debut).
Played for Transvaal 1967-68 to 1978-79.
HS: 44 Transvaal v Eastern Province, Port Elizabeth, 1974-75.
BB: 6-61 Transvaal v Rhodesia, Bulawayo, 1974-75.

VAREY, David William

RHB.
Born: Darlington, County Durham, 15 October 1961.
Education: Birkenhead School; Pembroke College, Cambridge.

Debut for Lancashire: 1984 v Warwickshire, Nuneaton.
44 matches for Lancashire 1984-87.
HS for Lancashire: 112 v Oxford University, Oxford, 1985.
Played for Cambridge University 1981-83 (Blue 1982-83).
HS: 156* Cambridge University v Northamptonshire, Cambridge, 1982.
Full first-class record: 2,723 runs (27.23); 2 centuries; 25 catches; 1 stumped.

David Varey, whose twin brother Jonathon played opposite him, for Oxford, in the 1982 and 1983 University matches at Lord's, promised well as a cultured opening bat but failed to realise his potential and left in 1987. He now plays for Cheshire, in the Minor Counties Championship, and for Oxton CC.

WADSWORTH, Ernest

RHB; RF (round-arm).
Born: Manchester, 30 September 1850.
Died: Hale, Bowdon, Cheshire, 7 January 1918, aged 67.

First-class debut: 1871, Lancashire v Derbyshire, Old Trafford.

7 matches for Lancashire 1871-79 (professional).

HS: 30 v Derbyshire, Derby, 1876.

Ernest Wadsworth, a local professional who batted usefully without establishing himself was, by trade, an organ builder in Oxford Road, Manchester.

WALKER, Roger

RHB; WK.

Born: Bury, Lancashire, 18 September 1846.

Died: Reading, Berkshire, 11 November 1919, aged 73.

Education: Rossall.

First-class debut: 1874, Lancashire v Derbyshire, Old Trafford.

2 matches for Lancashire 1874-75 (amateur).

HS: 19 v Derbyshire (debut).

Roger Walker, of Bury CC, was a friend of the Hornbys and became a Lancashire committee member in 1880. A better Rugby footballer than cricketer, he played for England five times.

WALL, Henry

RHB; RF (round-arm).

Born: Wigan, Lancashire, 21 April 1852.

Died: Southport, Lancashire, 13 October 1914, aged 62.

Education: Privately at Wigan.

First-class debut: 1877, Lancashire v Sussex, Old Trafford.

3 matches for Lancashire 1877 (amateur).

HS: 15 v Sussex (debut).

A mining engineer, Wall played for Wigan CC. His brothers, Thomas and William, also played for Lancashire.

WALL, Thomas

RHB; RA (slow round-arm); WK.

Born: Wigan, Lancashire, 27 November 1841.

Died: Wigan, 18 April 1875, aged 33.

Education: Privately at Wigan.

First-class debut: 1868, Lancashire v Surrey, The Oval.

2 matches for Lancashire 1868 (amateur).

HS: 37 v MCC, Lord's, 1868.

An amateur from Wigan CC, his brothers, Henry and William Wall, also played for Lancashire.

WALL, William

RHB; WK.

Born: Wigan, Lancashire, 8 January 1854.

Died: Southport, Lancashire, 18 April 1922, aged 68.

Education: Privately at Wigan.

First-class debut: 1877, Lancashire v Derbyshire, Derby.

1 match for Lancashire 1877 (amateur).

HS: 17* v Derbyshire (debut).

William Wall, a newspaper proprietor in Wigan, was brother of Henry and Thomas Wall of Lancashire.

WALLWORK, Mark Andrew

RHB; WK.

Born: Urmston, Lancashire, 14 December 1960.

Education: Eccles Grammar School; Newcastle upon Tyne University.

First-class debut: 1982, Lancashire v Yorkshire, Headingley.

1 match for Lancashire 1982.

Did not bat.

Wallwork, a wicketkeeper from Farnworth CC, found the competition a little too keen.

WALSH, George

Batsman.
Born: Over Darwen, Blackburn, Lancashire, 16 February 1852.
Died: Darwen, Lancashire, 22 May 1904, aged 52.
Education: Rugby School.
First-class debut: 1874, Lancashire v Derbyshire, Old Trafford.
2 matches for Lancashire 1874-77 (amateur).
HS: 15 v Derbyshire (debut).

George Walsh also played for Cheshire.

WALTON, Matthew

Opening batsman.
Born: Cross Cliff, Glossop, Derbyshire, 10 December 1837.
Died: Glossop, 7 January 1888, aged 50.
First-class debut: 1867, Lancashire v Yorkshire, Middlesbrough.
1 match for Lancashire 1867 (amateur).
HS: 6 v Yorkshire (debut).

A little-known professional with Glossop, his son, William Walton, played for Derbyshire.

WARBURTON, Leslie

RHB; RFM.
Born: Haslingden, Lancashire, 30 April 1910.
Died: Gloucester, 11 February 1984, aged 73.
First-class debut: 1929, Lancashire v Minor Counties, Old Trafford.
6 matches for Lancashire 1929-38 (amateur).
HS: 74* v Surrey, The Oval, 1929.
BB: 3-47 v Yorkshire, Headingley, 1936.
Played for North v South in Test Trial at Lord's in 1936.

Les Warburton was persuaded to prefer the security of life as a bank clerk to the possibilities of disappointment as a professional cricketer. He had a superb record in the Leagues, however, notably with Haslingden, Littleborough (for he achieved the double in 1937) and East Lancashire. Outside cricket and work he had a variety of hobbies, being an accomplished performer on violin and piano, amongst other more eccentric hobbies. Although Warburton's career figures do not impress too much, his League record suggests he could have reached a very high standard indeed in the first-class game.

WARD, Albert

RHB; LB.
Born: Waterloo, near Leeds, Yorkshire, 21 November 1865.

Died: Heaton, Bradford, Yorkshire, 6 January 1939, aged 73.
Debut for Lancashire: 1889 v MCC, Lord's.
330 matches for Lancashire 1889-1904 (professional). Benefit 1902 (£1,739).
HS for Lancashire: 185 v Kent, Gravesend, 1891.
BB: 6-29 v Derbyshire, Glossop, 1899.
1,000 runs (9); 1,511 (37.77) 1900 best.
Carried bat throughout an innings 5 times: 140*/281 v Gloucestershire, Bristol, 1893; 45*/97 v Australians, Old Trafford, 1893; 75*/168 v Leicestershire, Old Trafford, 1895; 109*/337 v Hampshire, Southampton, 1899; 83*/262 v Middlesex, Lord's, 1899.

Against Derbyshire, Derby, 1897, moved from 54* to 162 before lunch on second day of match.
7 Tests for England 1893 to 1894-95. HS: 117 v Australia, Sydney, 1894-95. Test record: 487 runs (37.46); 1 century; 1 catch.
Toured Australia with A.E.Stoddart's team 1894-95.
HS: 219 Stoddart's team v South Australia, Adelaide, 1894-95.
First-class debut: 1886, Yorkshire v Middlesex, Bradford.
4 matches for Yorkshire 1886.

Albert Ward

Full first-class record: 17,783 runs (30.08); 29 centuries; 168 catches. 71 wickets (34.83).

Albert Ward started off unimpressively with his native Yorkshire but, having taken a teaching post in Lancashire and qualified by residence, he was an immediate success with his new county. A tall and very sound batsman, his defensive technique, straight and positive, and his driving ability made him an ideal opener and an automatic choice for his adopted county for 14 season.

He was also a talented bowler of leg-breaks, although never taking a first-class wicket until he was over 30. Here was simply a case of lack of opportunity. Ward aquitted himself so well in Test cricket that it is surprising he played so rarely. After being leading scorer in his only full series, and scoring 93 in the final Test, he never again played for England. Perhaps he was entitled to feel embittered. If so, he never showed it.

WARD, Frank
RHB; RM.
Born: Carlisle, Cumberland, 9 January 1865.
Died: details unknown.

First-class debut: 1884, Lancashire v Kent, Old Trafford.
47 matches for Lancashire 1884-96 (professional).
HS: 145 v Kent, Old Trafford, 1890.
BB: 4-14 v Somerset, Taunton, 1893.

Stylish Frank Ward never quite fulfilled his promise, although as batsman and bowler he did some useful things. He was engaged by Leyland CC in 1885 and eventually went as professional to Rossall School. Eventually he emigrated to New Zealand, from where no details of his death have ever emerged. Ward was a convivial social companion with a liking for strong drink and good food and rumours of his having become a centenerian or near can almost certainly be discounted.

WARDLE, Charles
RHB; RF (round-arm).
Born: Arnold, Nottinghamshire, 20 February 1837.
Died: Arnold, Nottinghamshire, 10 August 1907, aged 70.
First-class debut: 1867, Lancashire v Yorkshire, Middlesbrough.
3 matches for Lancashire 1867-72 (professional).
HS: 7* v Derbyshire, Derby, 1872.

Wardle had various professional engagements, at Mappley Park, Old Trafford, Bowdon and Cheetham Hill.

WASHBROOK, Cyril
RHB.
Born: Barrow, near Clitheroe, Lancashire, 6 December 1914.
Education: Clitheroe Grammar School.
First-class debut: 1933, Lancashire v Sussex, Old Trafford.
500 matches for Lancashire 1933-59 (professional). Capped 1933. Benefit (£14,000, then a record) 1948. Testimonial (£1,520) 1959. Captain 1954-59.
HS: 251* v Surrey, Old Trafford, 1947.
Also scored 228 v Oxford University, Oxford, 1935; 219* v Gloucestershire, Bristol, 1938; 211* v Somerset, Old Trafford, 1952; 209* v Warwickshire, Edgbaston, 1951; 204* v Sussex, Old Trafford, 1947; 200 v Hampshire, Old Trafford, 1948.
1,000 runs (16); 1,950 (78.00) 1947 best.
Scored 100 in each innings, 172 and 121* v Sussex, Eastbourne, 1947.
Carried bat, 49*/124 v Worcestershire, Old Trafford, 1935.
100 runs first morning during 124 v Glamorgan, Old Trafford, 1938.

Added 350* for 1st wicket with Winston Place v Sussex, Old Trafford, 1947.
37 Tests for England 1937-56. HS: 195 v South Africa, Johannesburg, 1948-49 (adding 359 for the first wicket with Len Hutton, still a record opening stand for all Tests by England). Test record: 2,569 runs (42.81); 6 centuries; 12 catches.

Tours: MCC to Australia and New Zealand 1946-47, 1950-51; MCC to South Africa 1948-49. Full first-class record: 34,101 runs (42.67); 76 centuries; 212 catches; 7 wickets.

Stocky, broad-shouldered and a man who strutted rather than walked, Cyril Washbrook was a quick-footed opener, devastating against any aspiring quick bowler short in length or wayward in direction. He scored all around the wicket but his best shots were perhaps the cut and the hook. In the field he was one of the greatest cover-points of his time. When his Test career seemed over he was persuaded by fellow selectors, whose team he had just joined, to return to the England side against South Africa;

the reluctant hero repaid them with 98. As Lancashire's captain he was not everyone's ideal leader. He lacked rapport with younger players and confirmed that his values were not always theirs. He was a splendid committee man, however, and in 1988 received the ultimate honour of the county presidency.

WASIM AKRAM

LHB; LFM.
Born: Lahore, Pakistan, 3 June 1966.
Education: Islamia College, Lahore.
Debut for Lancashire: 1988 v Nottinghamshire, Trent Bridge.
30 matches for Lancashire 1988.
HS for Lancashire: 116* v Somerset, Old Trafford, 1988.

BB for Lancashire: 7-53 v Northamptonshire, Northampton, 1988.
32 Tests for Pakistan 1984-85 to date. HS: 123 v Australia, Adelaide, 1989-90 (also highest in

first-class cricket). BB: 6-62 (11-60 in match) v Australia, Melbourne, 1989-90. Test record: 665 runs (20.15); 1 century; 11 catches; 111 wickets (26.72). 97 limited-overs matches for Pakistan.

First-class cricket in Pakistan since 1984-85, for PAC and Lahore.

BB: 7-42 World XI v MCC, Scarborough, 1989. Full first-class record: 1,953 runs (21.46); 2 centuries; 28 catches; 273 wickets (25.06).

A sometimes devastating left-armed pace man and often effective with the bat, Lancashire are hopeful of outstanding all round service from Wasim Akram.

WATERTON, Stuart Nicholas Varney
RHB; WK.
Born: Dartford, Kent, 6 December 1960.
Education: Gravesend School; London School of Economics.
Debut for Lancashire: 1990, Lancashire v Nottinghamshire, Southport.
1 match for Lancashire 1990.
HS: 3 v Nottinghamshire (debut and only innings).
First-class debut: 1980, Kent v Yorkshire, Sheffield.
25 matches for Kent 1980-85.
15 matches for Northamptonshire 1986-87.
Full first-class record: 757 runs (19.84); 79 catches; 15 stumped.

Waterton, a much-travelled wicketkeeper, plays for Oxfordshire in the Minor Counties Championship.

WATKINSON, Michael
RHB; RM.
Born: Westhoughton, Lancashire, 1 August 1961.
Education: Rivington and Blackrod High School, Horwich.

Mike Watkinson is caught for 19 by Derbyshire's Bruce Roberts at Buxton in 1984.

First-class debut: 1982, Lancashire v Kent, Old Trafford.
158 matches for Lancashire 1982-1990. Capped 1987.
HS: 138 v Yorkshire, Old Trafford, 1990.
BB: 7-25 v Sussex, Lytham, 1987.
Full first-class record: 4,952 runs (24.63); 2 centuries; 81 catches; 341 wickets (32.65).

Mike Watkinson is perhaps a much underrated all-rounder whose best is to come.

WATSON, Alexander

RHB; OB.
Born: Coatbridge, Lanarkshire, 4 November 1844.
Died: Old Trafford, Manchester, 26 October 1920, aged 75.

First-class debut: 1871, Lancashire v Derbyshire, Derby.
283 matches for Lancashire 1871-93 (professional). Benefit (£1,011) 1885.
HS: 74 v Derbyshire, Old Trafford, 1883.
BB: 9-118 v Derbyshire, Old Trafford, 1874.
Achieved hat-trick v Kent, Castleton, 1876.
100 wickets (1); 100 (14.82) 1887.

Full first-class record: 4,492 runs (12.58); 277 catches; 1,383 wickets (13.32).

Alec Watson, one of the first county professionals from Scotland, was a wily and dead-accurate off-spinner, yet started off as a round-arm fast bowler. He was associated with the Drumpellier club in his early years and was then engaged by the Edinburgh Caledonian club. He came to Lancashire to play for Rusholme and was then a professional at Old Trafford. Such was Watson's success it is possibly a minor mystery that he never played a Test. The fact that he was Scottish may, perhaps, have weighed against him, but a more likely reason was his slightly suspect action. Perhaps had there been no Crossland, Watson would have been sacrificed. In later years Sandy Watson coached at Marlborough and was a sports outfitter in Manchester.

WATSON, Frank Bramley

RHB; RM.
Born: Nottingham, 17 September 1898.
Died: Warrington, Lancashire, 1 February 1976, aged 77.
First-class debut: 1920 v Warwickshire, Old Trafford.
456 matches for Lancashrie 1920-37 (professional).
HS: 300* v Surrey, Old Trafford, 1928.
Also scored 236 v Sussex, Hove 1928; 223 v Northamptonshire, Old Trafford, 1928; 207 v Worcestershire, Worcester 1929.
BB: 5-31 v Hampshire, Old Trafford, 1923.
1,000 runs (12); 2,541 (63.52) 1928 best. Also 2,137 (46.45) 1929; 2,031 (45.13) 1930.
Lancashire record 2nd-wicket stand of 371 (highest for all wickets for County) with Ernest Tyldesley v Surrey, Old Trafford, 1928.
Tour: MCC to West Indies 1925-26.
Full first-class record: 23,596 runs (36.98); 50 centuries; 292 catches; 407 wickets (32.14).

Frank Watson was not the most attractive batsman to play for Lancashire. Indeed, those who saw him often prefer to recall every other batsman but him. For many years, however, Watson was invaluable in a 'sheet-anchor' role who usually waited for the bad ball, which was unerringly hooked or driven to the boundary. Ill health and an eye injury shortened his career, not before his impressive career record had made perhaps more of a mark than the way it was acquired.

WATSON, Roger Graeme

LHB; ROB.
Born: Rawtenstall, Lancashire, 14 January 1964.

Education: Fearns Seconardy School, Bacup.
First-class debut: 1982, Lancashire v Somerset, Taunton.
2 matches for Lancashire 1982-85.
HS: 18 v Oxford University, Oxford, 1985.

WEBB, Sidney

RHB; RM.
Born: Brompton, Middlesex, 1 February 1875.
Died: Ilford, Essex, 4 April 1923, aged 48.
Debut for Lancashire: 1899 v Sussex, Old Trafford.
73 matches for Lancashire 1899-1903 (professional).
HS: 38* v Yorkshire, Old Trafford, 1899.
BB: 8-36 v MCC, Lord's. 1902.
100 wickets (1); 112 (23.18) 1901 best.
First-class debut: 1897, Middlesex v Nottinghamshire, Trent Bridge.
9 matches for Middlesex 1897-98.
Played for Griqualand West 1904-05 whilst coaching in South Africa.
Full first-class record: 554 runs (7.01); 59 catches; 302 wickets (20.17).

Sid Webb joined Lancashire after playing for his native Middlesex and his results were so impressive that it is something of a surprise that he left the county before the age of 30. Possibly his fielding was below par; certainly his batting was not good, but overall it seems to be a

mystery. Webb had a number of professional engagements. Before joining the Manchester groundstaff he was at Newport (Mon) and Taunton with Somerset. In 1903-04 he went to South Africa and joined Western Province CC.

WEBSTER, Fred

LHB; LFM.
Born: Accrington, Lancashire, 7 May 1897.
Died: Burnley, Lancashire, 28 July 1931, aged 34.
First-class debut: 1925, Lancashire v Northamptonshire, Northampton.
2 matches for Lancashire 1925-27 (professional).
HS: 10 v Northamptonshire (debut).

BB: 3-34 v Gloucestershire, Bristol, 1927.

Fred Webster was a professional with Leyland Motors and Lowerhouse.

WHARMBY, George Edward

RHB; RM.
Born: Sutton-in-Ashfield, Nottinghamshire, 7 December 1870.
Died: Rustington, Sussex, 15 November 1951, aged 80.
Debut for Lancashire: 1894 v MCC, Lord's.
6 matches for Lancashire 1894 (professional).
HS: 11 v Oxford University, Old Trafford, 1894.
BB: 3-35 v Sussex, Old Trafford, 1894.
First-class debut: 1891, Nottinghamshire v MCC, Lord's.
4 matches for Nottinghamshire 1891-93.

George Wharmby played most successfully for Bedfordshire in the Minor Counties Championship 1902-23. Other engagements are as follows:; Lasswade CC, Bedford School, Manchester CC, RAF Cranwell. He was also professional with Coventry and North Warwickshire, when he was 'mine host' of a neighbouring pub, the Bull's Head.

WHARTON, Alan

LHB; RMF.
Born: Heywood, Lancashire, 30 April 1923.

Education: Colne Grammar School.
First-class debut: 1946, Lancashire v Cambridge University, Cambridge.
392 matches for Lancashire 1946-60. (professional). Capped 1946. Benefit £4,352) 1958.
HS: 199 v Sussex, Hove, 1959.

BB: 7-33 v Sussex, Old Trafford, 1951.
1,000 runs (9); 2,157 (40.60) 1959 best.
Shared unbroken 1st-wicket stands with Jack Dyson in both innings v Leicestershire, Old Trafford, 1956, when Lancashire won by 10 wickets.
79 matches for Leicestershire 1961-63. Capped 1961.
1 Test for England 1949 v New Zealand, Headingley. HS: 13.

Alan Wharton was an atractive left-handed batsman who perhaps achieved his best work as an opener. He was also a useful seam bowler who sometimes perhaps surprised himself with regard to penetration and effectiveness. He was unlucky to have only one chance in Test cricket. Wharton, an educated man, a JP and in some views a distruptive influence in the dressing-room, left the county after refusing the 2nd XI leadership and went on to score valuable runs for Leicestershire. He also played Rugby League for Salford.

WHATMOUGH, Thomas

RHB; RF (round-arm).
Born: Manchester, 26 March 1844.
Died: Newton Heath, Manchester, 19 March 1911, aged 66.
First-class debut: 1871, Lancashire v Derbyshire, Old Trafford.
2 matches for Lancashire 1871 (professional).
HS: 28* v Derbyshire (debut).
BB: 2-52 v Derbyshire (debut).

Until 1873, Whatmough was engaged with Manchester CC. He subsequently moved to Stockport and played for Cheshire.

WHEWELL, John William

RHB; WK.
Born: Rishton, Lancashire, 8 May 1887.
Died: Blackpool, Lancashire, 2 July 1948, aged 61.
First-class debut: 1921, Lancashire v Leicestershire, Old Trafford.
12 matches for Lancashire 1921-27. (professional).
HS for Lancashire: 12 v Hampshire, Bournemouth, 1922.
HS: 25 Players v Gentlemen, Blackpool, 1924.
Full first-class record: 54 runs (4.90); 14 catches; 7 stumped.

Whewell, a 'jack-in-the-box' character, was engaged at Blackpool.

WHITEHEAD, Ralph

RHB; RMF.
Born: Ashton-under-Lyne, Lancashire, 16 October 1883.
Died: Winwick, Lancashire, 23 August 1956, aged 72.
First-class debut: 1908, Lancashire v Nottinghamshire, Old Trafford.
107 matches for Lancashire 1908-14 (professional). Capped 1908.
HS: 131* v Nottinghamshire, Old Trafford, 1908.
BB: 8-77 v Yorkshire, Hull, 1914.

Ralph Whitehead made an amazing start to his county career, scoring 131* in his first innings,

but was later called five times by umpire Tom Brown for doubtful deliveries. Fortunately Whitehead, a tall and graceful batsman and lively swing bowler, got over the trauma and showed valuable all-round form until World War One. As a professional, Whitehead played in the Lancashire League for Enfield and East Lancashire.

WHITEHEAD, Thomas

RHB.
Born: 1852.
Died: Brindle, Preston, Lancashire, 2 November 1937.

First-class debut: 1884, Lancashire v Kent, Maidstone.
1 match for Lancashire 1884 (professional).
HS: 8 v Kent (debut).

Tom Whitehead was a professional at Liverpool.

WHITELEY, Peter

RHB; SLA.
Born: Rochdale, Lancashire, 12 August 1935.
Died: Crompton, Lancashire (whilst playing golf), 28 October 1989, aged 53.
First-class debut: 1957, Lancashire v Nottinghamshire, Old Trafford.

5 matches for Lancashire 1957-58 (professional).
HS: 32 v Hampshire, Old Trafford, 1957.
BB: 3-70 v West Indians, Old Trafford, 1957.

Whiteley played variously for Crompton, Milnrow and Harrogate.

WHITESIDE, John Parkinson

RHB; WK.
Born: Fleetwood, Lancashire, 11 June 1861.
Died: Leicester, 8 March 1946, aged 84.
First-class debut: 1888, Lancashire v Sussex, Old Trafford.
6 matches for Lancashire 1888-90. (professional).
HS for Lancashire: 12 v MCC, Lord's, 1890.
215 matches for for Leicestershire 1894-1906 (professional).
HS: 50 Leicestershire v Hampshire, Leicester, 1899.

Full first-class record: 1,362 runs (6.16); 340 catches; 98 stumped.

John Whiteside was an excellent wicketkeeper who gave Leicestershire valuable service for many years. Whiteside was also engaged at Lord's from 1887 to 1920, when he was granted a benefit.

WHITTAKER, David

LHB; LM.
Born: Church, Lancashire, 25 October 1857.
Died: Rishton, Lancashire, 17 December 1901, aged 44.
First-class debut: 1884, Lancashire v Gloucestershire, Old Trafford.
9 matches for Lancashire 1884-88 (professional).
HS: 26 v Somerset, Taunton, 1884.

BB: 1-26 v Somerset, Taunton, 1884.

David Whittaker, who played for Rishton, Enfield and Ramsbottom, was a left-handed all-rounder whose last match, for Lancashire v Surrey at Old Trafford in 1888, occured because Joe Eccles cried off and Whittaker was at the game as a spectator. He played on the first day in borrowed gear and contributed a 'pair'. Poor Whittaker came to a sad end, his body being found in a canal at Rishton.

WHITTAKER, Edwin

RHB; WK.
Born: Ashton-under-Lyne, Lancashire, 4 December 1834.
Died: Matlock, Derbyshire, 25 June 1880, aged 45.
Education: Wesley College, Sheffield.
Debut for Lancashire: 1865 v Middlesex, Old Trafford.
11 matches for Lancashire 1865-68 (amateur).
HS: 39 v Middlesex (debut).
BB: 1-26 v Middlesex, Old Trafford, 1866.

Edwin Whittaker, whose first-class debut was for The North v The South at Old Trafford, in 1863, played for Ashton-underLyne CC, eventually becoming President.

WILKINSON, Leonard Litton

RHB; LBG.
Born: Northwich, Cheshire, 5 November 1916.
First-class debut: 1937, Lancashire v New Zealanders, Old Trafford.
63 matches for Lancashire 1937-47 (professional). Capped 1938.
HS: 48 v Worcestershire, Old Trafford, 1938.
BB: 8-53 v Hampshire, Old Trafford, 1939.
100 wickets (1); 145 (22.97) 1938.
Hat-trick v Sussex, Hove, 1938.
3 Tests for England 1938-39. HS: 2 v South Africa, Johannesburg, 1938-39. BB: 2-12 v South Africa, Durban, 1938-39. Test record: 3 runs (3.00); 7 wickets (38.71).
Tour: MCC to South Africa 1938-39.
Full first-class record: 321 runs (7.64); 53 catches; 282 wickets (25.25).

Len Wilkinson's wonderful form in 1938 marked him down as the best young spinner in England; a total of 151 wickets in all first-class matches by a 21-year-old spinner was unprecedented in modern cricket. However, Wilkinson seemed to lose his edge midway through the MCC tour of South Africa and he never regained it. A hand injury also hindered him in 1939 but Wilkinson's own theory for his loss of form was that he strove for perfection. Wilkinson's form after the war was disastrous, and cartilage trouble was no help.

His career started with Heaton, and later he was engaged with Burnley and Barrow. It is fair to say that in later years he has been virtually forgotten; he lost his bowling completely before he was 30, yet he did take over 150 wickets when he was only 21. And he did play for England.

WILSON, Alan

RHB; WK.
Born: Newton-le-Willows, Lancashire, 24 April 1920.
First-class debut: 1948, Lancashire v Australians, Old Trafford.
171 matches for Lancashire 1948-62 (professional). Capped 1951. Testimonial (£4,023) 1962.
HS: 37* v Leicestershire, Old Trafford, 1958.

Alan Wilson, nicknamed 'Ranji', which was presumably a tongue-in-cheek comment on his batting ability, was a most talented wicketkeeper who was always being replaced at Old Trafford,

Debut for Lancashire: 1966, Lancashire v Essex, Colchester.
260 matches for Lancashire 1966-79. Capped 1968. Benefit (£62,429) 1979.
HS: 198 v Glamorgan, Liverpool, 1976.
BB: 7-52 v Middlesex, Old Trafford, 1968.
1,000 runs (7); 1,492 (38.25) 1971 best.
First-class debut: 1964, Yorkshire v Somerset, Middlesbrough.
5 matches for Yorkshire (professional) 1964.
63 matches for Derbyshire 1980-83. Capped 1980. Captain 1981-82.
Played for Eastern Province (South Africa) 1971-72 to 1973-74.
12 Tests for England 1972-78. HS: 90 v Australia, The Oval, 1972 (debut). Test record: 454 runs (21.61); 6 catches.
13 limited-overs matches for England.
Tours: England to India, Pakistan and Sri Lanka 1972-73; England to New Zealand 1974-75; International Wanderers to Rhodesia 1975-76.
Full first-class record: 17,453 runs (33.82); 30 centuries; 283 catches; 298 wickets (30.93).

and then brought back when the successor fell by the wayside. 'Ranji' was a first-rate team man, and a most popular player. After his final departure he played for Stockport.

WINDER, George Alexander
RHB.
Born: Bolton, Lancashire, 16 July 1850.
Died: Fairmile, Ottery St Mary, Devon, 1 February 1913, aged 62.
Education: Rossall; Cambridge University.
First-class debut: 1869, Lancashire v MCC, Lord's.
2 matches for Lancashire 1869 (amateur).
HS for Lancashire: 9 v Surrey, The Oval, 1869.
1 match for Cambridge University 1871.
1 match for Gentlemen of North v Gentlemen of South, Lillee Bridge, 1871.
HS: 22 Gentlemen of North (above match).
Full first-class record: 64 runs (9.14); 1 catch.

This most attractive batsman saw his cricket career destroyed when, in January 1872, whilst out shooting, his gun went off accidentally, and so badly was his left hand injured that it had to be amputated. Despite that handicap, he continued to play minor cricket for many years afterwards.

WOOD, Barry
RHB; RM.
Born: Ossett, Yorkshire, 26 December 1942.

Barry Wood was a really brave and combative cricketer, the sort of player any captain longs for. A sound batsman, he was most suited to opening since he preferred the pace bowlers, who were sometimes hooked savagely if they misbehaved. He was also a lively medium-pacer with an interesting action which involved a mighty

Barry Wood, pictured with the 1978 squad. Back row (left to right): Wood, Arrowsmith, Trim, Scott, Abrahams, Reidy. Middle row: Savage (coach), Clive Lloyd, Kennedy, Lyon, Hogg, Ratcliffe. Front row: David Lloyd, Hughes, Pilling, Hayes, Simmons, Lee.

leap on delivery. He was also an excellent fielder.

Sadly, though, Barry Wood was something of a controversial figure. In 1975 he, along with Hayes and Lever, 'struck' for more money on the morning of a county match. That Wood received a six-match suspension, as opposed to two matches for the others, suggests that Wood was regarded as the ringleader. More controversy followed in 1979 when, after a magnificent benefit, he demanded more money to re-sign for 1980. Lancashire declined and he joined Derbyshire.

At the County Ground, Wood was reasonably successful and helped Derbyshire to the 1981 NatWest Bank Trophy, their first major honour since 1936. But again there were rumblings in the dressing-room and this excellent county cricketer left under another cloud. He later played for Cheshire in the Minor Counties Championship.

WOOD, James
RHB; LB.
Born: Burnley, Lancashire, 26 June 1933.

Died: Blackpool, 30 June 1977, aged 44.
First-class debut: 1956, Lancashire v Oxford University, Oxford.

1 matches for Lancashire 1956 (professional).
Did not bat.
BB: 3-56 v Oxford University (debut).

James Wood, who played for Castleton Moor, Royton, Burnley and Blackley, was unlucky not to be given further opportunities for the county. His brother John (Aldershot) and father James (West Ham United) were both professional soccer players. James Wood the cricketer died at his home with terrible suddenness, aged only 44, sitting in his armchair.

WOOD, Reginald

LHB; LM.
Born: Woodchurch, Cheshire, 7 March 1860.
Died: Manly, New South Wales, 6 January 1915, aged 54.
Education: Charterhouse.
First-class debut: 1880, Lancashire v Kent, Old Trafford.
6 matches for Lancashire 1880-84 (amateur).
HS: 52 v Surrey, Old Trafford, 1881.
BB: 1-23 v Kent, Old Trafford, 1880.
Played for Victoria 1886-87.
1 Test for England 1886-87. Scored 6 and 0 v Australia, Sydney.
Full first-class record: 235 runs (15.66); 4 catches; 8 wickets (16.74).

Reginald Wood was a most interesting personality who eventually became one of England's least-known and most elusive Test players. Having emigrated to Australia, he played as a professional for East Melbourne and Albert CC (Sydney), as well as for Victoria. He was roped-in by England as deputy for Billy Barnes, who had hurt his hand whilst fighting with the Australian skipper. Wood eventually disappeared, finding life quite hard before his death in 1915.

WORSLEY, Duncan Robert

LHB; RM.
Born: Bolton, Lancashire, 18 July 1941.
Education: Bolton School; St Edmund Hall, Oxford.
First-class debut: 1960, Lancashire v South Africans, Blackpool.
62 matches for Lancashire 1960-67. Capped 1966.
HS for Lancashire: 120 v Sussex, Eastbourne, 1964.
BB: 4-21 v Leicestershire, Leicester, 1966.
Played for Oxford University 1961-64 (Blue each year). Captain 1964.
HS: 139 Oxford University v Middlesex, Oxford, 1961.

Full first-class record: 5,062 runs (26.09); 4 centuries; 37 wickets (41.08).

Duncan Worsley was a sound player with an impeccable background and a man who, in other circumstances than the period in which he played, might have been seen as a county captain. He also turned out for Bradshaw CC.

WOOLLEY, Albert

RHB; RFM.
Born: Salford, Manchester, 26 September 1902.
Died: Doncaster, Yorkshire, 5 January 1978, aged 75.
First-class debut: 1926, Lancashire v Northamptonshire, Kettering.
7 matches for Lancashire 1926 (professional).
HS: 24 v Sussex, Hove, 1926.
BB: 4-56 v Hampshire, Bournemouth, 1926.

Albert Woolley had professional engagements at Heaton and Thornham.

WORSLEY, William

RHB; WK.
Born: Wandsworth, London, 11 September 1869.
Died: Accrington, Lancashire, 13 November 1918, aged 49.
First-class debut: 1903, Lancashire v Warwickshire, Edgbaston.
136 matches for Lancashire 1903-13 (professional).
HS: 37* v Nottinghamshire, Trent Bridge, 1905.

Bill Worsley was an excellent wicketkeeper, though sometimes inclined to be 'flash' and, more important, subject to repeated hand injuries. Worsley also received star billing in one of Sir Neville Cardus' more pleasing pieces of cricket fiction, in Autobiography. He played for Accrington and Church before joining Lancashire.

WRIGHT, Egerton Lowndes

RHB; WK.
Born: Chorley, Lancashire, 15 November 1885.
Died: Barly, France, 11 May 1918 (killed in action), aged 32.
Education: Winchester; New College, Oxford.
Debut for Lancashire: 1905 v Gloucestershire, Bristol.
4 matches for Lancashire 1905-10 (amateur).
HS for Lancashire: 17 v Gloucestershire (debut).
Played for Oxford University 1905-08 (Blue each year). Captain 1907-08.
HS: 95 Oxford University v Cambridge University, Lord's 1905.

Full first-class record: 1,638 runs (24.81); 26 catches; 3 stumped.

A brilliant schoolboy batsman, Wright scarcely fulfilled his promise in the first-class game but enjoyed an excellent reputation as a cricketer at Oxford, where he also won a soccer Blue.

WRIGHT, Frank Wynyard

RHB.
Born: Woodstock, Oxfordshire, 6 April 1844.
Died: Eastbourne, Sussex, 15 February 1924, aged 79.
Education: Rossall; St John's College, Oxford.
Debut for Lancashire: 1869 v Surrey, Old Trafford.
15 matches for Lancashire 1869-75 (amateur).
HS: 120* v Sussex, Old Trafford, 1869.
BB: 2-44 v Sussex, Old Trafford, 1869.
Played for Oxford University 1863-65. (Blue 1863-64-65).
First-class debut: Gentlemen of North v Gentlemen of South, The Oval, 1861.
Full first-class record: 917 runs (17.30); 1 century; 3 wickets (52.00).

Frank Wright was a useful, batsman with a free style who may have done better had he played more often. Ordained into the Anglican Church, he became curate at Broughton, Manchester, but he subsequently took up tuition at Eastbourne. Whilst there, playing for the Masters v Colleges & Schools at Devonshire Park, in 1876, he scored 307* in one innings. His father, F.B.Wright, also played for Oxford University.

YATES, Calvert

Batsman.
Born: Oswaldtwistle, Lancashire, 28 November 1851.
Died: Church, Lancashire, 10 June 1904, aged 52.
First-class debut: 1882, Lancashire v Yorkshire, Old Trafford.
1 match for Lancashire 1882 (professional).
HS: 24 v Yorkshire (debut).

Calvert Yates appeared for 22 Colts of England v MCC, Lord's, 1880.

YATES, Gary

RHB; OB.
Born: Manchester, 20 September 1967.
Education: Oundle.
First-class debut: 1990, Lancashire v Zimbabwe, Old Trafford.
5 matches for Lancashire 1990.
HS: 106 v Nottinghamshire, Trent Bridge, 1990 (Championship debut).
BB: 4-94 v Sri Lankans, Old Trafford, 1990.

YATES, George

RHB; RF (round arm).
Born: Haslingden, Lancashire, 6 June 1856.
Died: Marple, Cheshire, 21 August 1925, aged 69.
First-class debut: 1885, Lancashire v Surrey, Liverpool.

92 matches for Lancashire 1885-94 (professional).
HS: 74 v Kent, Tonbridge, 1892.
BB: 4-112 v Yorkshire, Bradford, 1887.

George Yates was a stylish batsman who played for a number of years for Lancashire without really making a mark. He was engaged at Colchester in 1878, then Werneth and finally at Old Trafford in 1887.

The following two players appeared in limited-overs cricket for Lancashire without making their first-class debut.

BECKETT, Douglas Keith
RHB.
Born: Hampton Court, Middlesex, 29 August 1959.
Education: Cheadle High School; Manchester University.

Beckett made his limited-overs debut in 1980.

WORSICK, Alan
RHB; RM.
Born: Rawtenstall, Lancashire, 13 August 1943.
Education: Aston Grammar School.

Worsick appeared in the John Player League in 1978. He was professional with Accrington CC.

Career Averages in all First-Class Lancashire Matches 1865-1990

Name	Played	Matches	Inns	NO	Runs	HS	Ave	100s	Runs	Wkts	Ave	Best	Ct/St
Abrahams J.	1973-1988	251	388	52	9,980	201*	29.70	14	2,811	56	50.19	3/27	162
Ainscough T.	1894-1906	2	3	0	40	24	13.33	-	-	-	-	-	1
Ainsworth J.L.	1899	4	6	1	17	11	3.40	-	289	18	16.05	6/84	4
Alderson R.	1948-1949	2	2	0	55	55	27.50	-	-	-	-	-	-
Allott P.J.W.	1978-1990	196	214	50	2,814	88	17.15	-	12,918	535	24.14	8/48	113
Appleby A.	1866-1887	58	93	14	1,052	99	13.31	-	3,474	245	14.17	9/25	44/1
Arnold J.F.	1896	3	5	0	94	37	18.80	-	-	-	-	-	-
Arrowsmith R.	1976-1979	43	40	12	286	39	10.21	-	2,796	99	28.24	6/29	13
Ashworth J.T.	1871-1873	2	3	0	28	19	9.33	-	-	-	-	-	-
Atherton M.A.	1987-1990	39	66	10	2,679	191	47.83	8	1,975	56	35.26	6/78	29
Atkinson G.	1967-1969	62	99	9	2,468	124	27.42	5	24	1	24.00	1/19	23
Austin I.D.	1987-1990	31	40	11	704	64	24.27	-	1,610	54	29.81	5/79	2
Bailey D.	1968-1969	27	36	1	845	136	24.14	1	-	-	-	-	10
Baker G.R.	1887-1899	228	350	29	7,710	186	22.33	4	3,475	138	25.18	6/18	142
Banham S.T.	1939	1	-	-	-	-	-	-	-	-	-	-	1
Barber H.W.	1866-1867	3	6	0	41	15	6.83	-	-	-	-	-	3
Barber J.B.	1874-1876	3	6	3	39	12*	13.00	-	-	-	-	-	2
Barber R.W.	1954-1962	155	264	25	6,760	175	28.28	7	4,768	152	31.36	7/35	70
Barchard H.G.	1888	1	2	0	45	40	22.50	-	-	-	-	-	1
Barcroft P.	1956	3	3	0	40	29	13.33	-	-	-	-	-	1

Name	Played	Matches	Inns	NO	Runs	HS	Ave	100s	Runs	Wkts	Ave	Best	Ct/St
Bardsley R.V.	1910-1920	7	8	0	46	15	5.75	-	23	0	-	-	-
Bardswell G.R.	1894-1902	21	28	1	429	50	15.88	-	342	8	42.75	4/37	32
Barlow A.	1947-1951	74	87	20	707	44	10.55	-	-	-	-	-	104/47
Barlow E.A.	1932	7	8	1	84	40	12.00	-	389	12	32.41	4/33	4
Barlow R.G.	1871-1891	249	426	45	7,765	117	20.38	2	10,010	736	13.60	9/39	197
Barnes J.R.	1919-1930	89	136	22	3,271	123*	28.69	3	53	0	-	-	39
Barnes S.F.	1899-1903	46	58	20	452	35	11.89	-	4,459	225	19.81	8/37	20
Barrell B.	1911-1923	3	3	1	45	25	22.50	-	135	9	15.00	3/10	1
Barron W.	1945	1	2	0	3	2	1.50	-	-	-	-	-	-
Baucher F.W.	1903	1	2	0	12	8	6.00	-	-	-	-	-	-
Baxter A.D.	1933-1934	3	1	0	0	0	0.00	-	208	16	13.00	6/50	-
Beattie F.D.	1932	5	9	1	120	36	15.00	-	-	-	-	-	-
Beddow A.M.	1962-1966	33	54	3	775	112*	15.19	1	473	15	31.53	3/10	14
Bennett A.	1932-1933	16	14	1	238	51	18.30	-	865	24	36.04	4/49	12
Bennett H.S.	1894	1	2	0	16	11	8.00	-	-	-	-	-	4
Bennett R.	1962-1966	49	82	3	1,814	112	22.96	2	49	0	-	-	13
Benton C.H.	1892-1901	29	50	6	663	68	15.06	-	-	-	-	-	15
Berry R.	1948-1954	93	85	34	427	27*	8.37	-	5,900	259	22.77	10/102	53
Biddulph G.H.	1885	1	2	0	19	18	9.50	-	13	0	-	-	1
Bigg G.A.	1887	1	1	0	16	16	16.00	-	13	1	13.00	1/13	-
Bird G.	1880	1	2	0	0	0	0.00	-	-	-	-	-	-
Bird M.C.	1907	5	10	0	36	10	3.60	-	84	4	21.00	2/9	4
Birley F.H.	1870-1872	4	6	1	58	18	11.60	-	120	4	30.00	3/76	1
Birtwell A.J.	1937-1939	14	16	6	103	31	10.30	-	999	25	39.96	4/78	12
Blackledge J.F.	1962	26	41	4	569	68	15.37	-	10	0	-	-	9
Blackstock R.	1865	1	2	0	23	18	11.50	-	-	-	-	-	1
Blake W.	1877	1	1	0	26	26	26.00	-	-	-	-	-	-
Bleackley E.O.	1919	2	3	0	31	21	10.33	-	-	-	-	-	-

Name	Played	Matches	Inns	NO	Runs	HS	Ave	100s	Runs	Wkts	Ave	Best	Ct/St
Blomley R.	1903-1922	69	87	32	316	41	5.74	-	-	-	-	-	109/33
Boddington R.A.	1913-1924	52	75	19	663	58*	11.83	-	-	-	-	-	72/21
Boden R.G.	1907	1	2	0	8	5	4.00	-	-	-	-	-	-
Bolton A.	1957-1961	40	71	6	1,223	96	18.81	-	80	2	40.00	1/17	15
Bond J.D.	1955-1972	344	522	76	11,867	157	26.60	14	69	0	-	-	217
Booth A.	1950-1951	4	5	0	81	49	16.20	-	-	-	-	-	1
Booth B.J.	1956-1963	117	210	17	5,075	183*	26.29	5	3,183	106	30.02	7/143	47
Booth F.S.	1927-1937	140	157	25	1,330	54	10.07	-	11,180	457	24.46	7/59	56
Bousfield E.J.	1865-1878	12	21	2	279	32	14.68	-	-	-	-	-	20/5
Bowden E.	1914	4	6	0	27	10	4.50	-	453	12	37.75	6/78	5
Bower W.H.	1885-1886	4	6	0	45	23	7.50	-	-	-	-	-	1
Bowes J.B.	1938-1948	10	13	1	106	39	8.83	-	602	21	28.66	4/103	6
Bowling K.	1954	1	2	1	7	4*	7.00	-	-	-	-	-	-
Bowman R.	1957-1959	9	12	1	189	58	17.18	-	459	11	41.72	2/28	8
Boyes R.	1877	1	2	1	13	10	13.00	-	-	-	-	-	2
Bradbury T.F.	1881	1	2	1	6	6*	6.00	-	-	-	-	-	1
Braddock J.	1873	1	2	0	13	11	6.50	-	-	-	-	-	-
Brearley W.	1902-1911	106	145	23	749	38	6.13	-	12,907	690	18.70	9/47	44
Bramhall S.	1990	2	3	2	1	1*	-	-	-	-	-	-	1/2
Brierley T.L.	1946-1948	46	62	8	1,286	116*	23.81	1	12	0	-	-	61/19
Briggs J.	1879-1900	391	602	39	10,707	186	19.01	9	26,464	1,696	15.60	10/55	185
Briggs J.	1939	4	4	2	0	0*	-	-	391	10	39.10	4/48	2
Brocklebank J.M.	1939	4	4	1	5	4	1.66	-	279	5	55.80	3/61	2
Brooke F.R.R.	1912-1913	29	35	0	566	61	16.17	-	9	1	9.00	1/9	46/11
Brooks A.W.	1877	1	1	0	6	6	6.00	-	-	-	-	-	2
Broughton J.J.	1901-1902	6	7	0	153	99	21.85	-	69	2	34.50	2/28	3
Brown W.	1894	2	3	0	17	7	5.66	-	12	0	-	-	1
Brown W.	1919-1922	10	17	2	239	39	15.93	-	474	22	21.54	4/22	10

Name	Played	Matches	Inns	NO	Runs	HS	Ave	100s	Runs	Wkts	Ave	Best	Ct/St
Bulcock L.	1946	1	1	0	1	1	1.00	-	90	2	45.00	2/41	-
Bullough J.	1914-1919	8	8	3	24	17	4.80	-	573	13	44.07	5/123	2
Burrows W.	1867-1873	14	26	1	255	39	10.20	-	6	0	-	-	2
Burton C.	1956	2	1	0	0	0	0.00	-	80	0	-	-	2
Butterworth H.R.W.	1931-1936	25	34	5	584	107	20.13	1	1,392	36	38.66	6/85	15
Butterworth W.S.	1876-1882	9	14	1	73	22	5.61	-	-	-	-	-	4
Campbell G.A.	1866	1	2	0	18	10	9.00	-	-	-	-	-	-
Carlisle F.	1869	2	4	0	37	18	9.25	-	-	-	-	-	-
Chadwick E.L.	1875-1881	13	24	3	254	42	12.09	-	-	-	-	-	2
Chadwick M.R.	1983-1987	33	56	1	1,197	132	21.76	1	71	0	-	-	15
Champion A.	1886	1	2	0	4	4	2.00	-	-	-	-	-	1
Chappell I.M.	1963	1	1	0	3	3	3.00	-	-	-	-	-	-
Clarke J.	1905	1	1	0	0	0	0.00	-	35	0	-	-	-
Clayton G.	1959-1964	183	277	49	4,382	84	19.21	-	-	-	-	-	390/32
Cockbain I.	1979-1983	46	78	9	1,456	98	21.10	-	14	0	-	-	22
Cole T.G.O.	1904	1	1	0	0	0	0.00	-	-	-	-	-	1
Collins R.	1954-1962	119	181	18	3,332	107*	20.44	2	4,782	159	30.07	6/63	79
Cook L.W.	1907-1923	203	258	91	2,051	54*	12.28	-	17,537	821	21.36	8/39	136
Cook W.	1905-1907	11	17	3	307	46	21.92	-	946	51	18.54	7/64	4
Cooke N.H.	1958-1959	12	16	0	242	33	15.12	-	93	3	31.00	2/10	2
Cooper F.	1946	4	8	2	96	33*	16.00	-	-	-	-	-	2
Copeland W.	1885	1	2	1	21	21*	21.00	-	23	1	23.00	1/23	-
Corlett S.	1871-1875	2	3	0	6	4	2.00	-	-	-	-	-	-
Coulthurst J.	1919	1	-	-	-	-	-	-	-	-	-	-	-
Coward C.	1865-1876	36	65	2	912	85	14.47	-	44	0	-	-	12
Coward F.	1867-1868	7	13	1	35	9	2.91	-	-	-	-	-	4
Cownley J.M.	1962	2	4	0	45	25	11.25	-	36	2	18.00	2/36	1
Crabtree F.	1890	1	1	0	1	1	1.00	-	-	-	-	-	1

Name	Played	Matches	Inns	NO	Runs	HS	Ave	100s	Runs	Wkts	Ave	Best	Ct/St
Crabtree H.	1902-1908	5	8	0	116	49	14.50	-	34	0	-	-	1
Cragg J.S.	1908	1	2	0	10	9	5.00	-	-	-	-	-	-
Craig E.J.	1961-1962	6	11	1	214	89	21.40	-	-	-	-	-	5
Craig W.R.	1874	1	2	0	8	7	4.00	-	-	-	-	-	-
Cranston K.	1947-1948	50	57	9	1,928	155*	40.16	2	3,267	142	23.00	7/43	32
Crawley J.P.	1990	3	3	1	103	76*	51.50	-	-	-	-	-	1
Crawley M.A.	1990	1	2	0	90	48	45.00	-	25	0	-	-	-
Croft C.E.H.	1977-1982	49	50	10	433	46*	10.82	-	3,604	136	26.50	7/54	8
Crooke F.J.	1865	1	2	0	55	35	27.50	-	-	-	-	-	-
Crosfield S.M.	1883-1899	90	140	13	1,909	82*	15.03	-	111	2	55.50	1/1	46
Crossland J.	1878-1885	71	109	21	1,002	48*	11.38	-	3,125	245	12.75	7/14	29
Cudworth H.	1900	1	1	0	4	4	4.00	-	-	-	-	-	-
Cumbes J.	1963-1971	9	5	4	5	5	5.00	-	563	19	29.63	4/42	3
Cuttell W.R.	1896-1906	213	294	30	5,389	137	20.41	5	14,890	760	19.59	8/105	128
Davidson I.C.	1985-1987	2	4	0	14	13	3.50	-	85	4	21.25	2/24	2
Davies H.D.	1924-1925	11	15	0	260	46	17.33	-	-	-	-	-	4
Dean H.	1906-1921	256	354	118	2,448	49*	10.37	-	22,828	1,267	18.01	9/31	115
DeFreitas P.A.J.	1989-	33	46	5	1,175	102	28.65	2	1,687	69	24.44	7/21	9
Deighton J.H.G.	1948-50	7	9	1	206	79	25.75	-	509	20	25.45	5/52	3
de Trafford C.E.	1884	1	1	0	0	0	0.00	-	-	-	-	-	2
Dewhurst R.	1872-1875	13	22	1	267	59	12.71	-	-	-	-	-	8
Dickinson T.E.	1950-1951	4	5	3	10	9	5.00	-	98	3	32.66	1/20	2
Dixon J.	1878	1	2	0	2	2	1.00	-	-	-	-	-	-
Dobell P.	1886-1887	7	12	1	96	28	8.72	-	-	-	-	-	1
Douthwaite H.	1920-1921	3	5	0	85	29	17.00	-	-	-	-	-	1
Duckworth G.	1923-1938	424	455	170	4,174	75	14.64	-	66	0	-	-	634/288
Dunlop G.C.H.	1868	1	2	0	17	16	8.50	-	-	-	-	-	-
Durandu A.	1887	1	1	0	5	5	5.00	-	-	-	-	-	-

Name	Played	Matches	Inns	NO	Runs	HS	Ave	100s	Runs	Wkts	Ave	Best	Ct/St
Dyson J.	1954-1964	150	242	35	4,433	118*	21.41	1	4,447	161	27.62	7/83	55
Eccles A.	1898-1907	123	196	20	4,179	139	23.74	4	30	0	-	-	80
Eccles H.	1885-1886	5	7	0	37	14	5.28	-	-	-	-	-	1
Eccles J.	1886-1889	47	75	5	1,787	184	25.52	2	38	0	-	-	16
Eckersley P.T.	1923-1935	256	293	45	4,588	102*	18.50	1	145	1	145.00	1/7	113
Edge C.A.	1936-1938	8	5	2	2	1	0.66	-	759	25	30.36	4/71	2
Edge H.E.	1913	1	1	0	3	3	3.00	-	101	0	-	-	4
Edmonds J.W.	1975	1	-	-	-	-	-	-	82	3	27.33	3/52	-
Edrich E.H.	1946-1948	33	40	4	854	121	23.72	2	-	-	-	-	37/14
Edrich G.A.	1946-1958	322	479	55	14,730	167*	34.74	24	199	2	99.50	1/19	320
Elliott H.	1930	1	1	0	4	4	4.00	-	-	-	-	-	2/1
Ellis J.	1892-1898	6	9	1	56	26*	7.00	-	240	21	11.42	8/21	-
Ellis S.	1923-1924	8	7	1	57	25	9.50	-	525	14	18.00	5/21	-
Ellis W.	1920-1923	36	55	4	846	138*	16.58	1	-	-	-	-	14
Engineer F.M.	1968-1976	175	262	39	5,942	141	26.64	4	10	0	-	-	429/35
Entwistle R.	1962-1966	48	79	4	1,554	85	20.72	-	-	-	-	-	16
Fairbrother N.H.	1982-1990	172	273	38	9,905	366	42.14	20	385	5	77.00	2/91	104
Fairclough P.M.	1911-1923	20	27	14	140	19	10.76	-	1,158	52	22.26	7/27	9
Fallows J.A.	1946	25	22	1	171	35	8.14	-	-	-	-	-	10
Farnsworth A.W.	1919	1	2	0	3	3	1.50	-	-	-	-	-	-
Farrar H.	1955	1	-	-	-	-	-	-	25	0	-	-	-
Farrar H.L.	1904	1	2	0	28	25	14.00	-	-	-	-	-	-
Farrimond W.	1924-1945	134	142	38	2,202	63	21.17	-	16	0	-	-	232/65
Findlay W.	1902-1906	58	82	20	1,223	81	19.72	-	15	0	-	-	101/12
Fitton J.D.	1987-1990	36	41	12	519	44	17.89	-	3,065	57	53.77	6/59	10
Folley I.	1982-1990	135	157	49	1,465	69	13.56	-	8,733	280	31.18	7/15	58
Fowler G.	1979-1990	204	342	23	11,877	226	37.23	26	211	6	35.16	2/34	118/5
Gaddum F.D.	1884	1	2	0	15	10	7.50	-	14	0	-	-	1

Name	Played	Matches	Inns	NO	Runs	HS	Ave	100s	Runs	Wkts	Ave	Best	Ct/St
Gallian J.E.R.	1990	1	1	1	17	17*	-	-	65	1	65.00	1/50	-
Garlick R.G.	1938-1947	44	56	7	753	50	15.36	-	2,797	120	23.30	6/27	16
Garnett H.G.	1899-1914	144	231	17	5,599	139	26.16	5	224	8	28.00	2/18	174/14
Gibson A.B.E.	1887	2	4	0	25	16	6.25	-	-	-	-	-	-
Gooch P.A.	1970	4	3	1	0	0*	0.00	-	252	6	42.00	4/52	3
Good A.J.	1973-1976	8	8	2	10	6	1.66	-	482	17	28.35	5/62	1
Goodwin F.	1955-1956	11	10	4	47	21*	7.83	-	715	27	26.48	5/35	7
Goodwin F.H.	1894	3	6	1	14	10	2.80	-	47	0	-	-	-
Goodwin K.	1960-1974	122	149	42	618	23	5.77	-	-	-	-	-	227/26
Green D.M.	1959-1967	135	242	10	6,086	138	26.23	4	1,849	41	45.09	3/6	40
Green L.	1922-1935	152	173	28	3,575	110*	24.65	1	299	9	33.22	2/2	36
Greenhalgh E.W.	1935-1938	14	18	5	366	53*	28.15	-	282	3	94.00	2/75	2
Greenhough T.	1951-1966	241	298	79	1,868	76*	8.52	-	15,540	707	21.98	7/56	81
Greenwood P.	1948-1952	75	92	15	1,270	113	16.49	1	5,090	208	24.47	6/35	22
Gregson W.R.	1906	5	7	1	62	26	10.33	-	428	24	17.83	5/8	-
Grieves K.J.	1949-1964	452	696	73	20,802	224	33.39	26	6,769	235	28.80	6/60	556/1
Grimshaw G.H.	1868	1	2	0	11	11	5.50	-	-	-	-	-	-
Haggas S.	1884-1885	3	5	0	59	18	11.80	-	-	-	-	-	-
Haggas W.	1903	2	2	0	6	4	3.00	-	-	-	-	-	3
Haigh C.H.	1879-1887	24	33	3	435	80	14.50	-	-	-	-	-	11
Hall A.E.	1923-1924	9	10	4	11	5*	1.83	-	630	24	26.25	6/23	-
Hallam A.W.	1895-1900	71	93	25	570	31*	8.38	-	4,063	211	19.25	6/28	44
Halliday T.M.	1925-1929	41	55	11	996	109*	22.63	1	16	0	-	-	12
Hallows C.	1914-1932	370	569	62	20,142	233*	39.72	52	784	19	41.26	3/28	135
Hallows J.	1898-1907	138	202	27	4,997	137*	28.55	8	6,610	279	23.69	9/37	57
Hardcastle F.	1867-1869	3	6	1	23	9	4.60	-	-	-	-	-	1
Hardcastle W.M.	1869-1874	4	7	0	33	11	4.71	-	-	-	-	-	1
Hargreaves F.W.	1881	1	1	0	0	0	0.00	-	-	-	-	-	2

Name	Played	Matches	Inns	NO	Runs	HS	Ave	100s	Runs	Wkts	Ave	Best	Ct/St
Harper G.M.	1883	1	1	0	1	1	1.00	-	-	-	-	-	-
Harrison F.	1936	3	3	1	4	2*	2.00	-	118	4	29.50	2/30	3
Harrop J.	1874	1	2	0	5	5	2.50	-	14	0	-	-	-
Harry F.	1903-1908	69	106	9	1,528	88	15.75	-	3,795	207	18.33	9/44	37
Hartley A.	1907-1914	112	185	9	4,963	234	28.20	6	61	1	61.00	1/39	39
Hartley C.R.	1897-1909	106	168	11	3,729	139	23.75	4	53	0	-	-	56
Hartley F.	1924-1945	2	1	0	2	2	2.00	-	44	1	44.00	1/44	-
Hartley G.	1871-1872	3	3	0	37	24	12.33	-	-	-	-	-	2
Harwood B.	1877	1	2	2	0	0*	-	-	16	1	16.00	1/16	2
Hawkwood C.	1931-1935	24	26	5	596	113	28.38	1	92	1	92.00	1/63	9
Hayes F.C.	1970-1984	228	339	48	10,899	187	37.45	22	11	0	-	-	150
Hayes K.A.	1980-1986	18	24	1	586	117	25.47	1	25	0	-	-	6
Hayhurst A.N.	1985-1989	42	63	6	1,185	107	20.78	1	1,644	49	33.55	4/27	10
Head F.S.	1868-1869	6	10	0	75	24	7.50	-	-	-	-	-	2
Heap J.G.	1884	2	2	0	0	0	0.00	-	4	0	-	-	2
Heap J.S.	1903-1921	210	312	41	5,146	132*	18.98	1	9,513	412	23.08	9/43	76
Hegg W.K.	1986-1990	85	121	19	2,215	130	21.71	2	7	0	-	-	204/26
Henriksen S.	1985-1986	3	4	3	17	10*	17.00	-	105	2	52.50	1/26	2
Hewitson J.	1890	4	5	0	99	56	19.80	-	235	14	16.78	6/57	1
Heys W.	1957	5	7	0	74	46	10.57	-	-	-	-	-	5/3
Hibbard H.	1884	1	2	0	7	4	3.50	-	54	2	27.00	2/35	-
Hibberd G.	1867	1	2	1	4	2*	4.00	-	37	0	-	-	1
Hibbert W.J.	1900-1901	14	22	4	445	79	24.72	-	116	3	38.66	2/41	5
Hickmott W.E.	1923-1924	34	35	9	272	31*	10.46	-	2,042	82	24.90	5/20	23
Hickton W.	1867-1871	24	42	9	373	55	11.30	-	2,024	144	14.05	10/46	13
Higgs K.	1958-1969	306	374	131	2,655	60	10.92	-	23,661	1,033	22.90	7/19	155
Highton E.F.W.	1951	1	1	0	6	6	6.00	-	49	1	49.00	1/49	1
Higson P.	1929-1931	3	3	2	22	13*	22.00	-	-	-	-	-	2

Name	Played	Matches	Inns	NO	Runs	HS	Ave	100s	Runs	Wkts	Ave	Best	Ct/St
Higson T.A.	1905-1923	5	7	1	123	42	20.50	-	58	1	58.00	1/18	1
Higson T.A. Jnr	1936-1946	20	20	1	153	32*	8.05	-	302	6	50.33	1/14	6
Hildyard L.D.	1884-1885	8	13	1	174	39	14.50	-	-	-	-	-	6
Hill R.W.D.	1871	1	2	0	8	5	4.00	-	-	-	-	-	1
Hillkirk J.R.	1871-1877	30	46	4	596	56*	14.19	-	-	-	-	-	17/1
Hilton C.	1957-1963	91	110	35	537	36	7.16	-	7,039	263	26.76	6/38	28
Hilton J.	1952-1953	8	7	0	99	33	14.14	-	152	2	76.00	2/27	5
Hilton M.J.	1946-1961	241	294	35	3,140	100*	12.12	1	17,419	926	18.81	8/19	187
Hird S.F.	1939	1	-	-	-	-	-	-	-	-	-	-	-
Hodgson G.	1928-1933	56	52	17	244	20	6.97	-	4,107	148	27.75	6/77	37
Hodgson G.	1965	1	1	0	1	1	1.00	-	-	-	-	-	3
Hogg W.	1976-1980	44	40	12	120	19	4.28	-	2,960	122	24.26	7/84	8
Holden C.	1890	3	5	1	43	27*	10.75	-	11	0	-	-	1
Holding M.A.	1981	7	8	2	66	32	11.00	-	715	40	17.87	6/74	2
Holgate G.	1866-1867	8	15	1	281	65	20.07	-	-	-	-	7/9	-
Holland J.	1900-1902	12	21	4	324	63	19.05	-	-	-	-	-	6
Hollins F.H.	1902-1904	12	18	0	290	114	16.11	-	-	-	-	-	7
Hollins J.C.H.L.	1914-1919	20	30	0	454	65	15.13	-	99	1	99.00	1/45	8
Holroyd E.	1878	1	2	0	6	4	3.00	-	-	-	-	-	1
Holroyd J.	1927-1933	11	9	5	33	18*	8.25	-	652	23	28.34	5/47	2
Hopwood J.L.	1923-1939	397	571	54	15,519	220	30.01	27	14,905	672	22.18	9/33	197
Hornby A.H.	1899-1914	283	426	40	9,441	129	24.45	8	168	1	168.00	1/21	211/1
Hornby A.N.	1867-1899	292	467	28	10,649	188	24.25	10	94	3	31.33	1/2	217/2
Hornby C.L.	1877	1	2	0	4	4	2.00	-	3	1	3.00	1/3	2
Hornby E.C.	1885-1887	9	13	1	229	82	19.08	-	98	3	32.66	1/15	6
Horridge L.	1927-1929	3	3	1	33	11*	16.50	-	79	3	26.33	2/46	2
Horrocks R.	1880-1882	6	10	0	116	61	11.60	-	-	-	-	-	1
Horrocks W.J.	1931-1933	15	19	3	371	100*	23.18	1	44	0	-	-	4

Name	Played	Matches	Inns	NO	Runs	HS	Ave	100s	Runs	Wkts	Ave	Best	Ct/St
Houldsworth W.H.	1893-1894	10	16	1	156	21	10.40	-	-	-	-	-	2
Houlton G.	1961-1963	20	33	2	688	86	22.19	-	6	0	-	-	5
Howard B.J.	1947-1951	32	45	3	996	109	23.71	2	-	-	-	-	29
Howard K.	1960-1966	61	82	35	395	23	8.40	-	3,175	104	30.52	7/53	57
Howard N.D.	1946-1953	170	234	29	5,526	145	26.95	3	23	0	-	-	131
Howard R.	1922-1933	8	9	2	166	88*	23.71	-	18	0	-	-	4
Howe R.	1876-1877	3	6	0	24	13	4.00	-	-	-	-	-	4
Hubback T.R.	1892	4	6	1	63	33	12.60	-	-	-	-	-	1
Huddleston W.	1899-1914	183	258	32	2,765	88	12.23	-	12,007	684	17.55	9/36	149
Hudson B.	1886-1888	5	6	0	207	98	34.50	-	59	3	19.66	2/14	-
Hudson G.N.	1936	2	2	1	1	1	1.00	-	82	0	-	-	1
Hughes D.P.	1967-1990	428	558	104	10,015	153	22.05	8	18,726	632	29.62	7/24	318
Hulton C.A.G.	1869-1882	8	12	3	80	19	8.88	-	-	-	-	-	6
Hulton H.A.H.	1868	2	4	1	13	6	4.33	-	-	-	-	-	-
I'Anson J.	1896-1908	57	76	9	986	110*	14.71	1	3,072	148	20.75	7/31	29
Iddison R.	1865-1870	16	31	5	621	106	23.88	1	875	56	15.62	6/29	14
Iddison W.H.	1867-1868	4	8	0	46	19	5.75	-	95	1	95.00	1/33	1
Iddon J.	1924-1945	483	683	90	21,975	222	37.05	46	14,214	533	26.66	9/42	207
Ikin J.T.	1939-1957	288	431	51	14,327	192	37.70	23	8,005	278	28.79	6/21	329
Ingleby C.W.	1899	1	2	1	40	29	40.00	-	17	0	-	-	-
Irani R.	1990	1	-	-	-	-	-	-	73	2	36.50	1/12	-
Isherwood F.	1881	1	1	0	0	0	0.00	-	-	-	-	-	-
Jackson E.	1871-1885	15	23	4	105	11	5.52	-	-	-	-	-	21/14
Jacques T.R.	1937	2	2	0	4	2	2.00	-	70	1	70.00	1/45	1
Jefferies S.T.	1983-1985	32	47	7	1,167	93	29.17	-	2,568	87	29.51	8/46	5
Jervis W.S.	1874	1	2	0	6	6	3.00	-	4	0	-	-	1
Jesty T.E.	1988-1990	55	89	16	2,532	98	34.68	-	126	1	-	1/20	15
John H.C.R.	1881	1	1	1	15	15*	-	-	13	0	-	-	-

Name	Played	Matches	Inns	NO	Runs	HS	Ave	100s	Runs	Wkts	Ave	Best	Ct/St
Jolley W.T.	1947	2	2	1	21	13	21.00	-	132	5	26.40	4/31	5
Jones C.L.	1876-1888	5	10	1	52	20*	5.77	-	6	1	6.00	1/6	-
Jones J.L.	1910	4	5	4	10	7*	10.00	-	-	-	-	-	5
Jordan J.	1955-1957	62	75	7	754	39	11.08	-	-	-	-	-	104/24
Jowett G.E.	1885-1889	19	32	2	507	58	16.90	-	55	0	-	-	11
Kaye J.L.	1867	1	2	0	21	20	10.50	-	16	0	-	-	-
Kelly E.A.	1957	4	6	2	38	16*	9.50	-	284	4	62.00	3/77	1
Kelly J.M.	1947-1949	6	11	3	150	58	18.75	-	14	0	-	-	3
Kemble A.T.	1885-1894	76	112	13	1,050	50	10.60	-	-	-	-	-	97/45
Kemp G.	1885-1892	18	33	2	355	109	11.45	1	-	-	-	-	6
Kennedy A.	1970-1982	149	241	20	6,232	180	28.19	6	398	10	39.80	3/58	85
Kentfield R.W.	1888	2	4	0	39	18	9.75	-	94	2	47.00	2/52	-
Kenyon M.N.	1919-1925	91	127	30	1,435	61*	14.79	-	-	-	-	-	20
Kermode A.	1902-1908	76	102	22	631	64*	7.88	-	7,260	321	22.61	7/44	33
Kershaw J.E.	1877-1885	33	54	3	575	66	11.27	-	-	-	-	-	12
Kevan J.H.	1875	2	4	0	12	12	3.00	-	-	-	-	-	-
Kewley E.	1875	1	2	0	3	3	1.50	-	-	-	-	-	1
King B.P.	1946-1947	37	56	3	1,505	145	28.39	2	-	-	-	-	18
Knowles A.	1888	1	2	0	6	6	3.00	-	-	-	-	-	1
Knox G.K.	1964-1967	52	92	3	1,698	108	19.07	3	161	2	80.50	1/10	38
Krikken B.E.	1966-1967	2	2	0	4	4	2.00	-	-	-	-	-	5
Lancashire O.P.	1878-1888	97	158	10	1911	76*	12.91	-	-	-	-	-	32
Lancaster T.	1894-1899	27	40	11	554	66	19.10	-	1,456	66	22.06	7/25	6
Landon C.W.	1874-1875	6	10	0	121	47	12.10	-	69	2	34.50	1/10	1
Latchford J.R.	1930-1932	7	10	0	154	63	15.40	-	181	4	45.25	1/6	4
Lawson G.F.	1979	1	2	0	19	17	9.50	-	88	5	17.60	4/81	-
Lawton A.E.	1912-1914	12	20	1	269	52	14.15	-	259	14	18.50	4/33	9
Lawton W.	1948	2	2	0	3	3	1.50	-	64	1	64.00	1/0	1

Name	Played	Matches	Inns	NO	Runs	HS	Ave	100s	Runs	Wkts	Ave	Best	Ct/St
Leach E.L.C.	1923-1924	12	15	0	161	79	10.73	-	-	-	-	-	3
Leach H.	1881	1	1	0	33	33	33.00	-	-	-	-	-	1
Leach J.	1866-1877	5	9	0	103	34	11.44	-	-	-	-	-	1
Leach R.	1868-1876	3	5	0	35	14	7.00	-	-	-	-	-	-
Leach R.C.	1885	1	2	0	49	39	24.50	-	-	-	-	-	-
Leach W.E.	1885	5	9	1	208	56	26.00	-	11	0	-	-	1
Lee P.G.	1972-1982	152	119	54	500	25	7.69	-	11,817	496	23.82	8/34	18
Leese C.P.	1911	1	2	0	16	10	8.00	-	-	-	-	-	-
Leese E.	1880-1884	8	11	1	146	62	14.60	-	-	-	-	-	1
Leese J.F.	1865-1881	24	42	1	556	44	13.56	-	94	5	18.80	3/49	14
Leigh J.	1887	1	2	0	2	1	1.00	-	-	-	-	-	-
Leventon E.C.	1867	1	2	0	6	6	3.00	-	24	2	12.00	2/24	-
Lever P.	1960-1976	268	285	59	3,073	83	13.59	-	17,647	716	24.64	7/70	89
Lister W.H.L.	1933-1939	158	210	17	3,561	104*	18.45	2	74	1	74.00	1/10	69/2
Littlewood G.H.	1902-1904	14	19	5	129	42	9.21	-	1,123	58	19.36	7/49	12
Littlewood G.W.	1885	3	6	1	28	8*	5.60	-	-	-	-	-	4/3
Lloyd C.H.	1968-1986	219	326	42	12,764	217*	44.94	30	1809	55	32.89	4/48	161
Lloyd D.	1965-1983	378	605	70	17,877	195	33.41	37	7,007	234	29.94	7/38	311
Lloyd G.D.	1988-1990	22	34	3	1,260	117	40.64	3	77	-	-	-	12
Lloyd R.A.	1921-1922	3	5	0	100	51	20.00	-	-	-	-	-	2
Lomax J.G.	1949-1953	57	78	2	1,137	78	14.96	-	2,519	81	31.09	5/18	28
Lyon J.	1973-1979	84	89	18	1,010	123	14.22	1	-	-	-	-	153/11
McDonald E.A.	1924-1931	217	215	31	1,868	100*	10.15	1	22,079	1,053	20.96	8/53	78
McFarlane L.L.	1982-1984	35	34	18	115	15*	7.18	-	2,563	73	35.10	6/59	6
McIntyre H.	1884	1	1	1	1	1*	-	-	-	-	-	-	1/2
McIntyre W.	1872-1880	72	112	20	758	66	8.23	-	5,141	441	11.65	8/31	53
MacKinnon D.W.	1870-1871	3	5	0	65	24	13.00	-	72	5	14.40	3/13	3
MacLaren A.C.	1890-1914	307	510	37	15,772	424	33.34	30	247	1	247.00	1/44	349

Name	Played	Matches	Inns	NO	Runs	HS	Ave	100s	Runs	Wkts	Ave	Best	Ct/St
Maclaren F.G.	1903	1	2	0	19	19	9.50	-	7	0	-	-	-
MacLaren G.	1902	2	4	0	7	3	1.75	-	13	2	6.50	1/5	-
MacLaren J.A.	1891-1894	4	4	0	9	6	2.25	-	-	-	-	-	4
MacLeod K.G.	1908-1913	75	124	9	2,619	131	22.77	4	2,019	81	24.92	6/29	88
MacLeod K.W.	1987	6	6	0	92	31	15.33	-	409	17	24.05	5/8	1
McNairy R.	1925	1	1	1	4	4*	-	-	73	1	73.00	1/23	-
Makepeace J.W.H.	1906-1930	487	757	64	25,207	203	36.37	42	1,971	42	46.92	4/33	194
Makinson D.J.	1984-1988	35	39	17	486	58*	22.09	-	2,486	70	35.51	5/60	9
Makison J.	1865-1873	5	9	0	131	45	14.55	-	73	4	18.25	4/49	7
Malone M.F.	1979-1980	19	16	3	181	38	13.92	-	1,421	64	22.20	7/88	1
Marchbank W.J.	1869-1870	4	7	1	20	15	3.33	-	-	-	-	-	1/2
Marner P.T.	1952-1964	236	391	38	10,312	142*	29.21	10	4,116	109	37.76	5/46	200
Marriott C.S.	1919-1921	12	16	2	78	16	5.57	-	967	34	28.44	8/98	3
Martin P.J.	1989-	12	9	3	64	21	10.66	-	1,001	23	43.52	4/68	6
Massey W.M.	1883	1	2	0	6	5	3.00	-	-	-	-	-	1
Matthews C.D.	1988	3	3	0	38	31	12.66	-	225	7	32.14	4/47	-
Matthews D.M.	1936-1938	7	8	0	130	46	16.25	-	-	-	-	-	1
Mayall J.	1885	1	1	0	0	0	0.00	-	-	-	-	-	1/2
Maynard C.	1982-1986	91	120	21	1,934	132*	19.53	1	8	0	-	-	145/23
Melhuish F.	1877	3	6	0	32	13	5.33	-	-	-	-	-	-
Melling J.	1874-1876	3	5	0	39	20	7.80	-	16	0	-	-	4
Mellor H.	1874-1875	2	4	0	28	17	7.00	-	-	-	-	-	-
Mendis G.D.	1986-1990	114	195	22	7,177	203*	41.48	13	82	0	-	-	39
Miller F.N.	1904	1	2	0	37	37	18.50	-	-	-	-	-	1
Miller H.	1880-1881	5	8	0	84	27	10.50	-	202	10	20.20	5/46	1
Mills J.	1889	1	1	0	1	1	1.00	-	-	-	-	-	-
Mills W.G.	1871-1877	6	11	1	57	26	5.70	-	97	6	16.16	3/52	4
Milne R.O.	1882	1	1	1	7	7*	-	-	-	-	-	-	-

Name	Played	Matches	Inns	NO	Runs	HS	Ave	100s	Runs	Wkts	Ave	Best	Ct/St
Mold A.W.	1889-1901	260	347	114	1,675	57	7.15	-	23,384	1,543	15.15	9/29	104
Moore F.	1954-1958	24	26	7	151	18	7.94	-	1,516	54	28.07	6/45	11
Moorhouse E.	1873-1875	5	9	3	75	34	12.50	-	-	-	-	-	8/3
Moorsom L.H.	1865	1	2	0	12	7	6.00	-	-	-	-	-	-
Mortimer R.G.	1891	1	1	1	22	22*	-	-	-	-	-	-	-
Mugliston F.H.	1906-1908	7	11	0	117	35	10.63	-	-	-	-	-	10
Murphy A.J.	1985-1988	13	13	6	18	5	2.57	-	993	24	41.37	4/115	6
Musson F.W.	1914-1921	16	27	1	510	75	19.61	-	-	-	-	-	12/4
Napier, Revd J.R.	1888	2	3	1	48	37	24.00	-	102	11	9.27	4/0	-
Nash G.	1879-1885	54	80	24	295	30	5.26	-	2,503	202	12.39	8/14	35
Nasir Zaidi S.M.	1983-1984	19	22	9	313	51	24.07	-	827	19	43.52	3/27	15
Nelson J.	1913	1	2	0	7	5	3.50	-	-	-	-	-	-
Norbury D.V.	1919-1922	14	23	0	594	100	25.82	1	448	23	19.47	4/28	4
Nutter A.E.	1935-1945	70	90	16	2,200	109*	29.72	1	4,453	152	29.29	6/66	55
Nutter E.	1885	1	1	0	18	18	18.00	-	-	-	-	-	-
Oakley W.	1893-1894	20	31	8	131	24	5.69	-	638	37	17.24	6/50	20
Oldfield N.	1935-1939	151	220	24	7,002	147*	35.72	12	85	2	42.50	1/0	32
Ollivant A.	1873-1874	2	3	1	36	24*	18.00	-	-	-	-	-	-
Openshaw W.E.	1879-1882	4	5	0	29	16	5.80	-	-	-	-	-	1
Ormrod J.A.	1984-1985	27	47	3	1,253	139*	28.47	1	-	-	-	-	13
O'Shaughnessy S.J.	1980-1987	100	161	27	3,567	159*	26.61	5	3,947	110	35.88	4/66	52
Palmer S.	1879-1880	6	9	0	28	8	3.11	-	11	0	-	-	4
Parker W.	1904	2	3	0	66	40	22.00	-	175	4	43.75	2/47	-
Parkin C.H.	1914-1926	157	189	27	1,959	57	12.09	-	14,526	901	16.12	9/32	107
Parkin R.H.	1931-1939	20	18	4	231	60	16.50	-	845	23	36.73	3/52	4
Parkinson H.B.	1922-1923	15	18	5	34	8	2.61	-	-	-	-	-	14/3
Parkinson L.W.	1932-1936	88	112	13	2,132	93	21.53	-	5,654	192	29.44	6/112	45
Parr F.D.	1951-1954	48	51	10	493	42	12.02	-	-	-	-	-	70/20

Name	Played	Matches	Inns	NO	Runs	HS	Ave	100s	Runs	Wkts	Ave	Best	Ct/St
Parr H.B.	1872-1876	10	14	0	167	61	11.92	-	-	-	-	-	4
Patterson B.P.	1984-1990	70	61	24	187	29	5.05	-	5,496	202	27.20	7/49	12
Patterson W.S.	1874-1882	7	11	1	132	50	13.20	-	241	24	10.04	7/30	3
Paul A.G.	1889-1900	95	150	15	2,958	177	21.91	4	146	2	73.00	1/7	73/1
Payne J.	1898	1	2	0	0	0	0.00	-	48	0	-	-	-
Payne J.H.	1883	9	15	3	158	33	13.16	-	-	-	-	-	4/1
Paynter E.	1926-1945	293	445	47	16,555	322	41.59	36	1,250	24	52.08	3/13	131
Pennington H.	1900	4	5	1	41	29*	10.25	-	-	-	-	-	2/3
Perry W.	1865	1	2	0	16	16	8.00	29	-	-	-	-	3/1
Pewtress A.W.	1919-1925	50	73	5	1,483	89	21.80	-	10	1	10.00	1/10	16
Phillips W.	1904-1908	10	18	3	109	18	7.26	-	-	-	-	-	17/2
Phillipson W.E.	1933-1948	158	202	46	4,050	113	25.96	2	13,508	545	24.78	8/100	81
Pilkington C.C.	1895	2	4	0	38	18	9.50	-	100	3	33.33	3/70	-
Pilling H.	1962-1980	323	525	65	14,841	149*	32.26	25	195	1	195.00	1/42	85
Pilling R.	1877-1889	177	258	86	1,854	78	10.77	-	-	-	-	-	333/153
Pilling W.	1891	1	1	1	9	9*	-	-	-	-	-	-	1/1
Place W.	1937-1955	298	441	43	14,605	266*	36.69	34	42	1	42.00	1/2	179
Poidevin L.O.S.	1904-1908	105	163	14	4,460	168*	29.93	8	1,786	46	38.82	8/66	133
Pollard R.	1933-1950	266	298	52	3,273	63	13.30	-	22,492	1,015	22.15	8/33	203
Porter E.H.	1874-1882	17	29	1	301	61	10.75	-	9	0	-	-	10
Potter G.	1902	10	17	1	449	86	28.06	-	-	-	-	-	3
Potter T.O.	1866	1	2	0	39	39	19.50	-	-	-	-	-	-
Potter W.H.	1870	1	2	0	23	12	11.50	-	-	-	-	-	-
Preston S.	1928-1930	5	4	2	46	33	23.00	-	212	6	35.33	2/42	1
Price A.	1885	1	2	0	8	8	4.00	-	-	-	-	-	1
Price E.J.	1946-1947	35	36	14	305	54	13.86	-	2.373	115	20.63	6/34	15
Pullar G.	1954-1968	312	524	45	16,853	167*	35.18	32	305	8	38.12	3/91	107
Radcliffe G.	1903-1906	7	11	0	171	60	15.54	-	-	-	-	-	2

Name	Played	Matches	Inns	NO	Runs	HS	Ave	100s	Runs	Wkts	Ave	Best	Ct/St
Radcliffe L.	1897-1905	50	67	22	275	25	6.11	-	-	-	-	-	69/34
Radford N.V.	1980-1984	24	33	8	549	76*	21.96	-	1,805	33	54.69	5/95	10
Rae R.B.	1945	1	1	0	74	74	74.00	-	29	0	-	-	-
Ramadhin S.	1964-1965	33	40	19	151	13	7.19	-	2,267	97	23.37	8/121	5
Ramsbottom H.J.	1868	1	2	0	1	1	0.50	-	11	0	-	-	-
Ratcliffe E.	1884	1	2	0	9	7	4.50	-	8	0	-	-	-
Ratcliffe R.M.	1972-1980	82	84	22	1,022	101*	16.48	1	5,411	205	26.39	7/58	23
Rawlinson E.B.	1867	1	2	1	15	14	15.00	-	-	-	-	-	3
Rawlinson W.	1870-1871	3	6	0	24	10	4.00	-	-	-	-	-	1
Rawstorne G.S.	1919	1	1	0	2	2	2.00	-	-	-	-	-	-
Reidy B.W.	1973-1982	107	162	26	3,641	131*	26.77	2	2,508	60	41.80	5/61	65
Reynolds F.R.	1865-1874	38	65	20	293	34*	6.51	-	1,823	94	19.39	6/92	29
Rhodes A.	1922-1924	17	25	3	382	70	17.36	-	475	15	31.66	2/24	9
Rhodes A.C.	1937-1938	8	10	4	11	6	1.83	-	619	22	28.13	4/37	1
Richmond W.	1868	1	2	0	1	1	0.50	-	-	-	-	-	-
Ricketts J.	1867-1877	34	66	4	1,120	195*	18.06	1	250	12	20.83	4/40	25/1
Rickman W.	1876	1	1	0	5	5	5.00	-	-	-	-	-	-
Ritchie D.M.	1924	1	1	0	3	3	3.00	-	-	-	-	-	2
Roberts J.F.E.	1957	2	4	2	5	5	2.50	-	90	0	-	-	-
Roberts R.	1872-1874	10	16	0	100	20	6.25	-	-	-	-	-	9/5
Roberts W.B.	1939-1949	114	113	39	810	51	10.94	-	7,971	382	20.86	8/50	58
Robinson P.A.	1979	1	1	0	15	15	15.00	-	58	2	29.00	2/57	-
Robinson W.	1880-1888	115	186	10	3,597	154	20.43	4	61	0	-	-	48
Rogerson G.H.	1923	12	20	1	340	47*	17.89	-	-	-	-	-	3
Roper E.	1876-1886	28	47	2	586	65	13.02	-	-	-	-	-	6
Rowland D.	1868	1	2	0	0	0	0.00	-	23	0	-	-	-
Rowlands L.S.	1903-1910	6	10	4	27	9	4.50	-	322	16	20.12	4/29	2
Rowley A.B.	1865-1871	12	21	3	282	63*	15.66	-	603	24	25.12	5/71	9

Name	Played	Matches	Inns	NO	Runs	HS	Ave	100s	Runs	Wkts	Ave	Best	Ct/St
Rowley E.B.	1865-1880	81	131	8	1,626	78	13.21	-	17	0	-	-	23/1
Rowley E.B. Jnr	1893-1898	16	25	4	553	65	26.33	-	-	-	-	-	4
Royle, Revd V.P.F.A.	1873-1891	74	120	8	1,754	81	15.66	-	114	2	57.00	1/22	34
Rushton F.	1928-1929	6	5	0	59	28	11.80	-	362	10	36.20	4/30	2
Rushton T.H.	1870	1	1	0	7	7	7.00	-	-	-	-	-	-
Rutter F.J.	1868	2	4	1	15	8*	5.00	-	11	0	-	-	1
Sanderson L.	1884	1	1	0	0	0	0.00	-	-	-	-	-	-
Sanderson R.W.B.	1870	1	2	0	7	6	3.50	-	-	-	-	-	1
Savage J.S.	1967-1969	58	64	33	197	19	6.35	-	3,051	114	26.76	5/1	9
Sawyer C.M.	1884	2	2	1	21	11*	21.00	-	65	0	-	-	-
Schofield J.	1876	4	6	2	27	11	6.75	-	-	-	-	7/1	-
Scholfield F.B.	1911	1	2	1	17	17	17.00	-	2	0	-	-	-
Schultz S.S.	1877-1882	9	17	3	215	42*	15.35	-	23	0	-	-	6
Scott C.J.	1977-1982	46	51	13	262	27*	6.89	-	-	-	-	-	94/10
Scott W.A.	1874	1	2	1	14	9	14.00	-	-	-	-	-	-
Seymour A.	1869	1	2	0	45	25	22.50	-	-	-	-	-	1
Sharp J.	1899-1925	518	776	70	22,015	211	31.18	36	11,821	434	27.23	9/77	231
Shelmerdine G.O.	1919-1925	31	45	4	980	105	23.90	1	97	0	-	-	12
Shore C.	1886	1	2	0	3	3	1.50	-	11	0	-	-	-
Shuttleworth K.	1964-1975	177	179	62	1,929	71	16.48	-	11,097	484	22.92	7/41	84
Sibbles F.M.	1925-1937	308	311	79	3,436	71*	14.81	-	20,538	932	22.03	8/24	176
Silcock W.	1899-1902	6	7	1	82	43	13.66	-	367	5	73.40	2/62	5
Simmons J.	1968-1989	429	530	142	8,773	112	22.61	5	26,489	985	26.89	7/64	325
Sladen A.R.	1903-1904	2	3	0	8	5	2.66	-	175	6	29.16	3/77	1
Slater R.	1865	1	2	0	0	0	0.00	-	3	0	-	-	-
Smalley J.	1869	2	4	0	24	17	6.00	-	-	-	-	-	-
Smith A.	1867-1871	4	8	3	56	30	11.20	-	-	-	-	-	5/3
Smith A.P.	1886-1894	48	76	5	1440	124	20.28	2	517	29	17.82	5/49	31

Name	Played	Matches	Inns	NO	Runs	HS	Ave	100s	Runs	Wkts	Ave	Best	Ct/St
Smith C.	1893-1902	167	234	50	2,248	81	12.21	-	18	1	18.00	1/18	312/119
Smith C.S.	1951-1957	45	55	4	768	67	15.05	-	2,815	101	21.63	5/39	17
Smith D.J.	1951-1952	3	4	0	26	14	6.50	-	205	4	51.25	1/19	2
Smith J.	1865-1869	6	12	1	153	40*	13.90	-	290	12	24.16	4/46	4
Smith R.	1893	1	1	0	6	6	6.00	-	11	0	-	-	-
Smith S.	1952-1956	38	54	4	865	72*	17.30	-	-	-	-	-	10
Smith T.	1867	2	3	0	18	12	6.00	-	36	1	36.00	1/8	2
Snellgrove K.L.	1965-1974	105	170	16	3,906	138	25.36	2	27	3	9.00	2/23	35
Speak G.J.	1981-1982	5	6	4	27	15*	13.50	-	230	1	230.00	1/78	3
Speak N.J.	1987-1990	13	23	1	644	138	29.27	1	26	1	26.00	1/26	9
Spencer H.	1914	2	3	1	5	4	2.50	-	139	3	46.33	1/0	5
Spooner A.F.	1906-1909	18	33	1	500	83	15.62	-	-	-	-	-	8
Spooner R.H.	1899-1921	170	280	14	9,889	247	37.17	25	554	5	110.80	1/5	106
Standring K.B.	1955-1959	8	14	2	110	41	9.16	-	375	11	34.09	3/44	1
Stanning H.D.	1906-1908	33	54	1	898	86	16.94	-	3	0	-	-	10
Stanning J.	1900-1903	4	7	0	97	33	13.85	-	-	-	-	-	1
Stanworth J.	1983-1990	37	38	11	236	50*	8.74	-	-	-	-	-	52/10
Statham J.B.	1950-1968	430	501	98	4,237	62	10.51	-	27,470	1,816	15.12	8/34	171
Staziker M.W.	1970	2	2	2	1	1*	-	-	269	1	269.00	1/114	-
Steel A.G.	1877-1893	47	72	5	1960	105	29.25	1	3,134	238	13.16	9/63	29
Steel D.Q.	1876-1887	22	35	1	560	82	16.47	-	-	-	-	-	8/2
Steel E.E.	1884-1903	40	58	4	861	69*	15.94	-	2,598	122	21.29	8/32	37
Steel H.B.	1883-1896	22	37	3	765	100	22.50	1	-	-	-	-	8
Stephenson F.	1875-1877	2	4	1	0	0*	0.00	-	17	1	17.00	1/17	2
Stoddart W.B.	1898-1899	15	25	4	294	43*	14.00	-	899	37	24.29	6/121	5
Stone D.H.	1949-1950	6	8	2	86	46	14.33	-	472	9	52.44	4/30	1
Storer E.	1865-1878	6	11	5	46	23	7.66	-	245	15	16.33	5/12	2
Sugg F.H.	1887-1899	235	387	24	9,620	220	26.50	15	259	10	25.90	2/12	131

Name	Played	Matches	Inns	NO	Runs	HS	Ave	100s	Runs	Wkts	Ave	Best	Ct/St
Sullivan J.	1963-1976	154	241	32	4,286	81*	20.50	-	2,216	76	29.15	4/19	85
Sutcliffe R.J.	1978	1	2	2	10	10*	-	-	37	1	37.00	1/37	-
Swire S.H.	1865-1868	5	9	1	93	18*	11.62	-	37	0	-	-	1
Tattersall R.	1948-1960	277	312	128	1,786	58	9.70	-	20,316	1,168	17.39	9/40	118
Tattersall R.H.	1971	2	-	-	-	-	-	-	219	1	219.00	1/44	-
Taylor F.	1874-1888	52	85	4	1,451	96	17.91	-	73	3	24.33	1/4	23
Taylor F.	1920-1922	15	18	6	188	29*	15.66	-	1,026	40	25.65	6/65	7
Taylor J.	1871-1873	3	6	0	52	33	8.66	-	13	0	-	-	-
Taylor M.L.	1924-1931	95	112	15	2,216	107*	22.84	1	26	0	-	-	42
Taylor R.J.	1898	2	3	0	6	6	2.00	-	96	2	48.00	1/25	-
Taylor T.J.	1981-1982	4	4	1	2	2	0.66	-	238	5	47.60	2/63	-
Tebay K.	1961-1963	15	27	2	509	106	20.36	1	-	-	-	-	3
Teggin A.	1886	6	8	0	31	9	3.87	-	176	16	11.00	6/53	4
Tennent H.N.	1865-1870	2	3	0	45	21	15.00	-	-	-	-	-	-
Tennent W.M.	1867	1	2	0	3	3	1.50	-	-	-	-	-	-
Thomas A.	1966	1	2	0	4	4	2.00	-	7	0	-	-	22/8
Thomas R.	1894-1902	20	22	5	60	17	3.52	-	-	-	-	-	-
Thornber H.	1874	1	2	0	0	0	0.00	-	-	-	-	-	20
Tindall S.M.	1894-1898	42	62	1	1,039	86	17.03	-	28	1	28.00	1/11	24
Tinsley A.	1890-1895	58	91	10	1,348	65	16.64	-	7	0	-	-	27
Tinsley H.J.	1894-1896	4	6	0	57	18	9.50	-	-	-	-	-	2
Titchard S.P.	1990	3	5	0	129	80	25.80	-	-	-	-	-	-
Tranter E.	1875-1876	3	5	0	9	5	1.80	-	94	3	31.33	2/11	2
Trim G.E.	1976-1980	15	25	0	399	91	15.96	-	13	0	-	-	10
Tyldesley G.E.	1909-1936	573	850	93	34,222	256*	45.20	90	332	6	55.33	3/33	275
Tyldesley H.	1914-1922	4	7	3	63	33*	15.75	-	101	3	33.66	2/37	1
Tyldesley J.D.	1910-1922	116	169	16	2,885	112*	18.85	3	8,092	309	26.18	7/34	97
Tyldesley J.T.	1895-1923	507	824	52	31,949	295*	41.38	73	170	2	85.00	1/4	311

Name	Played	Matches	Inns	NO	Runs	HS	Ave	100s	Runs	Wkts	Ave	Best	Ct/St
Tyldesley R.K.	1919-1931	374	435	47	6,126	105	15.78	1	24,139	1,449	16.65	8/15	322
Tyldesley W.K.	1908-1914	87	137	7	2,979	152	22.91	3	383	8	47.87	2/0	52
Unsworth J.	1871	2	3	0	25	23	8.33	-	75	3	25.00	3/52	2
Van der Knapp D.S.	1967	1	-	-	-	-	-	-	69	2	34.50	2/24	-
Varey D.W.	1984-1987	44	70	7	1,752	112	27.80	1	6	0	-	-	14/1
Wadsworth E.	1871-1879	7	13	0	69	30	5.30	-	13	0	-	-	1
Walker R.	1874-1875	2	4	1	27	19	9.00	-	-	-	-	-	1/1
Wall H.	1877	3	4	0	24	15	6.00	-	-	-	-	-	2
Wall T.	1868	2	4	0	48	37	12.00	-	17	0	-	-	1
Wall W.	1877	1	2	1	17	17*	17.00	-	-	-	-	-	2/2
Wallwork M.A.	1982	1	-	-	-	-	-	-	-	-	-	-	3
Walsh G.	1874-1877	2	3	0	16	15	5.33	-	-	-	-	-	-
Walton M.	1867	1	2	0	6	6	3.00	-	-	-	-	-	-
Warburton L.	1929-1938	6	5	1	159	74*	39.75	-	217	5	43.40	3/47	1
Ward A.	1889-1904	330	544	47	15,392	185	30.96	24	2,380	65	36.61	6/29	140
Ward F.	1884-1896	47	74	6	986	145	14.50	1	538	27	19.92	4/14	11
Wardle C.	1867-1872	3	5	2	25	7*	8.33	-	17	0	-	-	4
Washbrook C.	1933-1959	500	756	95	27,863	251*	42.15	58	268	4	67.00	1/4	182
Wasim Akram	1988-1990	30	48	4	967	116*	21.97	1	2,355	100	23.55	7/53	5
Watkinson M.	1982-1990	158	232	31	4,952	138	24.63	2	11,108	341	32.57	7/25	81
Watson A.	1871-1893	283	423	88	4,187	74	12.49	-	17,516	1,308	13.39	9/118	261
Watson F.B.	1920-1937	456	664	48	22,833	300*	37.06	49	12,811	402	31.86	5/31	287
Watson R.G.	1982-1985	2	3	0	33	18	11.00	-	-	-	-	-	-
Waterton S.N.V.	1990	1	1	0	3	3	-	-	-	-	-	-	4
Webb S.	1899-1903	73	94	27	513	38*	7.65	-	5,226	265	19.72	8/36	57
Webster F.	1925-1927	2	3	1	12	10	6.00	-	122	7	17.42	3/34	1
Wharmby G.E.	1894	6	8	2	29	11	4.83	-	209	8	26.12	3/35	2
Wharton A.	1946-1960	392	589	55	17,921	199	33.55	25	7,094	225	31.52	7/33	223

Name	Played	Matches	Inns	NO	Runs	HS	Ave	100s	Runs	Wkts	Ave	Best	Ct/St
Whatmough T.	1871	2	4	2	42	28*	21.00	-	79	3	26.33	2/52	1
Whewell J.W.	1921-1927	12	13	5	19	12	2.37	-	-	-	-	-	12/3
Whitehead R.	1908-1914	107	158	36	2,571	131*	21.07	4	7,260	300	24.20	8/77	37
Whitehead T.	1884	1	1	0	8	8	8.00	-	20	0	-	-	-
Whiteley P.	1957-1958	5	8	2	86	32	14.33	-	266	9	29.55	3/70	2
Whiteside J.P.	1888-1890	6	8	0	25	12	3.12	-	-	-	-	-	6/7
Whittaker D.	1884-1888	9	14	1	128	26	9.84	-	46	1	46.00	1/26	4
Whittaker E.	1865-1868	11	21	2	232	39	12.21	-	125	1	125.00	1/26	3
Wilkinson L.L.	1937-1947	63	61	24	296	48	8.00	-	6,091	232	26.25	8/53	49
Wilson A.	1948-1962	171	186	59	760	37*	5.98	-	-	-	-	-	287/59
Winder G.A.	1869	2	4	0	23	9	5.75	-	-	-	-	-	1
Wood B.	1966-1979	260	424	56	12,969	198	35.24	23	6,910	251	27.52	7/52	200
Wood J.	1956	1	-	-	-	-	-	-	103	4	25.75	3/56	1
Wood R.	1880-1884	6	9	2	167	52	23.85	-	72	4	18.00	1/23	3
Woolley A.	1926	7	9	0	61	24	6.77	-	351	11	31.90	4/56	9
Worsley D.R.	1960-1967	62	108	9	2,508	120	25.33	2	904	27	33.48	4/21	37
Worsley W.	1903-1913	136	167	63	628	37*	6.03	-	-	-	-	-	239/45
Wright E.L.	1905-1910	4	8	0	53	17	6.62	-	-	-	-	-	3
Wright, Revd F.W.	1869-1875	15	22	2	416	120*	20.80	1	156	3	51.66	2/44	12/9
Yates C.	1882	1	2	0	28	24	14.00	-	-	-	-	-	-
Yates, George	1885-1894	92	135	15	1,632	74	13.60	-	934	30	31.13	4/112	41
Yates, Gary	1990	5	4	2	165	106	82.50	1	420	8	52.50	4/94	1